221.93
P31   Pearlman, Moshe.
          Digging up the Bible.

221.93
P31   Pearlman, Moshe.
          Digging up the Bible.

Temple Israel Library
Minneapolis, Minn.

———

Please sign your full name on the above card.

Return books promptly to the Library or Temple Office.

Fines will be charged for overdue books or for damage or loss of same.

Digging up the Bible

ENDPAPERS The view from Mount Sinai.
OVERLEAF Archaeological excavation of a
Dead Sea cave.

Digging up the Bible

The stories behind the great archaeological
discoveries in the Holy Land

MOSHE PEARLMAN

William Morrow and Company, Inc.
New York   1980

Also by Moshe Pearlman

Collective Adventure
Mufti of Jerusalem
Adventure in the Sun
The Army of Israel
The Capture and Trial of Adolf Eichmann
Ben Gurion Looks Back
Historical Sites in Israel (co-author)
The Zealots of Masada
Jerusalem: A History of 40 Centuries (co-author)
Pilgrims to the Holy Land
In the Footsteps of Moses
The Saga of Moses
In the Footsteps of the Prophets
The Maccabees

Library of Congress Catalog Card Number
79–48063

ISBN 0–688–03677–5

Set, printed and bound in Great Britain by
Fakenham Press Limited, Fakenham, Norfolk

Contents

זור חיים
CISTER

1 The Hunt

IT WAS THE greatest hunt in history, mounted on the largest scale, at the most lavish cost, pursued over the longest period across the broadest area by the most remarkable assembly of hunters ever committed to a search for buried riches. The best of them were endowed with brilliant minds and the spirit of adventure, and had spent years preparing themselves for the task. Many were to end their lives in disappointment, condemned to oblivion. Only the few made triumphant finds which brought rewards of immeasurable value to the civilized world. But much treasure remained underground, a challenge to the probing spade and questing intellect of the future.

The hunt started in earnest one hundred and fifty years ago. It is still on. Indeed, it is more intense than ever, for the new generation of hunters, spurred by the excitement of the chase after an elusive but worthwhile quarry, are favoured by the accumulated wisdom from the trials and errors of their predecessors, and by the new devices and sophisticated skills of the modern world. They are aware of the hazards. But they venture forth with the confidence that their trowels will strike treasures that others have missed.

It is a strange hunt, with a strange target. Even stranger are the huntsmen. They have, on occasion, turned up gold and silver; but gold and silver are not primarily what they are after. They have brought out of the depths of the earth finely-fashioned jewels and ornaments; but these, too, while affording spontaneous joy, have held only modest interest for the diggers. Often, a broken goblet, a shattered lamp, part of a primitive spindle, a fragment of a pottery jar with strange markings scratched on its surface, have caused more excitement – and proved of more abiding worth – than a precious gem.

This special group of hunters are the biblical archaeologists. They

OPPOSITE Qumran, on the shore of the Dead Sea, the settlement of the Jewish sect who on the eve of their destruction by the Romans in the first century AD hid their sacred scrolls in the nearby caves to save them from pagan destruction.

7

may share with the more common treasure-hunter the adventure and the hardships, the sense of hopeful expectation in the search, and the overwhelming thrill of discovery. But there the similarity ends. The biblical archaeologists are not out for material gain, nor is theirs the exploration for private wealth – their finds end up in public museums or institutions of higher learning. The objective of these archaeologists is knowledge, knowledge of the biblical past. The treasures they seek lie buried beneath the dust and rubble of millennia, the remains of the people who lived in the land of the Bible in biblical times.

It is and has been a formidable quest, requiring erudition and physical endurance. The most successful of the scholars engaged in this enterprise, digging through four and three and two thousand years of debris, have made discoveries which give immediate reality to the biblical word. They have brought to light objects associated with the leading figures and events recorded in the Scriptures. The result has been to add another dimension to our understanding of the text, content and background of the Bible, and to expand our knowledge of the military, political, religious and social patterns of ancient times, as well as the development of language.

The physical digging itself is only part of the archaeological story. Long before they reach the excavation sites, the scholars are to be found in their studies poring over texts in a variety of ancient Near Eastern tongues to prepare the strategy and tactics of their expeditions. They then proceed to the target areas they have selected on the basis of their scholarly findings to test their speculations on the ground. Will these sites indeed prove to hold within them the remains of buried biblical cities, as their studies suggest? If so, will their excavations turn up illuminating finds, keys to a broader understanding of the ancient records?

The digging season usually lasts several summer months – major expeditions often continue for several seasons – and the teams of scholars and labourers dig and sift under the fierce sun through the accumulated debris right down to bedrock, marking and classifying every object found on the way. Each day is one of suspense. The season over, back home go the archaeologists to unravel the complex intellectual puzzles posed by the products of their excavations. They examine every artefact, as well as the diagrams and data they recorded on every ruined structure they unearthed, and apply their knowledge and flair to assess their value as clues which can enable them to reconstruct the history of the site. As open-minded scholars, they account themselves successful if their material finds make possible the recovery of a fragment of the past. As biblical archaeologists, they account themselves fortunate if these finds match, illustrate, expand and shed new light on the biblical narrative. For the Bible, we must remember, is a very succinct record, expressed in spare, often cryptic, style. (Hebrew is a very compact language.) Moreover, written for its contemporaries, who knew the land and the times in which they lived, a single word or phrase was enough, whereas we, living three thousand years later and often thousands of miles away, encounter much in the Bible that is obscure. Anything found by the archaeologist which can help fill in the contemporary background heightens our level of understanding.

It is now evident that the ideal archaeologists must possess an array of unusual talents. They must be scholars and men of action, theorists and pragmatists, with a soaring imagination but with feet firmly on the ground. They must be historians, with a specific familiarity with the history of the Near Eastern peoples in biblical times. They must know their biblical geography, and possess a keen eye for terrain. They must be linguists, with a good knowledge of Hebrew and an acquaintanceship with the classics and ancient Sumerian, Egyptian, Accadian, Ugarit and Aramaic. They must now – since a revolutionary discovery made at the end of the last century – be pottery experts. They must also have read, with a critical mind, the detailed accounts of the excavations of all their archaeological predecessors.

With all these qualities as a solid base, they must also, above all, have the curiosity of the true scientist – asking themselves questions, taking nothing for granted – and the powers of observation and reasoning of a Sherlock Holmes. They must, indeed be scholarly detectives, able to spot, and recognize, the flimsiest clue and discern the direction in which it points.

The supreme archaeological treasure, of course, is a body of writing, for this is a direct communication from the past to the present. Writings are not simply clues. They are the direct utterances of the biblical generations, speaking to us of their lives and thoughts, their codes and chronicles, telling us at times of some dramatic biblical event which may enlarge upon the brief mention in the Scriptures. Several such formidable texts have been discovered in the last 150 years – apart from the most recently brought to light and more popularly known, though less ancient, Dead Sea Scrolls, which were written on parchment a mere 2,000 years ago. The much earlier writings, from the 2nd and 1st millennia BC, were preserved for so long and found in excellent condition because they had been written long before parchment, paper and printing were conceived. The 'paper' in those days was virtually indestructible, the words being etched on stone, or scratched or written with primitive ink on pottery shards, or

impressed on clay tablets, and looking to the layman of our times like rows of meaningless signs or geometric strokes. Deciphering these ancient tongues – except for Hebrew, which has been in continuous use since the biblical age – was like cracking the most elaborate code, for with these early writings one had first to discern a pattern in the individual symbols to perceive a glimmer of a clue to the script and to be able to distinguish the words; only thereafter was it possible to plumb the secret of their meaning. This often took years to accomplish. The results of such work were stupendous.

But such discoveries were – and are – rare. Archaeologists embark on their explorations with only the faint hope that their search will be crowned by a literary find. They are happy if they dig up indirect communications from the past – the material remains of the peoples of antiquity, the ruins of their buildings, their fortifications, a level of ashes indicating the destruction of their city by fire, their weapons, their tools, their domestic utensils, the desiccated remnants of food in their silos, their water installations, their altars – the list is long. These serve as tangible illustrations to their human story in the Scriptures, showing us how they lived, fought, hunted, farmed, worshipped, died. Today, with greater knowledge and more advanced techniques than in the last century, humble finds, rejected as worthless by earlier scholars, such as the clay sealing of a wine jar, or a broken vessel, can serve as valuable clues to the secret of a site. Thus, the modern archaeologist may discern a vital fact in the most paltry object he unearths; for, as one of them observed, nothing is so poor as not to have a story to tell to one who knows – and it is the business of the archaeologist to know.

Modest or spectacular, most archaeological discoveries add vividness to our grasp even of familiar episodes in the Bible. Recent Jerusalem excavations uncovered the charred wrist-bone of a young woman flattened against the remains of a doorpost near the Temple Mount, evoking the poignant scene during the destruction of the city of a terrified housewife cowering at the door of her flaming house when the conquering enemy troops entered ancient Jerusalem and put it to the torch. Similarly, the grim mood in the aftermath of the Israelite defeat by the Philistines in the battle of Mount Gilboa some 3,000 years ago was almost palpable when archaeologists laid bare the ruins of Philistine temples in Bethshan. It was there, the Bible records, that the body of king Saul was 'fastened to the wall'.

There are countless other archaeological discoveries which add this dimension of reality to the written biblical word: the uncovering of city walls and gates built by king Solomon; king Ahab's House of Ivories; intricate ninth-century BC water systems, complete with shafts and tunnels, which are briefly recorded in the Bible; impressive structures which perfectly fit the account in the vision of the prophet Ezekiel – and which had been dismissed as imaginary until the archaeological revelation; tablets bearing missives from a sixth-century BC Judean army officer conveying the feelings of his beleaguered troops on the eve of the biblical battle at Lachish; an elaborate tomb by a pretentious court official which aroused the wrath of the prophet Isaiah – which now explains a

OPPOSITE Cuneiform (wedge-shaped) writing carved on stone found in a royal palace at Nimrud, at one time the Assyrian capital. Many such inscriptions discovered and deciphered in the middle of the last century, brought to light accounts of biblical events hitherto known only from the Old Testament.

hitherto obscure biblical passage, as well as the moral patterns of the period.

An almost fictional quality is added to the story of biblical archaeology by the role played by pure chance. 'Dry holes' have been dug by seasoned archaeologists, while some discoveries were stumbled upon by lucky illiterates – of course without realizing the value of their finds. Two in particular were made by unschooled youths. It was a Bedouin shepherd lad looking for a goat that had strayed into a cave in the craggy Judean hills in 1947 who came upon sealed jars containing the first of the Dead Sea Scrolls, the most important documentary treasures of the century. And the discovery in 1880 of an eighth-century BC Hebrew inscription on the wall of the water tunnel in Jerusalem built by king Hezekiah, as recorded in the Bible, was made by a boy who had fallen into the water just beneath it and spotted it when he emerged. There have also been sundry instances of unexpected encounters with biblical finds by Israeli bulldozers at work on building programmes and road construction sites.

These, however, are random episodes of chance which fall outside the framework of systematic archaeology. But even within that framework, when one scholar makes a discovery where another had drawn a blank, it is difficult to avoid the feeling that chance does somehow play a part. A distinguished explorer in the mid-nineteenth century carried out a trial dig at the site of Jericho, and missed – by only a few yards – an ancient city wall which made headlines when it was discovered by another archaeologist one hundred years later. One scholar in 1928 failed to unearth a vital clue in Galilee which was discovered in 1956 – only thirty yards away – and which transformed prevailing theories about the date of the Exodus. Another experienced archaeologist in the 1960s searched for scrolls along the dried up valleys near the Dead Sea for two successive seasons, and found nothing. A scholar in the following year examined the same locations, and discovered a treasury of second-century writings.

Luck or judgement? To the layman, the foregoing examples appear to be products of chance. Most serious archaeologists, however, discount the element of luck. They ascribe results solely to the quality of knowledge and thinking behind the effort. Failure is due to a flawed or missing thread in the calculation.

But whether or not there is any role for luck, all would agree that the prime ingredients for archaeological success are sound preparation, well-planned excavation, and sagacious reasoning in the interpretation of the finds. Having a flair helps. What one scholar may dismiss as insignificant may be detected by a more imaginative scholar as a vital clue. This has happened time and again on several biblical sites.

The archaeological pioneers of the last century were often lone explorers with only primitive aids to help them meet the tough intellectual and physical challenges. The modern archaeologists usually head large expeditions and command sophisticated facilities. Where a scholar in the 1970s helicoptered through a Judean gorge with a speed camera in hand to spot potential excavation sites likely to yield biblical treasures, his counterpart a hundred years ago rode through the land on horseback, camel and donkey, and trudged over likely sites with a measuring rod.

At the basic level of investigation, however, disparity vanishes. In 1838 a scholar identified a Bible-recorded conduit in Jerusalem's Kidron valley by crawling laboriously through it, much of the way up to his chin in water and sliding along the slimy bottom. In 1960 an archaeological team dangled over an abyss on a rope ladder from the edge of a steep cliff to enter and crawl through to the inner recesses of a musty cave to search for – and find – ancient documents.

There is a special quality to biblical archaeology unmatched by archaeological exploration anywhere else. Digs have been undertaken in many parts of the world. Nowhere have they been so numerous or carried out on so extensive a scale as in the Bible

Ancient writings were often found in the least accessible places. Archaeologists Binyamin Mazar (seated) and Nahman Avigad are here seen copying – and subsequently deciphering – rock inscriptions in the forbidding mountain country of southern Sinai.

lands. The reason is simple: it is the only region of antiquity of which there is a written historical record that has been familiar to so many people in every generation for so long. That record is the Bible, whose tenets form the basis of western civilization, and almost half the human race have either read or heard it – or at least parts of it – or handled a copy of it in one of its hundreds of translations.

The Bible is not only a religious work and a unique code of ethics, but also the narrative of the birth and development of the Hebrew nation. It tells in very human terms and in timeless prose the story of the triumphs and tribulations of the Hebrews, beginning with the patriarchs Abraham, Isaac and Jacob some 3,700 years ago. The chronological highlights of this historic account, which is illustrated by a profusion of highly dramatic episodes, are the Hebrew bondage in Egypt, the Exodus, and the Covenant ceremony on Mount Sinai in the thirteenth century BC; the Joshua conquest of the Promised Land of Israel some forty years later; the settlement of the land and the period of the Judges in the twelfth and eleventh centuries BC; the united kingdom of Israel under David and Sol-

Moses and the burning bush, from an illustrated medieval French bible.

omon; the divided kingdoms of Israel and Judah which followed – and which included the centuries of the great prophets – down to the destruction of Jerusalem and the First Temple in the sixth century BC, the Jewish exile to Babylon, and the dramatic return to Jerusalem fifty years later. The last of the Old Testament books was written in the fourth century BC, though part of the Book of Daniel belongs to the second-century BC period of the Maccabees, a period covered by two books in the Apocrypha. The New Testament Scriptures followed the Crucifixion of Jesus in the first century AD.

Israel's independence was wiped out in the year AD 70 (to be restored after 1,900 years, in our own time) when Jerusalem and the Second Temple were destroyed and a great number of the Jews were forcibly exiled from their land. But the biblical record in its original Hebrew remained intact, and the Jews carried it with them to whichever country they had wandered. This 'portable homeland', as they called it, was to preserve the special identity of the Jewish people ever after.

Throughout almost the entire 1st millennium BC, the Old Testament was known only in Hebrew and only to the Jews. (Jesus, for example, and his contemporary followers had studied the Bible in Hebrew.) In the third century BC, a start was made on the translation of the Old Testament into Greek, at the initiative of the Alexandrian Jewish community and with the blessing of the Egyptian ruler, Ptolemy II Philadelphus. It was called the Septuagint. This was the first translation, and the only one in existence for the next 400 years. Then came additional translations, notably into Syriac and Coptic. These were followed by several Latin versions, which contained, however, textual corruptions. Since the Old Testament, together with the New, constituted the Bible of the Christian Church, the ecclesiastical authorities resolved towards the end of the fourth century AD that a uniform and reliable text should be prepared on which it could base its teaching. The project was entrusted to the scholarly Saint Jerome, who was then living and working in Bethlehem, and who possessed the required mastery of Greek and Hebrew. Basing himself on the original Hebrew and on the Septuagint, he produced the standard Latin translation, commonly known as the Vulgate. Translations into other languages followed, and the numbers mounted as century followed century, making the Bible the most translated work. Today, it appears in almost every language and dialect in the world, including such exotic tongues as Chinese and Sanskrit, Japanese and American Indian. (In one American Indian dialect, Cherokee, it is said that the tribal chief, Sequovah, devised a special alphabet for the translation and printing of parts of the Bible.)

Thus it was that the story of biblical thought, life and times

An Old Testament page in Icelandic. The Bible has been translated into almost every language.

15

became the most widely known work ever to appear in the history of man. One of the results is that the major biblical characters, places and events have become part of the cultural landscape of hundreds of millions of people in the world. The pious and the non-believer alike have heard of Abraham, of Moses and Joshua, David and Solomon, Isaiah and Jeremiah. They have heard of the Exodus, of the 'parting of the Red Sea', of the Ten Commandments. They have heard of Jerusalem and Jericho and the river Jordan, though they may not know exactly where they are. It is natural, therefore, that there should be more popular as well as scholarly interest in biblical archaeology than in excavations carried out in any other land.

If the idea of digging up the land of the Bible crossed anyone's mind early in the last century, it was no doubt dismissed as a futile undertaking. Where and how would the archaeologists start their search? They would know what to look for, but where would they look? Most of the places which had been the scenes of historic events no longer existed outside the pages of the Bible. They had vanished long ago, destroyed, later re-settled, again wiped out, eventually abandoned, and are now covered by the dust and debris of millennia; their exact locations, and often their names, are forgotten.

They had been known for more than 1,000 years BC and right up to AD 70 by the Jewish inhabitants of the land. But with the Roman conquest in that year following the bitter five-year Roman–Jewish war, with widespread destruction of cities and villages, and the exile of Jewish survivors, most of the biblical Hebrew names were buried with the decimated sites, echoed only through the lips of Jews at prayer wherever they were. Moreover, in the year AD 135, at the instigation of Rome's emperor Hadrian, many city-names were changed from the Hebrew in an attempt to erase all trace of Jewry's connection with its land. Even the name of Jerusalem was changed to Aelia Capitolina, and this lasted until the fourth century AD when it was restored by the emperor Constantine. Hadrian also eradicated the Hebrew name of the land of Israel and Judah, calling it Palestine, after the Philistines who had harried the Israelite tribes a millennium earlier, and this name stuck. Further name-changes occurred after the successive imperial conquests in subsequent centuries.

Thus, the scholars of 150 years ago were faced with a large number of unknowns. They knew, of course, about the general geography of biblical Israel from descriptions in the Bible. They knew its conspicuous natural features, the principal mountains and valleys, lakes and rivers. They knew them by their biblical names, and they knew their locations. They could do the same with the outstanding biblical cities, notably Jerusalem, but also landmark sites like Acre and Jaffa, Jericho and Hebron; for though they had dwindled in size and population since early Israelite times, these cities had enjoyed a continuous history of settled habitation.

But what of the countless other sites where the drama of significant biblical events had been enacted but which had long ceased to exist? Where exactly was Shiloh, which had held the Ark of the Law in the twelfth and eleventh centuries BC, had been the principal meeting place of the Israelite tribal confederacy which preceded the monarchy, and which had thereafter lain desolate for some 3,000 years? Where was Hazor, which had been a formidable strategic city in Upper Galilee, the 'head of all those kingdoms' in those times, where Joshua fought the key battle in his northern campaign? No-one had lived on the site for more than two millennia, and there was now no trace of it. How could one start digging when there was no apparent surface sign of where it had been? What of Gezer, one of the chariot cities built by king Solomon, which had lasted right down to the first century BC and been abandoned thereafter? Where was Megiddo, scene of so many biblical and post-biblical battles that its name was perpetuated in the corrupted form of apocalyptic Armageddon? Where exactly was the Judean town of Lachish, so important in biblical times that its destruction was the subject of a grim but illuminating wall relief in the palace of the victorious Sennacherib at Nineveh? Where were Samaria, Beth-shan, Ashkelon, Gath, Dan, and the host of other places which figure prominently in the biblical record and which could yield the secrets of their past to the spade of the archaeologist if only he knew where to dig.

Not that the scholars were ignorant of the general whereabouts of these sites. They knew from the biblical accounts the regions in which they were situated. But this was hardly enough. A single region might once have held hundreds of flourishing townlets and villages, but centuries of erosion and neglect had long turned it into a barren stretch of desolation, unmarked by human activity. How, then, would the archaeologist determine the site of special biblical interest he was anxious to excavate?

It must be remembered, too, that cities in the biblical age were nowhere near as large as they are today. Even a modest modern metropolis sprawls over several miles. In early times, an important town would be confined to less than fifty acres, so it was essential for the biblical archaeologist to be able virtually to pinpoint the buried city he sought to unearth. This was infinitely more difficult than the task that will face the general archaeologist in America or

The parting of the Red Sea, one of the Old Testament episodes depicted in relief on a Christian sarcophagus now in the Lateran Museum in Rome.

any European country in the year 4980. Let us suppose – hopefully, an unlikely example – that medium-sized towns like England's Manchester, France's Lyons or Houston, Texas, are wiped out in the course of the next 1,000 years and never re-settled; that the records of the period have, however, been saved and preserved, as with Israel and the Bible; and that 2,000 years later, an archaeologist arrives in the desolate region in search of the past. He will be able to sink his spade anywhere within a radius of ten to twenty miles in this wilderness with the reasonable assurance of unearthing some artefact or ruin of today's metropolis.

The early biblical explorer was not so favoured. His target area was small and the region in which it was set was extensive. Thus, unless he had good grounds for thinking that he could identify its exact location, he could spend a lifetime on a hit-or-miss probing of the area and strike nothing.

Clearly, the prerequisite of biblical archaeology was the identification of the sites. But how was this to be done when they bore no apparent external signs, and when in fact their specific identity would be established – or questioned – only after excavation?

The answer was given by an American of prodigious scholarship 150 years ago: the process of site-identification would begin with theoretical deduction based on all the available written sources, and this would be followed by exploration. The man was Edward Robinson, a Connecticut Yankee with a passion for learning and doing. He was born in Southington in 1794 to a clergyman-farmer and raised on the Bible in a home where it was said 'the intellectual and the practical were closely linked'. In the year 1838, at the age of forty-four, he set forth on a journey to the Holy Land equipped

18

with telescope, thermometer, compass and measuring tape, an
all-embracing mastery of biblical studies, copies of the Bible in
English, Hebrew, Greek and Latin, sharp eyes and critical judgement. His principal object was to prepare a work on the physical
geography of Palestine and the identification of biblical sites.

The result of his pioneer researches, published three years later
and hailed by his contemporaries as 'epoch-making', was to lay the
foundations for modern archaeology in the Holy Land. Even
though he did some probing but no actual excavation, it was he
who told the future scholarly diggers where to look – and how.

2 The Devout Sceptic

IT WAS A happy conjunction of paradoxical human qualities that led Edward Robinson to his scientific breakthrough, the rediscovery of biblical geography. If the combination of intellectual and man of action was unusual, more so was faith and doubt – and Robinson was both believer and sceptic. He believed devoutly in the authenticity of the biblical narrative; but he applied a sternly critical mind towards everything written about the land of the Bible subsequent to Scriptural times. It was this above all that fired his ambition to visit Palestine, check the facts for himself, and perhaps discover on the spot the answers he could not find in the books.

Strange, too, how Robinson, frail as a youth, found the physical capacity in middle age to tackle the gruelling hardships of exploration in the primitive Palestine of the first half of the last century. It took tough physique, stamina, endurance and a cool head to meet the trials and danger of covering long stretches over rough terrain on camel, horse and foot through lawless regions controlled by corrupt and un-neighbourly petty chieftains. Yet Robinson rose admirably to the arduous challenge, and recalled, with wry amusement, that as a boy on his father's farm – clergymen in those days received slender stipends, and Robinson senior supplemented his income by farming – the delicate young Edward was spared the hard physical chores and set to weaving, a skill at which he became expert. But already in those youthful years he showed signs of the persistence which was to mark his later work of topographic investigation, when he exploited every minute of the day. He was a druggist's assistant and part-time teacher in his teens, law clerk and tutor in mathematics and Greek upon graduation, and farm manager and editor of classical translations in his early twenties.

He then resolved to give himself over completely to biblical studies. His first step was to master the Bible in its original tongue.

OPPOSITE David slays Goliath, one of Lorenzo Ghiberti's fifteenth-century bronze reliefs of biblical scenes on the door of the Baptistry in Florence known as the 'Gate of Paradise'. It was Robinson who identified the vale of Elah where the duel took place.

He left the farm to learn Hebrew for two years under a celebrated Hebraist, Professor Moses Stuart, at the Theological Seminary of Andover, Massachusetts. He was taught the language there for the next three years; travelled to Germany to study with the famed biblical scholar, orientalist and lexicographer Heinrich Friedrich Wilhelm Gesenius [1786–1842]; returned to full-time study and academic work in America; and was appointed professor of biblical literature at New York's Union Theological Seminary in 1837. Before taking up his new teaching duties, he insisted on making the journey of exploration that was to give him a permanent niche in the history of biblical scholarship.

He set sail in July 1837, sojourned in England, Germany, Italy and Greece for meetings with fellow scholars on his route east, proceeded to Egypt, crossed the Sinai peninsula to Akaba, turned north to Beersheba, then on to Hebron, and arrived in Jerusalem in April 1838. After a complete tour of Judea, he continued northwards through Samaria to Nazareth, Tiberias and the Jordan valley, traversed Galilee, and arrived in Beirut two months later. He made a second journey in 1852, also for two months, and concentrated his investigations this time on Galilee and Samaria. This resulted in considerable additions to the material gathered on his first journey which had been published in 1841.

Despite their comparative brevity, the two journeys yielded a prodigious volume of scholarly and hitherto unknown data which was to prove so important to the later surveys and archaeological excavation of the country. Numerous biblical sites, missed or inaccurately located by travellers during the previous fifteen centuries, were identified by Robinson. That he discovered so much in so short a time was due to his wide-ranging scholarship, his faculty for remembering all he had read, and, in no small measure, to the industrious way in which he pursued his task. He observed every detail of topographic interest; inspected and measured the remains he came across of every ancient building, wall, pool, well, aqueduct which might prove useful clues to the past; and no matter how long the distance he had covered nor how fatiguing the day, he would never retire to bed before writing up his notes. And very full and illuminating notes they were. In proposing the identification of a site, he would give a brief account of its history and biblical context, describe its location and surroundings, give the reasoning behind his proposal, and comment critically on its mention in – or absence from – the writings of the more reputable of the early travellers.

An example of the way he went about his task, and of the physical effort and scholarly resources it demanded, may be seen from his account of a minor discovery. This was his exploration

Edward Robinson, the Connecticut Yankee who began it all. His pioneer work in locating long-lost cities of the Bible laid the foundations for biblical archaeology.

The entrance to the Siloam
Tunnel, the aqueduct built by
king Hezekiah at the end of
the eighth century BC to bring
water into the city of
Jerusalem.

23

of what turned out to be the subterranean aqueduct in Jerusalem constructed by king Hezekiah at the end of the eighth century BC. In his notes written after his preliminary visit to the tunnel, Robinson first presented the biblical references to it, and the historical background. It is recorded in 2 Kings 20:20 that Hezekiah 'made a pool, and a conduit, and brought water into the city'; and 2 Chronicles 32:30 states; 'This same Hezekiah also stopped the upper watercourse of Gihon, and brought it straight down to the west side of the city of David.' The Gihon spring, which has always been Jerusalem's main source of water, lay in the Kidron valley just outside the city wall. It was thus vulnerable to a besieger, who could cut off the water supply – and Jerusalem at the time of Hezekiah was threatened by Assyrian invaders. To safeguard Jerusalem's water source, the king constructed this underground aqueduct, which carried the water from Gihon by gravity flow beneath the city ramparts and into a depression inside the city which would serve as a reservoir. This reservoir was the 'pool' he made, fed by the 'conduit', and it was known as the Pool of Siloam [Shiloah, in Hebrew].

Robinson recalled in his notes, that 'the Son of Sirach' [Ben-Sirah, in Hebrew] – the third-century BC author of the Apocryphal Book of Ecclesiasticus – 'also informs us that "Hezekiah strengthened his city, and brought in water into the midst of it; he dug with iron into the rock, and built fountains for the waters"' (Ecclesiasticus 48:17). Robinson adds that 'Josephus also mentions the fountain of Gihon.'

Continuing his preamble to the account of his actual exploration of the tunnel, Robinson says that after the reference by historian Josephus in the first century AD, there is no word of it for the next millennium and a half, not indeed until it is 'mentioned by Quaresmius, writing about AD 1625. He relates the unsuccessful attempt of his friend Vinhouen to explore it.... But he gives no definite information respecting the canal [the tunnel]. . . . The canal seems to have been again forgotten, or at least overlooked, for another century.' He adds that four other travellers whose writings he had read, 'Monconys, Doubdan, Le Brun, and Maundrell, all of whom were no careless observers, are wholly silent as to its existence. . . . Slight and imperfect notices of it again appear in the eighteenth century, and more in the nineteenth. All these, however, are . . . confused and unsatisfactory.'

Robinson was determined to be neither confused nor unsatisfactory. Recalling the references in his reading, making enquiries among the local peasants, and hearing from them that 'a passage existed quite through between the two fountains' – the Gihon and the Pool of Siloam – he and his companion decided 'to examine it

OPPOSITE ABOVE A wall relief from the palace of Sennacherib in ancient Nineveh, discovered by Britain's Austen Henry Layard in 1849, showing the Assyrian emperor receiving booty from the Judean city of Lachish shortly after its capture.

OPPOSITE BELOW The prophet Jeremiah depicted on a medieval German medallion. Jeremiah's warnings on the eve of the destruction of Judah were echoed in the sixth-century BC 'Letters of Lachish' discovered by British archaeologist John Llewelyn Starkey in 1935,

ourselves, should a fit opportunity occur'. It occurred on the afternoon of 27 April 1838, and in the notes Robinson wrote later that night, he recorded that they went 'to Siloam, in order to measure the reservoir . . . and the water in the basin being low, we embraced this opportunity for accomplishing our purpose. Stripping off our shoes and stockings and rolling our garments above our knees we entered with our lights and measuring tapes in our hands. The water was low, nowhere over a foot in depth. . . . The bottom is everywhere covered with sand, brought in by the waters. The passage is cut wholly through the solid rock, everywhere about two feet wide; somewhat winding, but in a general course NNE. For the first hundred feet, it is fifteen to twenty feet high . . . gradually becoming lower and lower as we advanced. At the end of 800 feet, it became so low, that we could advance no further without crawling on all fours, and bringing our bodies close to the water. As we were not prepared for this, we thought it better to retreat, and try again another day from the other end. Tracing therefore upon the roof with the smoke of our candles the initials of our names and the figures 800, as a mark of our progress on this side, we returned with our clothes somewhat wet and soiled.'

It was not until 'three days afterwards (30 April), that we were able to complete our examination and measurement of the passage'. This time they decided to start from the Gihon spring:

. . . and having measured the external distance (1,100 feet) down to the point east of Siloam, we concluded that as we had already entered 800 feet from the lower end, there could now remain not over three or four hundred feet to be explored. We found the end of the passage at the upper fountain [Gihon] rudely built up with small loose stones. . . . Having caused our servants to clear away these stones, and having clothed (or rather unclothed) ourselves simply in a pair of wide Arab drawers, we entered and crawled on, hoping soon to arrive at the point which we had reached from the other fountain [Siloam]. The passage here is in general much lower than at the other end; most of the way we could indeed advance upon our hands and knees; yet in several places we could only get forward by lying at full length and dragging ourselves along on our elbows. . . .

There are here many turns and zigzags. . . . The way seemed interminably long. . . . But at length, after having measured 950 feet, we arrived at our former mark of 800 feet traced with smoke upon the ceiling. This makes the whole length of the passage to be 1,750 feet; or several hundred feet greater than the direct distance externally – a result scarcely conceivable, although the passage is very winding. We came out again at the fountain of Siloam.

Particularly remarkable in the light of a later discovery is Robinson's theory as to how the tunnel had been excavated by Hezekiah's quarrymen. He had discerned while crawling through

PREVIOUS PAGES The first-century BC structure built by king Herod, with additions from later periods, above the traditional site of the Cave of Machpelah, tomb of the biblical Patriarchs.

OPPOSITE Remains of the city gate built in the tenth century BC by king Solomon at Megiddo.

29

the conduit that the chisel strokes in the southern half ran in the opposite direction to those in the northern half. He had also noticed that 'at the upper end, the work was carried along' on one level, and 'at the lower end, the excavation would seem to have been begun on a higher level' and later corrected. He therefore reached the conclusion that: 'In constructing this passage, it is obvious that the workmen commenced at both ends, and met somewhere in the middle.'

His theory was dramatically confirmed by pure chance forty-two years later. On a hot day in June in 1880, some Jerusalem school-boys were cooling off in the Pool of Siloam when one of them ventured into the conduit, waded along for some distance, slipped, and fell into the water. As he rose, groping around for support, his hand touched a smooth surface in the otherwise rough rocky wall of the tunnel near the water level, and it had strange markings cut into it. (It had probably been submerged when Robinson had gone through and had thus escaped his observant eye.) The boy's story reached the ears of a local German missionary and archaeology enthusiast, who promptly went to the conduit,

The interior of Hezekiah's tunnel. Robinson and his companion, often 'crawling on all fours' through the slime, were the first to examine and measure the 1,750-foot rock-hewn passage which had been quarried more than 2,500 years earlier to ensure Jerusalem's water supply in time of siege.

The Siloam inscription, written in classical Hebrew on a wall of the tunnel to mark its completion, describes the novel way in which the engineering feat was accomplished.

inspected the markings and realized that they were ancient writing. Some of the lines were still under water, so the level was lowered by cleaning the bottom of the tunnel, and the missionary and others then copied the markings by candle-light, made a squeeze and a plaster cast, and brought them to the attention of the scholarly world.

On examination by experts, these markings were found to be part of an inscription in classical Hebrew prose. The language style, script and content pointed to its having been written during the period which covered the reign of king Hezekiah. The words were inscribed on a prepared surface of the rock, like the surface of a tablet. The top part of the inscription was missing, but six lines remained, enough to tell the story of how the tunnel had been dug – as Robinson had surmised – by two teams of miners starting at opposite ends, working towards each other and meeting near the middle. It is now known as the Siloam inscription. In its standard English translation it reads as follows:

... when the tunnel was driven through. And this was the way in which it was cut through: – while ... were still ... axes, each man toward his fellow, and while there were still three cubits to be cut through, there was heard the voice of a man calling to his fellow, for there was an overlap in the rock on the right and on the left. And when the tunnel was driven through, the quarrymen hewed the rock, each man toward his fellow, axe against axe; and the water flowed from the spring toward the reservoir for 1,200 cubits, and the height of the rock above the heads of the quarrymen was 100 cubits.

31

When he is describing the re-discovery of long-forgotten biblical sites, like Hezekiah's tunnel, Robinson shows a satisfying surprise and no derision whatsoever at the failure of the more learned of his predecessors to spot them. But he is less tolerant of geographical inaccuracy and unfounded surmise; and an uncritical acceptance by the gullible of what he considers pure fantasy or fabrication finds him positively abrasive. This is especially true when he examines the basis for the supposed location of venerated Christian sites in the country. Here he seems to be moved by an infinite faith in God but little in man, including man committed to the service of the Lord, the local priesthood, custodians of holy places.

It was to Jerusalem in particular that he brought what was perhaps the single major fault in an otherwise unexceptionable scientific objectivity: a marked prejudice against the Roman Catholic and Eastern clergy, which sprang no doubt from the austere puritanism of his New England upbringing. This was certainly a grave scholarly lapse; but it may conceivably have sharpened the cutting edge of his scepticism and prompted meticulous investigation to establish factual accuracy.

There was indeed much that needed establishing. While devouring the available literature on the land of the Bible in his earlier days, Robinson had been struck by its severe limitations. The information was inadequate, incomplete, riddled with inconsistencies, and much was of doubtful authenticity. Chiefly to blame, he thought, were the pilgrim journals, with their tales and legends that 'the monks and churchmen' in Palestine had been relaying to visitors for centuries as gospel truth. But even the useful contributions of the few reputable travellers whom he respected had left him with questions which were not satisfactorily explained.

He had long known why the information was incomplete. While the highways of the Holy Land were well trodden, the byways had largely been lost to sight and memory since the mass exile of the Jews from their land in the first century AD. And many of the sites which had been the scenes of dramatic biblical episodes lay along these forgotten byways. There had been some serious early attempts to recover them, notably in the fourth century by bishop Eusebius of Caesarea, in his compilation of biblical topography, the *Onomasticon*, and by Saint Jerome, who expanded and translated it from Greek to Latin in that century. Robinson thought well of these works, for they had been written not by visiting pundits on brief stays but by scholars who lived in the land, and who gave the location of biblical sites and a description of their condition which he said were 'of the highest importance'. But even Eusebius and Jerome were writing after a gap of three centuries, and so, says

Robinson, their findings 'can be regarded in an historical respect only as a record of the traditions current in their day'. And some of those traditions were manifestly false, even though they were so much closer in time to the biblical events. An outstanding example is Jerome's mistaken location of the two hills, one of 'blessing' and one of 'cursing', where Joshua assembled the Israelite tribes, in accordance with the words of Moses: 'These shall stand upon mount Gerizim to bless the people' who follow the Lord's commandments, 'And these shall stand upon mount Ebal to curse' those who disobey. Jerome put the mounts near Jericho. They are in fact on either side of biblical Shechem (near today's Nablus).

Nevertheless, Robinson acknowledges that the traditions in the time of Eusebius and Jerome 'were then in general far less corrupted than in the lapse of subsequent centuries'. And he cites 'ecclesiastical tradition' as the reason for the 'corruption' that continued over the next 1,500 years. The 'carriers' were the Christian pilgrims. Pilgrimage had started soon after the launching of the formidable church-building programme by Constantine the Great, the first Roman emperor to shed paganism and adopt Christianity. He raised it from the status of a faith of scattered minority groups to the official religion of his empire, and thereby did much to secure its future. But it was his mother, queen Helena, who conceived the plan of commemorative Christian monuments in the Holy Land – three centuries after the death of Jesus – which attract believers and non-believers the world over to this day.

Helena had met bishop Macarius of Jerusalem by chance at a convocation of the first ecumenical council of the Christian Church convened by Constantine at Nicaea (in today's Turkey) and was much moved by his words. The bishop told her of the sorry state of the faith in the land of its birth, and urged that the noblest act to further the new religion would be to mark, commemorate and preserve the sites hallowed by Jesus. A year later, with the blessings of her son, Helena journeyed to Jerusalem, and together with Macarius determined – arbitrarily, thought Robinson – the locations where Jesus had been crucified and buried. They decided that the two sites were close to each other, and over them Constantine built a great basilica, the Church of the Holy Sepulchre, which became the most sacred shrine in Christendom.

It was indeed an impressive edifice. No expense had been spared. In a letter to bishop Macarius commissioning the building, Constantine had written:

It is fitting that your sagacity do so order and make provision for everything necessary, that not only shall this basilica be the finest in the world, but that the details also shall be such that all the fairest structures in every city may be surpassed by it. . . .

33

From Jerusalem, queen Helena and bishop Macarius went to Bethlehem, and determined the site of the grotto where Jesus was born. Constantine's erection of the Church of the Nativity followed.

These two magnificent shrines quickly drew pilgrims from afar. To provide accommodation and prayer halls for them and for the growing Christian community, wealthy Christians followed Constantine's example and built monasteries, convents, hospices, churches and chapels in and around Jerusalem, Bethlehem, the Judean desert, and Galilee, on sites thought to have been those mentioned in the New Testament as having an association with Jesus. Each in turn found its place on the itinerary of later pilgrims.

The cloisters in the Church of the Nativity in Bethlehem, on the site of the original fourth-century structure built by Constantine.

With the pilgrims came the stories. Robinson, reading the pilgrim journals, thought he knew how the legends had been created, nurtured, and embellished in the repetition, and had become fixed traditions as the centuries rolled by. The pilgrims were lodged in the monasteries and hospices, and came under the care of local monks, who also served as local guides. Not all were scholarly; not a few were credulous, almost none doubted his own omniscience. The response 'I don't know' was not part of their vocabulary. They were there to satisfy the curiosity of the pilgrims, and no-one was left unsatisfied. The visitors insisted on being shown exactly where all the events in the Gospels had happened, and who better than the local ecclesiastical guides to tell them? They had no need to ask about the sites of Calvary and the Resurrection, for these were marked by the Church of the Holy Sepulchre. But where was Gethsemane? Where had the judgement of Jesus taken place? Could they please be shown the spot where Pontius Pilate had stood? What was the route along which Jesus had borne the Cross?

It seemed evident to Robinson that when pressed by such questions, the early monks resorted to invention, and their utterances were passed on by their successors with fervent conviction. Such, for example, was the reply given by a religious dragoman in the fifth century to a pilgrim who had asked the significance of a depression he had noticed in a stone in Jerusalem. He was told that it was made by the palm of Jesus when he stopped for a moment and supported himself against it on his grim journey to Calvary.

The pilgrims left the Holy Land with their hearts filled with awe and their heads with wondrous tales which they relayed to their families and friends when they got home. Some of them kept diaries, wrote journals, committed to published paper all they had heard from their mentors, for the edification of other Christians and as guides to future travellers. The stories would be repeated in the successive travel accounts by later pilgrims. Thus had traditions beome more deeply rooted as time flowed on.

Actually, much of the pilgrim writing makes enchanting reading for the layman; but it was of little use to Robinson the scholar and offensive to Robinson the puritan. Arriving in Palestine, he found his earlier scepticism bitterly confirmed, and he railed against 'the righteous quacks' who purveyed the material which found its way into the travel journals, charging them with 'mistaken piety . . . credulous superstition, not unmingled with pious fraud'. The fourth century, he pointed out, had 'been particularly fruitful . . . in the dressing out of the traditions or rather legends', and thereafter, it 'became a passion among the multitudes of priests and monks' to hand them on, so that 'the inventions of succeeding ages continued upon these foundations'. Thus, 'all the reports and accounts ... have come to us from the same impure source'. This led the devoutly religious Robinson with the biblical text as his anchor, to the sweeping conclusion that: 'All ecclesiastical tradition respecting in and around Jerusalem and throughout Palestine IS OF NO VALUE, except so far as it is supported by circumstances known to us from the Scriptures or from other contemporary testimony.' The capitals are his, and the whole sentence appears in italics!

Robinson the linguistic scholar was able to discern another tradition, largely ignored, which he thought could be a key to the identification of biblical sites: the preservation of ancient place-names on the lips of the common people. This, he said, was 'a truly national and native tradition' which was

not derived in any degree from the influence of foreign convents or masters, but drawn in by the peasant with his mother's milk, and deeply seated in the genius of the Semitic languages. The [biblical] Hebrew names of places continued in their Aramaic form long after the times of the New Testament; and maintained themselves ... in spite of the efforts made by Greeks and Romans to supplant them by others derived from their own tongues.

There were many such failed efforts. The Old Testament town of Lod became Diospolis under the Romans in the year AD 200, but the inhabitants preserved the original Hebrew name in the slightly modified Lydda. Acco was renamed Ptolemais in the third century AD – the Ptolemais of Paul in the New Testament – but soon reverted to the similar-sounding Acca or Acre. Emmaus became Nicopolis, also in the third century AD, but was preserved as Imwas. Kfar Saba for a time bore the name Antipatris. Beth-shan had been renamed Scythopolis. Most of 'the high-sounding names' given to these sites in Hellenistic and Roman times, said Robinson, 'have perished', disappearing with the fall of the Roman government, while the original Hebrew names 'which they were intended to supplant, are still current among the people'. Only two have remained: Nablus, which is a corruption of the Greek Neapolis, for biblical Schechem; and Sabastiye, from the Greek Sebastos.

The fact is that Greek names were just as difficult to pronounce and transcribe by the local population as was their language by the Seleucid and Roman occupiers; but the inhabitants had no such difficulty with Hebrew names, for the language they spoke was Aramaic, and Aramaic and Hebrew were cognate Semitic tongues. The alphabet, basic grammar, roots and even the sounds were very similar. Moreover, many elements of Hebrew, including the geographic names of the country, had long been absorbed into the

Aramaic spoken in Palestine. Thus, even after the mass expulsion of the Jews, the original Hebrew place-names could always be recognized in their Aramaic form.

Aramaic continued to be spoken for some time after the Moslem conquest in the seventh century AD before it was finally superseded by Arabic. But Arabic, too, was a kindred Semitic tongue, and this language had also absorbed much of Aramaic, as Aramaic had drawn on much of Hebrew. The word 'one', for example, is 'achad' in Hebrew and 'wachad' in Arabic; 'five' is 'hamisha' and 'hamsa' respectively; 'king' is 'melech' and 'malik'; and 'peace' is 'shalom' in Hebrew and 'salaam' in Arabic. It is easy to see, therefore, that many a biblical Hebrew place-name would be echoed in its Aramaic and later in its Arabic form right up to Robinson's time. And indeed, Robinson discerned on his travels in the country that the ancient Hebrew names which had 'found a ready entrance' first into Aramaic and then into Arabic 'have thus lived on upon the lips of the Arabs, whether Christian or Muslim, townsmen or Bedouin, even unto our own day, almost in the same form in which they have also been transmitted to us in the Hebrew Scriptures'.

Why had this tradition of the native nomenclature been overlooked, its existence almost unknown? Robinson says it was largely because most travellers were unfamiliar with the Arabic tongue, could therefore communicate with the local people only 'through the medium of illiterate interpreters', and also because they 'mostly followed only beaten paths'. Curiously enough, though this had always been true of the whole of Palestine, it began to be less true of the territory east of the Jordan at the beginning of the nineteenth century. Only a few years before Robinson's first visit, two pioneer explorers, both with a good knowledge of Arabic, had used this method of gathering information from the local inhabitants to identify ancient sites. They were Ulrich Jasper Seetzen, a German botanist, who had travelled extensively in Arabia and had also spent some time in eastern Palestine. The other was a Swiss orientalist, Johann Ludwig Burckhardt, who was able to learn much in his travels through the Arabian territories by wearing Arab dress and appearing as a Moslem under the name of Sheikh Ibrahim Ibn Abdullah. Robinson knew of their work and makes suitable acknowledgment, but adds that their methods were not followed in western Palestine until he himself applied them.

Robinson was able to get to know, appreciate the value and make use of native traditions by his happy choice of travelling companion, the Reverend Eli Smith, an American Protestant missionary based in Beirut. Smith, a friend and former pupil of Robinson, knew Arabic, was familiar with the ways of the native population and had a taste for geographical and historical research. He was also well acquainted with the onerous conditions of oriental travel at the time, as he had shortly before made extensive journeys to Persia and Armenia. He was as enthusiastic as Robinson himself about recovering the geography of Palestine, and had in fact noted down the place-names used by the local population wherever he had travelled on his missionary duties.

After completing their investigations in known centres like Jerusalem, Jericho, Hebron, Gaza, they would find out from the local people by what names they referred to the villages, ruined sites, streams, hills, and any other notable feature in the surrounding districts. They would then consult the Bible, their basic geographic guide, and if what they had been told was compatible with the biblical clues, they would set off on their horses to explore the byways, carefully recording times, compass bearings, temperatures and special features of the passing terrain as they rode to their targets.

They were aware of course of the danger of clinging fast to the language tradition. The conservation of ancient place-names in modern speech was not iron-clad. If the local Arabs called a village by a name which sounded like one in the Bible, it could not be assumed automatically that this was indeed the authentic location of that particular biblical site. There had to be corroborative evidence – the context of the biblical reference, Robinson's own topographic reasoning, a comparison of the recorded with the observed terrain, hints in the works of early scholars like Josephus, Eusebius, Jerome, or a casual description in the journal of a later pilgrim. Where such evidence existed, the local names could help to clinch a theory.

In acknowledging the debt to his companion for the important results of their researches, Robinson refers particularly to Eli Smith's 'tact in eliciting and sifting the information to be obtained from an Arab population'. When they spoke to the peasants in out-of-the-way villages, they framed their questions carefully and always bore in mind, as Robinson put it, that the 'amiable' Arab, encountering a foreign visitor, would usually give the answer he thought would please. They gave no hint of the biblical sites they sought, but, using the oblique approach, would elicit the current place-names in the region. Robinson indicates that he and Smith were like lawyers cross-examining a witness, but it was all done in a seemingly casual and unhurried way, characteristic of oriental meetings.

The talk may have been unhurried, but the results often saved time. After collecting the local names of several hamlets and ruins in the vicinity of Hebron for example, they compared them with

OPPOSITE Robinson's Arch, the name given to the stone projection from the western wall of Jerusalem's Temple compound which Robinson correctly identified as the springer to an arch built by Herod. But he mistook its function, a rare error detected only recently by archaeologists.

38

the long list of settlements within 'the inheritance of the tribe of the children of Judah' given in the Book of Joshua (Chapter 15) and found several which clearly bore the Arabic equivalent of the biblical sites. They then went to the top of a hill to the east of the city, looked down upon the area which contained these sites, marked their locations, and thereby, in a single session, added eight to the list of recognized biblical sites. These included 'Jattir, and Socoh. . . . And Anab, and Eshtemoh, and Anim' (Joshua 15:48, 50). Some had found no mention in any of the records since those of Jerome in the fourth century. A few had been marked on an early nineteenth-century map but without biblical identification.

Robinson and Smith had equally quick results in a similar way with more important sites a few hours' ride north and north-east of Jerusalem, providing a firmly based identification of such places as Anathoth, birthplace of the prophet Jeremiah, which also figures in Joshua; Gibeah, the family village of Saul, the first king of Israel; and Bethel, which figures frequently in Genesis, Joshua and Judges. They also identified Beth-shemesh, where the Ark of the Law was returned after its capture by the Philistines in the eleventh century BC; the vale of Elah where David fought his duel with Goliath; and the site of ancient Shiloh. And they were only a short distance off the exact location – as was later established – of Hebrew Megiddo. This is the commanding strategic site at the entrance to the valley of Jezreel which was the scene of countless biblical battles, and which is perpetuated in the corrupted Armageddon (from the Hebrew *Har Megiddo*, the mount of Megiddo).

Robinson is best known to the general public for his brilliant identification of a stone projection a few yards south of the Western Wall of Jerusalem's Temple compound, called to this day Robinson's Arch. It was of course noticed by previous travellers; but Robinson was the first to see that it was the springer to an arch, and that it supported a bridge mentioned by Josephus as having connected the Temple to the Upper City across the Tyropoean valley. (A few years ago, at Jerusalem's dramatic archaeological excavations directed by Professor Binyamin Mazar in the south-western corner of the Temple compound, further remains were found of this arch; but it was established that what it supported was not a bridge but a broad platform at the entrance to one of the western gates to the Temple mount, which was reached by a monumental staircase supported by a series of smaller arches.)

Robinson also recognized the remains of certain ancient structures of uncommon architectural design as ancient synagogues. It was he who spotted a ruin on the northern shore of the Sea of Galilee, known locally as Tel Hum, as the synagogue Capernaum (from the Hebrew *Kfar Nahum*) where Jesus was said to have preached one Sabbath (Mark 1:21; John 6:59). The identification of this site was confirmed by archaeological excavations carried out in 1905 by H. Kohl and C. Watzinger, and the structure was found to be one of the best preserved of the early Galilean synagogues.

There is a revealing episode recorded in Robinson's notes which shows the ingenuity and persistence with which he pursued a clue to confirm an identification. Exploring the southern part of the western fringe of the Judean hills, and after discovering biblical Maresha, one of the cities fortified by king Rehoboam in the tenth century BC, Robinson reached the ruins of a site with the local name of Bet Jibrin. This immediately suggested the preservation in its Arabic form of the original Hebrew Beth Guvrin, a village which rose to prominence in the Roman period after the decline of neighbouring Maresha. Robinson knew from the early Greek writings that Beth Guvrin had been converted into a fortified city, made the administrative centre of the region, and renamed Eleutheropolis in AD 200; but this name, like the other Hellenistic names, perished, while the original Hebrew name was preserved in the Aramaic and Arabic. Robinson was anxious to establish definitely whether this was or was not the site of Beth Guvrin-Eleutheropolis. He then remembered that Eusebius's *Onomasticon* had recorded that six miles from Eleutheropolis was a village called Yedhna. From talks with the local villagers Robinson and Smith gathered the names of sites in the region and among them was a hamlet called Idhna. This seemed close to the sound of Eusebius's Yedhna, so Robinson decided to test whether in fact this hamlet which nestled in the hills to the east of Beth Guvrin was indeed six miles away. He and Smith accordingly mounted their horses at six o'clock in the morning and set off towards Idhna. By the nature of the terrain they would be traversing, Robinson calculated that six miles on horseback without pause should take two hours to cover.

He wrote later, describing this scholarly adventure to test the soundness of his reasoning:

I know not when I have felt more the excitement of suspense, than while travelling this short distance. A question of some historical importance was depending on the circumstance whether we reached Idhna at eight o'clock. If so, our researches for the long-lost Eleutheropolis would be crowned with success; if not, we were again afloat and certain of nothing.

At 7.50 a.m. they came to the head of the valley, and as yet there was no sight of the hamlet. They began the ascent, and when they reached the top, 'the village lay before us, somewhat lower down on the other side, and precisely at eight o'clock we entered the place and dismounted at the house of the Sheikh'.

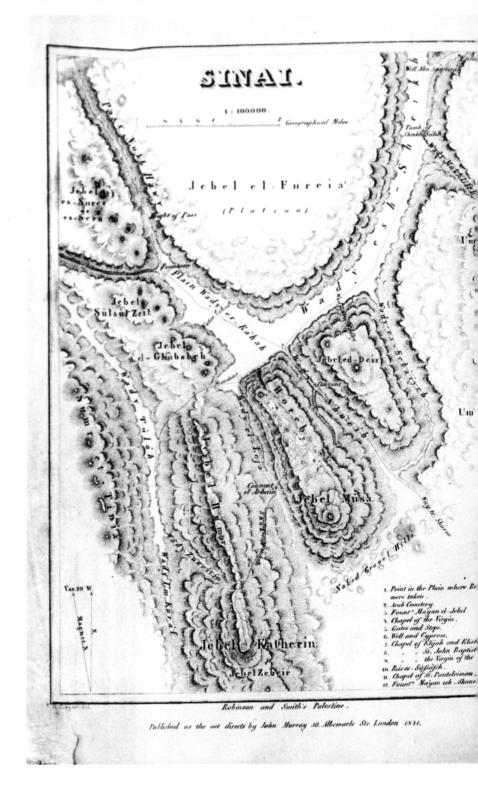

The title page of Volume I of Robinson's pioneer work, *Biblical Researches*.

BIBLICAL RESEARCHES

IN

PALESTINE,

MOUNT SINAI AND ARABIA PETRÆA.

A JOURNAL OF TRAVELS IN THE YEAR 1838,

BY

E. ROBINSON AND E. SMITH.

UNDERTAKEN IN REFERENCE TO BIBLICAL GEOGRAPHY.

DRAWN UP FROM THE ORIGINAL DIARIES, WITH HISTORICAL ILLUSTRATIONS,

BY EDWARD ROBINSON, D.D.

PROFESSOR OF BIBLICAL LITERATURE IN THE UNION THEOLOGICAL SEMINARY,
NEW YORK ;

AUTHOR OF A GREEK AND ENGLISH LEXICON OF THE NEW TESTAMENT,
ETC.

WITH NEW MAPS AND PLANS IN FIVE SHEETS.

VOL. I.

LONDON:
JOHN MURRAY, ALBEMARLE STREET.

MDCCCXLI.

Later surveys and actual excavations confirmed the accuracy of almost all the site-identifications by Robinson and Smith, and the debt to their researches is acknowledged by all subsequent scholarly explorers. There were three in particular, a German, a Frenchman and an Englishman, for whom Robinson's work served as a springboard, and whose own work in the next few years added thick scientific layers to the basis for the historical geography of Palestine established by the American pioneer. The first was Titus Tobler, whose careful investigations were to earn him the title of father of German Palestinian research, and who said of the studies of Robinson and Smith that they 'alone surpass the total of all previous contributions to Palestine geography from the time of Eusebius and Jerome to the early nineteenth century'. Curiously enough, Tobler started out as an amateur. As a young newly qualified doctor of medicine, he had made a pleasure trip to the Holy Land three years before Robinson, and was seized with the desire to explore it scientifically. He returned to Germany to equip himself for the task by plunging into all the literature on Palestine, and he was still at it when Robinson's three-volume *Researches* were published – they appeared simultaneously in English and German in 1841. As he read them, disappointed at first by the loss of the pioneer's crown, Tobler was enormously impressed by Robinson's discoveries and research methods, and heartened by the realization that much still remained to be done. He noted, for example, that puritan prejudice had kept Robinson from a thorough study of the venerated religious sites, and the brevity of his visit from a comprehensive survey. This is what he, Tobler, would do on extended explorations. A five-month visit to Palestine in 1845–6 resulted in the detailed recording of the topography of Jerusalem and its environs and the northern belt of Judea, with meticulous accounts of the construction and history of ruined and existing structures. His two volumes published in 1853 added to the current scientific knowledge of some seventy ancient sites. A third volume was the product of a lengthy exploration of Judea carried out in 1857.

Tobler's successor was France's H. V. Guérin, who carried out five scholarly campaigns, the first in 1852 and the last in 1875, which resulted in his massive seven-volume *Geographical, Historical and Archaeological Description of Palestine*, covering Judea, Samaria and Galilee. Though he did no digging, as did neither of his predecessors, he had an archaeological eye, and his detailed descriptions of the nature of the masonry, pillars and other building remains on the ancient ruined sites he spotted were to prove valuable clues to the archaeologists who came later.

It remained for the next explorer, England's Lieutenant Claude

Reignier Conder, heading an expeditionary team with ample time, resources and equipment, to carry out the most comprehensive surface exploration of the century, the monumental *Survey of Western Palestine*. The Palestine Exploration Fund had sent out the team to Palestine in 1871 under a Captain Stewart of the Royal Engineers, but he fell sick a few months later and was replaced by Conder in July 1872.

Accompanied by an archaeologist, an Arabic scholar, a sergeant and corporal as assistants, and the most advanced measuring instruments of the time, he criss-crossed the country, mapping and recording geographical information as he went. He had completed four-fifths of the survey by mid-1875 when he and his party ran into trouble, first from attacks by Arab brigands and soon after from an outbreak of cholera. They returned to England, and the exploration of the remaining area to be investigated was accomplished by Lieutenant Horatio Herbert Kitchener in 1877–8. This subaltern, who had joined Conder's team in 1874 at the age of twenty-four, would go on to make history as one of Britain's most illustrious soldiers. Indeed, so brilliant was his subsequent military record that it tended to overshadow his scholarly work on the historical geography of the Holy Land.

Many new identifications were proposed by Conder, and though a number were disputed, most were later confirmed by archaeologists. The great map he produced, published in 1880, covered an area of 6,000 square miles, from just beyond today's Lebanese frontier in the north to Sinai in the south, and from the river Jordan in the east to the Mediterranean in the west. It fixed the position of literally hundreds of ruined sites. It was now up to others, the archaeologists, to dig up the most promising of these sites, and confirm or question their biblical identification. On the completion of his enormous survey, Conder paid tribute to Robinson:

The results of his travels formed the groundwork of modern research, and showed how much could be done towards recovering the ancient topography. He proved that the old nomenclature clings to Palestine in an extraordinary manner and that in the memory of the peasant population the true sites have been preserved. . . . It is in his steps we have trod. With greater advantages, more time and more money, we have been able to more than double the number of his discoveries, but the cases in which we have found him wrong are few and far between.

One of the early biblical archaeologists, America's Frederick Jones Bliss, who carried out important excavations in Palestine in the 1890s, said this of the 'great quartet', Robinson, Tobler, Guérin and Conder:

The work of these four men shows a logical progression. Robinson established the correct principles of research. Tobler applied these more minutely, but over a limited geographical range. Guérin endeavoured with the same minuteness to cover the whole field – Judea, Samaria, Galilee – but was subjected to the limitations of an explorer travelling singly and with straitened resources. Conder, heading a survey expedition adequately manned and splendidly equipped, was enabled to fill in the numerous topographical lacunae left by his predecessors.

There was, however, a vital archaeological clue which all four either missed or ignored. This was the topographical feature known as a 'tel'. This is the Hebrew word (*tell* in Arabic) for a hillock or a pile of ruins, and it is now the standard archaeological term for an artificial mound formed by the accumulated debris from ancient settlements. It contains the remains of structures and artefacts of a succession of superimposed cities or villages, one buried beneath its successor, and finally the entire heap covered by earth and vegetation. The wind, rain and decay over many centuries, since the last and topmost city was destroyed or abandoned, give the tel a rounded shape rather like the broad lower part of a truncated cone, with a flat top and smooth sloping sides. To the untrained eye it looks like a natural feature of the landscape.

As a matter of fact Robinson saw such tels. Just outside Jericho, he wrote, was 'a high double-mound, or group of mounds, looking much like a tumulus, or as if composed of rubbish'. He was discerning enough to consider that this could well have been the site of ancient Jericho, for he said that 'the earliest city . . . would naturally have been near the fountain'. However, he then added: 'But any distinct traces of the former city are now hardly to be looked for.'

The first to recognize the nature and importance of a tel were archaeologists, but not biblical archaeologists, and not in Palestine. They were Heinrich Schliemann and Wilhelm Dorpfeld, who excavated in Greece from 1871 to 1890 and discovered Troy and Mycenae. They found that the mound at Troy consisted of the consecutive remains in a vertical series of seven ancient cities, each built on the ruins of its predecessor. But when they announced this, and even after their detailed reports were published, many scholars were sceptical. This was due partly to personal prejudice – a reluctance to credit so amazing a discovery to Schliemann, whom they regarded as an amateur. But it was also because they found it hard to imagine a pile of cities, one on top of the other, when it seemed to them that each new settlement would have cleared the remains of the last one and rebuilt in its place. Thus, even though by that time archaeologists had begun to dig up the Bible, the tels in Palestine were largely ignored.

But not by Englishman William Matthew Flinders Petrie, a

OPPOSITE Tel Megiddo, its shape characteristic of an archaeological mound in the land of the Bible. This tel held the remains of the strategic city built by Solomon at the entrance to the valley of Jezreel.

47

towering genius, 'the revered Nestor of archaeologists' as he was called by the comparable twentieth-century archaeological giant, America's William Foxwell Albright. Petrie was familiar with the tel, and knew that its formation was peculiar to the conditions of the ancient East. The main building materials in the early days of Palestine were sun-dried mud bricks bonded by chopped straw. Thus, when such mud structures were destroyed in battle, or abandoned and fell into decay after the flight of settlers at the threat of war, the crumbly material afforded a thick, ready, foundation platform, higher than the original city level, on which the next wave of settlers would build, whether they came a decade or centuries later. A tel of many such re-occupations might rise to a considerable height in the course of a millennium, whereas a similar development with cities of stone would produce a much lower mound; for the demolished structures could be rebuilt with re-used stone on the original foundations, or razed and built afresh, giving it much the same level as its predecessor.

Petrie carried out his first archaeological probe of a Palestinian tel in 1890, after ten years of stunning work in Egypt. The site he chose was a large mound in the rolling country between the coastal plain and the Judean foot-hills called Tel el-Hesi. Lying sixteen miles to the north-east of Gaza, it was thought at the time to contain the remains of biblical Lachish. In a scant six weeks, Petrie spotted the significance of the vital clue which led him to the ingenious discovery that was to add a dimension to archaeology and set its course thereafter: he discovered the secret for determining the history of a tel.

The biblical tel, as we have seen, consists of a series of strata, each stratum containing the remains and ruins of a specific period of ancient settlement. Petrie conceived a systematic method for the sequential dating of these strata. Being able to attach a date to the buried contents of an ancient site is the primary step for fathoming its mysteries. Accurate chronology is essential for the recovery of history, for history, to make sense, is not only what happened, but when. In a Palestinian tel, without a dating guide, diggers might expose the ruins of a structure of antiquity and have no other means of knowing whether it had been built by king Solomon in the tenth century BC or by the Maccabees 800 years later. Since the structure itself would be an added ingredient to the information on the history of its stratum, and therefore of the entire site, the history would be wrong. It would be like some archaeologist or historian in the distant future, hypothetically and without records, putting the Crusaders in the twentieth century and the Second World War in the twelfth. Before Petrie came along, the biblical archaeologists could only guess, and not always correctly. Petrie provided the guide.

Thus, if Robinson showed the archaeologist in broad terms where to dig, Petrie showed them the historical significance of what they had dug up. Robinson had recovered the geographical location of those ancient sites which had a recorded history. Petrie had now discovered the key to the alphabet of archaeology, making it possible to evaluate the tangible history that lay buried beneath those biblical sites.

His 'key' was the humblest of man-made objects, intrinsically worthless: a piece of pottery from a broken jar.

THE ROSETT
DECREE OF THE PRIESTS OF MEMPHIS
HONOURS ON PTOLEMY V EPIPHANES KING
THE INSCRIPTION IS IN THREE FORMS I IN THE

3 Breakthrough in Time

FLINDERS PETRIE would not have agreed that it was chance that brought him into the world of archaeology. He would have acknowledged only that it was chance that brought him into the world. Almost given up as still-born, he was brought round by the efforts of an experienced nurse who chanced to be present at his birth. He was also lucky to survive a punched-in skull when he was dropped on his head by another nurse shortly afterwards – he bore the mark on his temple till his dying day eighty-nine years later.

It was certainly chance, however, that brought him to Egypt in 1880 at the age of twenty-seven to carry out a survey of the great pyramid at Giza. But once there, it was his persistence and imaginative reasoning that led him to great discoveries when he widened the area of his investigations. Among the sites he excavated and discovered in the course of the next ten years were Tanis, called Avaris by the former Hyksos conquerors and later renamed Raamses (as mentioned in the Bible), the city rebuilt by the Hebrew slaves for pharaoh Rameses II; the long-lost city of Naukratis, an early Greek settlement in the Nile delta, where Petrie confirmed his identification by the discovery of inscriptions bearing its name; and Daphnae, near today's Canal, the Greek name for the biblical fortress town of Tahmanhes, where a few Jerusalem Jews, including the prophet Jeremiah, found refuge after the destruction of the First Temple in 587 BC. It was during his years as an Egyptologist that Petrie developed the ideas that were to enable him, when he came to excavate in Palestine in 1890, to spot the clue that led to his breakthrough in time – conceiving the system for attaching relative dates to the buried treasures of the past, a system which gave meaning to biblical archaeology.

If an inquiring mind is one of the marks of the infant prodigy, Petrie went one better: he searched and found the answers to his own queries. The broad range of his interests was evident when he

OPPOSITE The Rosetta Stone, inscribed in 196 BC in hieroglyphic, demotic and Greek, deciphered by Champollion in 1822.

51

was still a child, and this was greatly encouraged by an unusual family. At the age of three he tramped five miles with an aunt of seventy-two to see the relics of Admiral Nelson. At four he was entranced by the tales of an uncle just back, in 1857, from the Crimean war. The victories of Garibaldi were the remembered excitements of his seventh year. At eight he was being crammed by a tutor with French, Latin and Greek. A collapse soon cut that short, and thereafter he had no formal schooling. His learning was left to himself, and he took full advantage of this, reading endlessly – the books were on a variety of subjects, though few, unlike Robinson's, in the biblical fields – and becoming engrossed in his mother's two collections, one of ancient coins and the other of minerals and fossils. He was soon adding to them, ransacking the local marine stores for coins brought in by sailors after a voyage; fossil hunting in the summer weeks; and extracting garnet-granite and a soft rock called serpentine from the gutter-linings whenever he was out in the street. After reading the standard text-book on mineralogy at the time 'till I knew every page of it', he was led to chemistry and to an improvised do-it-yourself laboratory where he could test the more than one hundred mineral specimens he had acquired. In numismatics, he became so expert that by the age of fifteen he was already supplying the occasional rare Imperial Greek and Byzantine coins to the British Museum.

But long after he had established his reputation as the outstanding archaeologist of his day, he would amuse his students with the true story of having ventured his first archaeological opinion at the age of eight. It occurred when friends on a visit to the Petrie family were describing the unearthing of a Roman villa in the Isle of Wight. The boy was 'horrified at hearing of the rough shovelling out of the contents, and protested that the earth should be pared away, inch by inch, to see all that was in it and how it lay. All that I have done since,' he wrote when he was in his late seventies, 'was there to begin with, so true is it that we can only develop what is born in the mind. I was already in archaeology by nature.'

Archaeology may have been his inborn vocation, as he indicates, but the pursuit of it in Egypt and Palestine is attributed to the chance sight on a London bookstall of a volume called *Our Inheritance in the Great Pyramid*, written by Charles Piazzi Smyth, Astronomer Royal for Scotland and an old family friend. Petrie, barely thirteen at the time, bought it and brought it home, much to his father's delight. Petrie senior hankered after perfection – it was said of him that he 'would rather stay out in the rain than shelter in an imperfect house' – and had in fact abandoned medical studies because he found the methods irrational and unsatisfactory. He sought his longed-for perfection in primitive Christianity, and as a profession he chose surveying. He was therefore intrigued by Smyth's book, which had been inspired by the theory of a certain John Taylor linking the Old Testament in a novel way with the Great Pyramid. Taylor had argued that the pyramid had been built by members 'of the chosen race, the sons of Shem', enslaved by the abhorred Egyptian pagans; that its design was divinely inspired; and that it contained mysterious revelations about the human race, the key to which was to be found in its dimensions. Smyth's book developed the mathematics of Taylor's thesis, suggesting a direct correlation between the length, in inches, of the base of the pyramid, and the history of the world, in years, as might be worked out from the Bible: one inch to one year. So taken was Petrie's father with this extraordinary proposition that he thought of going to Egypt himself to take accurate measurements of the pyramid. He never did, but he encouraged his son to do so.

Young Flinders went, fifteen years later, years crowded with continued book study, as well as surveying the earthworks at no less than 150 sites in England (with the plans going to the British Museum), and correcting the recorded dimensions of ancient buildings by measuring them himself. Now, in 1880, at the age of twenty-seven, he had arrived in Egypt and was able to test Smyth's proposition, only to reach what he called the 'ugly little fact which killed the beautiful theory' he had first read when he was thirteen. Smyth had based his study on the generally accepted 9,140 inches as the length of the pyramid base. Petrie found that he was 71 inches out. It measured only 9,069 inches.

Such was the strange beginning to Petrie's astonishing career in archaeology. From there he went on to widen the horizons of

A detail of a restored Philistine pot which shows how shards are reassembled to reconstruct the pot and how the characteristics of its shape and decoration are used to identify it.

Egyptology over the next ten years. He then proceeded to Palestine to prise the secrets from Tel el-Hesi – and to make his breakthrough discovery.

His years of investigation in the land of the pharaohs were a fruitful preparation for spotting the hidden significance of what he was to find at this Palestinian tel. Wherever he excavated in Egypt, he kept coming across bits of shattered pottery, and they were also strewn in abundance on and around ancient sites where others had dug. They had been discarded as useless by scholars looking for early inscriptions; as without interest by treasure-seekers on the hunt for works of art; and as valueless by marauders and grave robbers throughout the centuries. Petrie applied his reasoning mind to these trivial objects, wondering whether they could tell him anything more of the past other than that they had been fashioned by an ancient potter. He conjured up a vision of a family in antiquity using these earthen vessels for cooking – pots were of earthenware in olden times – for plates, bowls, jugs, storage jars, lamps. Such vessels in daily use got broken, were thrown away and replaced by others, and they in turn broke and were replaced.

Musing upon this ancient scene, it occurred to him that these paltry domestic potsherds might indeed hold a message from those distant days. Pottery, after all, was made of ready-to-hand materials and therefore cheap and available to every household. The vessels themselves had a short life, since they broke easily and could not be mended. But the material, though brittle and breakable, was itself imperishable, neither rotting nor decomposing; and so these heaps of fragments, discarded at any time in the last 6,000 years, were still there in exactly the same state when dug up by a nineteenth-century archaeologist.

Petrie then took his reasoning one crucial step further. Not all the pottery he had encountered was the same. There were differences in shape, colour, type and location of handle, style of decoration, combination of kinds of clay, technique of manufacture (hand or wheel) and method of firing. He thought he knew why. Constant replacement after frequent breakage meant frequent improvement and change. Thus, every decade or generation, and certainly every century, would produce its own style, and each style would be specific to its particular period. These periods would be brief, nothing like the ages of antiquity covering vast stretches of time, like the Paleolithic, Mesolithic or Neolithic. A pottery vessel might thus be given a date of origin to within a few years – which in archaeology is virtually pin-pointing in time. A potsherd would no longer suffer the temporal anonymity of a flint tool – which might be 200,000 or 20,000 years old – or of a stone mortar, which could belong to any year between 12,000 and 4,000 BC.

A particular style of pottery could have been made only during one special and comparatively short period. And it would be feasible to make the general presumption, always allowing for a variety of possible exceptions, that the remains of an ancient city in which such pottery was found belonged to that period. Thus, if one could establish the time-span of one particular pottery style, and thus of the settlement remains in which it was embedded, one would also have a guide to the periods of the differently shaped or coloured or ornamented potsherds found in the earlier and later strata. If, said Petrie, the varied pottery styles found on an archaeological site could be classified and correlated with their corresponding periods, not only would the history of the site be known but it was also likely that the classification would apply to all the sites in the region. It would therefore be possible to establish a standard chronology for the relative dating of all levels of settlement based on the pottery objects found in each stratum.

This was the concept Petrie sought to apply at Tel el-Hesi when he came to excavate in 1890. If it proved correct, he thought it should be possible for the first time to recover the tangible history of a site – particularly in Palestine, where it could be compared with the detailed recorded history in the Bible. Moreover, the concept could have wider implications, giving reciprocity to the relationship between pottery and site-dating. Suppose, for example, the remains of an ancient city could be specifically dated by the rare discovery of an inscription, yet the pottery found therein was unfamiliar and missing from the list in the classification Petrie hoped would one day be compiled. Finding it in that stratum would give it the date. This pottery would then in its turn make possible the dating of other sites where it appeared and where other dating clues were absent.

Further rewards could flow from this mutual time-association between pottery and the settlement level in which it was embedded. Again, let us assume that a particular stratum at an archaeological site is found from its pottery to belong to a certain century BC, and that this stratum holds the remains of a fortified wall constructed in a particular way. A wall of such construction could then be held to belong to that very century, and could itself become a rough aid to dating when found on other archaeological sites.

Such wall-dating, however, would be far less precise than pottery-dating, and would need to be used with greater care, since changes in construction were far less frequent. A pottery style might have lasted for no more than a generation, but a particular type of city wall could well have been in use for one or more centuries, depending on how long its defence capacity could meet

ת הארכיאולוגיות

קופה הביזנטית

POTTERY TYPES CHARACTERISTIC

FROM THE CHALCC

640 C.E.

BYZANTINE PERIOD

330 C.E.

ROMAN PERIOD

63 B.C.E.

HELLENISTIC PERIOD

330 B.C.E.

PERSIAN PERIOD

586 B.C.E.

IRON AGE II

930 B.C.E.

IRON AGE I

1200 B.C.E.

LATE BRONZE AGE

1550 B.C.E.

MIDDLE BRONZE AGE II

1850 B.C.E.

MIDDLE BRONZE AGE I 2100 B.C.E.

EARLY BRONZE AGE

3100 B.C.E.

CHALCOLITHIC AGE

4000 B.C.E.

Petrie conceived the brilliant notion that pottery finds could be the key to archaeological daring. This chart is the product of his theory, relating pottery types to the periods of antiquity when they were manufactured.

כלי-חרס אופייניים
למן התקופה הכלקו...

ARIOUS ARCHAEOLOGICAL PERIODS
E BYZANTINE PERIODS

640 לספה"נ

תקופת התלמוד
(התקופה הביזנטית)

330 לספה"נ

המשנה וראשית התלמוד, תקופת בית הירודס
(התקופה הרומאית)

63 לפני ספה"נ

סוף תקופת כנסת הגדולה והחשמונאים
(התקופה ההלניסטית)

330 לפני ספה"נ

תקופת שלטון בבל, שיבת ציון וכנסת הגדולה
(התקופה הפרסית)

586 לפני ספה"נ

תקופת מלכי יהודה וישראל
(תקופת הברזל השניה)

930 לפני ספה"נ

תקופת השופטים וראשית המלוכה
(תקופת הברזל הראשונה)

1200 לפני ספה"נ

התקופה הכנענית המאוחרת והכבוש הישראלי
(תקופת הברונזה המאוחרת)

1550 לפני ספה"נ

תקופת האבות
(תקופת הברונזה התיכונה)

1850 לפני ספה"נ
התקופה הכנענית התיכונה א' 2000 לפני ספה"נ

התקופה הכנענית הקדומה
(תקופת הברונזה הקדומה)

3100 לפני ספה"נ

התקופה הכלקוליתית
(תקופת מתכת-אבן)

4000 לפני ספה"נ

57

the challenge of attack weapons by a threatening enemy. The development of more powerful armaments would bring with it the establishment of more formidable defensive ramparts. Advances in weaponry were more gradual in those days than they are in our atomic age, so an ancient city wall might have lasted long enough for several fashions in pottery to have been introduced and superseded, and samples of both early and late pottery styles might be found with the same type of structure. However, the difference in time between the styles of pottery, marking its first and its final appearance, would give its duration.

It was with these thrilling ideas whirling in his mind that Petrie appeared on the morning of 4 April 1890 at a small Judean hillock roughly midway between Gaza and Bethlehem known locally as Umm Lakis. It was thought to be the possible site of biblical Lachish – which was known to be in the area – because of the similarity in name. But Petrie was sceptical when he saw it; it did not seem large enough to hold the remains of what had been an important and well-fortified city in ancient days. Nevertheless he carried out a three-day probe which confirmed his doubt. 'It was', he wrote, 'only a shallow village of Roman age', many centuries after biblical times. He abandoned it and tested other sites nearby, plumping for a large and lofty mound a few miles away called Tel el-Hesi, which 'from its nearness to Umm Lakis it doubtless was the ancient Lachish'. To the untrained eye it looked like a natural hill.

Resolving to investigate it the following morning, he set up his tent and went to sleep for the night. He was disturbed only twice, once by a dog who had taken advantage of a gap in the canvas, and again by an intruder – Petrie saw 'a man's head and shoulders' in the gap. He was 'fumbling over the tool-bag, too heavy to carry off, and awkward to open. I challenged, he ran, and four bullets went over his head to improve his pace.' Petrie went back to sleep, awoke early, and set off to tackle the mound.

He could not have chosen a more appropriate site to test his theories. The entire east side of Tel el-Hesi, skirted by a wadi, was eroded, the product of torrents rushing down the normally dry river bed throughout the ages and overflowing its banks in annual flash-floods. It looked to Petrie as though a sixty-foot-thick chunk of hillock had been sliced away, exposing the edges of the strata containing the remains of the successive ancient settlements, from the first to the last. Nature had performed over the centuries a major part of the work of the archaeologist. Instead of having to start digging down from the top of the mound and removing each layer before finding what was buried in the next, Petrie could take in the cross-section at a glance. He was given, as he wrote later, 'at one stroke, a series of all the varieties of pottery over a thousand years' which he could then examine. With pocket knife in one hand and trowel in the other, he moved up and down the hill picking out and comparing the pottery pieces from the different levels.

'The site was ideal for gaining a first outline of archaeology,' he said, 'and I could begin by terracing along each level and getting out its pottery.' For the next six weeks, Petrie made vertical sections, and carefully noted the exact levels at which the various styles of pottery lay. The results soon confirmed his theory of the direct correlation between pottery and stratigraphy, namely, the chronological sequence of the strata in an ancient site; for he was able to show that each period had pottery which was characteristic of that period alone, and distinguishable by the trained archaeologist from corresponding articles of pottery belonging to earlier and later periods.

The additional importance of this discovery for scholars excavating a tel is that, while it is much like a multi-layered cake, the archaeological strata are not sharply defined, nor clearly demarcated, nor are they always flat, nor of the same thickness throughout. They often merge with each other, like the layers of a squashed cake, and are difficult to delineate. Petrie showed how pottery could help to define the course and limits of each stratum.

Petrie would have been the first to stress that 'help' is the operative word in that proposition, for the problem of determining the bounds – and therefore the date – of a stratum is not so simple. Pottery was a superb archaeological tool for the dating of an ancient settlement only when used with common sense, together with an examination of the soil and debris in which it was found, and of the contours of the terrain. Otherwise it could mislead. For example, the first settlement on any tel was usually established on a natural mound. Thus, the remains of its structures on the summit might well appear to poke through to the strata of its successors, for they would be at a higher level than even later structures built lower down the slope. One had to be careful not to ascribe automatically a later date to pottery, and therefore to its stratum, simply because it was found nearer to the surface. The archaeological circumstances of its location had also to be taken into account.

A more common trap for the archaeologist is of the kind that happened at early excavations in Jericho. An ancient wall had been built on the ruins of its predecessor, and had collapsed some time later. Then the ruins of the first wall were destroyed, and collapsed on top of it. The first wall and its potsherds were thus found by the archaeologists above the level of the later structure, which led them to the erroneous conclusion that they were of more recent date.

Another glaring example of correct pottery dating according to

Petrie's method, but its false application to the archaeological circumstances, occurred at the first excavations of Samaria in 1908–10. The archaeologists were 500 years out in their dating when they ascribed to the eighth century BC the huge round towers set at intervals against the walls of the acropolis, and attributed them accordingly to the reign of king Jeroboam II. A more thorough excavation in 1931–5 found them to be early Hellenistic, built in the third century BC. The earlier scholars had gone wrong because they had discovered pottery, correctly identified as belonging to the period of the Israelite kings, amidst the ruins of the towers. They had even narrowed down the date, equally correctly, to the eighth century BC, by following Petrie's inventive concept developed at Tel el-Hesi twenty years earlier. But they had failed to examine the nature of the ground in which the potsherds lay. The fact was that in preparing for the construction of the towers, the trenches for the foundations had been dug deeply – right through to the eighth-century strata. The foundations had then been laid, and the excavated earth with its pottery replaced as filling, with the eighth-century potsherds now on top. And that was how the earlier archaeologists found them – the more ancient pottery *above* the third-century foundations. The later scholars had carefully excavated, sifted and examined the filling and spotted immediately how the earlier mistake had occurred. Their own conclusions, and the true date, were confirmed by the discovery of typical Hellenistic pottery – again, classified according to the Petrie method – amidst the construction material of the towers. Thus, it was not Petrie's ideas that had misled, but the failure to set those ideas in their proper archaeological context.

Petrie at Tel el-Hesi had not intended to carry out a comprehensive archaeological campaign; but he had scarcely expected to get such illuminating results in only six weeks. Luck was with him in that part of the site was eroded and exposed, and he was thus able to test his pottery theory at once, with a glance, a probe and a certain amount of trenching. This successful practical application of his concept inaugurated the archaeological system of ceramic typology – classifying pottery according to type to serve as an index to chronology. Having thus marked out the archaeological path which all future scholars would follow, and improve, Petrie departed, and handed over the detailed excavation of the site to Frederick Jones Bliss, who devoted the next two years to it. Paying tribute to his mentor's 'brilliant campaign', Bliss acknowledged that in his recovery of the outline history of the site, he was aided primarily by Petrie's ingenious recognition of the great value of 'fragments of pottery of various ages'. And he added: 'As the site had yielded up all the secrets' that could be expected in Petrie's brief exploration, 'there was nothing left for me to do but to cut down the mound itself, layer by layer, in order to ascertain the number of occupations and the character of each'.

He could have done more, particularly since he was one of the few to acknowledge the significance of the new pottery criterion when others had scoffed. Despite this, as Albright pointed out forty years later, 'he failed to publish a correlation of Petrie's detailed treatment of sherds with his own stratigraphic results'. Had he done so, had he realized the importance of recording the styles of the most typical potsherds in each stratum, 'the essentials of Palestinian pottery chronology might have been fixed for good'.

The site of biblical Lachish, excavated by Starkey.

As it was, because of the hesitation even of scholars to seize upon a novel concept, it would be decades before the Petrie method became part of standard archaeological procedure.

Perhaps the oddest feature of the Petrie Tel el-Hesi experience was that while he made archaeological history at this very site, his identification was wrong. He had thought it was ancient Lachish. So did Bliss, who had followed with a detailed excavation. It was not. The true site of biblical Lachish was discovered forty-five years later to be a mound some miles away called Tel ed-Duweir. The dramatic identification was made, curiously enough, by a British archaeologist, John Llewelyn Starkey, who had learned his craft by working with Petrie at several archaeological sites in the 1920s, and in the course of his Lachish excavations made a sensational biblical find of Hebrew writings, associated with Nebuchadnezzar's Babylonian invasion of Judah in 587 BC.

As for Tel el-Hesi, the best current scholarship considers it to be Eglon, neighbour to Lachish and with a similar early history. Both make their first biblical appearance in the Book of Joshua: the rulers of both were among the five kings who fought the Israelites at Gibeon and were subdued, and both cities became part of the territory of Judah.

In view of his inaccurate identification it might be said that Petrie used brilliant means but gained a false end. The fact is, however, that the end Petrie had in mind was to put his pottery theory to the test – and to practical archaeological use. This he accomplished in his brief probe of the edges of the Tel el-Hesi site, and off he went to new archaeological pastures, leaving it to others to dig up the mound itself and elicit its story.

With Petrie's key to relative dating, and hence to the chronological sequence of the strata in a tel, one would now know which settlements were earlier or later than others. This of course was a vital step in the recovery of the history of an archaeological mound. But what of absolute dating? How would one know from the archaeological evidence alone the specific periods in which an ancient city flourished, was destroyed or abandoned, and re-settled? With the Petrie method, one would know from the pottery in ruins of structures built by king Herod, for example, that they were older than those found in Crusader remains. But how could one tell that the one settlement was Herodian and the other Crusader, that one was first century BC and the other more than a thousand years later?

True, an added beauty of the Petrie discovery was that once a piece of pottery of a particular type was embedded in an archaeological stratum which could be dated by other means, that

A group of eighth to sixth century BC seals unearthed at excavations in Palestine, which enabled scholars to narrow the date of the biblical ruins in which they were found.

pottery style would automatically become a key to the absolute dating of any level of settlement in which it was found. And once a single stratum could be given a specific date, it would be possible, through sequence dating, to chart the approximate periods of earlier and later strata. Further discovery at subsequent excavations, as well as more advanced and detailed classification of pottery types, would substitute precision for approximation. But what were these 'other means'? How was an absolute date to be discovered in the first place? How could one ever know that a settlement level in an archaeological excavation belonged specifically to, say, the fourteenth century BC and not the twentieth or the tenth – nor even to the thirteenth or fifteenth?

63

There are several ways, all of them rare, so that dating is still the principal problem facing the archaeologist and still the most intricate, despite the enormous progress made since Petrie's time. The primary archaeological clues to the precise dating of biblical ruins are ancient writings, coins, and seals. Least rare are the seals, and particularly seal impressions. They have been found at a number of archaeological sites in Palestine, for they were much used in the entire region for sealing official documents, for marking personal objects belonging to notables, and for sealing container jars carried on the international trade routes which passed through Palestine. The official seal usually bore a standard decoration, which varied from country to country and period to period, and often carried the name of the local king or a member of the royal family. Both the decoration and the name would be clues to its date. The most notable seal in the 2nd millennium BC, especially during the seventeenth and sixteenth centuries, was the scarab seal, of Egyptian origin, which bore on one side the figure of the venerated beetle, and on the other the royal name (sometimes together with a geometric, plant or animal design). However, scholars had to be careful in using such seals as automatic pegs for dating, since those bearing the name of a powerful ruler continued in use, and were reproduced, as amulets long beyond that king's reign.

Coins can be good pointers to the absolute dates of the strata in which they are found; but they are of value to the biblical archaeologist only for the final years of the Old Testament period, for they made their first appearance in the region at the end of the seventh century BC with a metal coin minted in Anatolia. The consecutive history of Jewish coinage begins only late in the second century BC, after independence was regained by the Maccabees. However, even for this late period, the drawback of the coin as a stratum dater lies in its intrinsic value. Like the seal, it could have continued in use or been hoarded by a family's descendants for generations, and would therefore be found by the archaeologist in a stratum more recent than its date of issue.

[Before continuing with ancient writings as an archaeological guide to absolute dating, it is worth saying a word on a novel non-archaeological technique which was recently introduced into the world of archaeology. It is the brain-child not of an archaeologist but of a nuclear chemist of staggering brilliance. It is called radiocarbon age dating, and it was conceived in the late 1940s by American Nobel prize-winner Willard Frank Libby. A professor of chemistry, he had spent the Second World War years on the Manhattan Project helping to develop the atom bomb. At the end of the war he returned to his peaceful laboratory, and one of the fruitful by-products of his research, ingeniously applied, provided a direct method of determining the absolute date of long-dead organic matter, such as burnt wood, bones, fossils, parchment and mummies. Libby arrived at the concept behind the technique by subtle and complex reasoning and esoteric knowledge of the cosmos. The technique is based on the fact that all living organisms contain a minute quantity of radio-active carbon, called Carbon 14 – 14 being its atomic weight, heavier than ordinary everyday carbon which is C 12. The C 14 content, being radio-active, emits particles (i.e. disintegrates) at a specific measurable rate which can be detected by a Geiger counter. While the organism is alive, the loss is counterbalanced by continued absorption of carbon from the atmosphere, so that the proportion of C 14 is kept constant. Upon death, with no further intake of C 14, the quantity that was there when life ceased continues to disintegrate at a fixed rate, slowly and steadily reducing its proportion to C 12. Libby showed that at this rate, the amount of radio-activity is reduced by one half in the course of 5,568 years (with a margin of error of plus or minus 200 years). Thus a Geiger counter testing a piece of wood lopped off a tree 5,568 years ago would emit half as many clicks as a branch cut down today. By applying the C 14 test to an organic object found in an archaeological stratum, one could tell how old it was. The success of this method was established in February 1948 when a committee of four American archaeologists submitted to Libby samples of organic antiquities with a known date. They included wood from the tombs of Egyptian pharaohs and ashes from a Roman encampment. Libby's results were within ten per cent of the dates that had already been determined by other means. Since then, the technique has been refined, and it has proved an invaluable dating device for prehistoric objects, so old that the margin of error is of minor significance. Unfortunately, it is of little help to the biblical archaeologist seeking to narrow the dates of an antiquity to the reign of a particular Israelite king or to some prominent episode in the Bible. What the carbon test can do, even with its margin of error, is serve as nemesis to would-be forgers trying to pass off a twentieth-century fake as a Dead Sea Scroll!]

To return from nuclear chemistry to archaeology, ancient writings are of course the best evidence for absolute dating; the ideal which every archaeologist yearns to attain is a dedicatory inscription recording the date when a monument or structure was erected. This is rare indeed. Most of such inscriptions in antiquity were unlike those we see today in the capitals of the world on statues of kings, presidents and generals, with names and dates in bold characters; nor were they like the dated scrolls which are occasionally sealed into the foundations of some prominent building – a boon to the archaeologist of the future. Ancient inscriptions

American Nobel prize-winner Willard Frank Libby, the nuclear scientist who invented the Carbon 14 technique for determining the absolute date of long-dead organic matter, an invaluable boon to the pre-history archaeologists.

were rarely so clear, at least not to us, thousands of years later. At best they may contain a reference to a monarch or to some outstanding occurrence from which the date may be deduced in a variety of complex ways requiring the joint skill of astronomers, mathematicians, historians and philologists.

Such deduction became possible with the discovery in the last century of documents belonging to Israel's neighbours in ancient times, notably the Babylonians and Assyrians in the north-east and the Egyptians in the south-west. Up to then, all that was known of these peoples were the references to them in the Bible. The Hebrew Old Testament was the only complete ancient record of a nation in this region, its language preserved without a break for some 3,000 years. These neighbours were part of the biblical background, but only in the last century were fragments of their own records brought to light. And they are particularly useful in helping to date the historical periods – and the archaeological finds – of the 2nd millennium BC, where the documentation was thin. These were the centuries of the patriarchs Abraham, Isaac and Jacob, down to Joshua and the Judges. The records were fuller for the centuries that followed, paralleling the biblical period from king David onward.

Among these ancient writings were what are known as kingslists, which gave the names of the successive kings in some of the early dynasties and the length of each reign. Philologists deciphered the unknown languages in which these lists were inscribed, providing the historians with the sequence of the rulers in the particular country and the duration of the dynasty. Mathematicians adapted the ancient local time-span and calendar to our own. What was still missing, however, was an absolute date. With the sequence in a kings-list, discovery of the date of a single ruler would make possible the specific dating of the other kings in the dynasty. This is where astronomers could help.

Astronomical observations were keenly followed by some of the ancient peoples. In Mesopotamia, for example, one of the subsidiary purposes was to discern signs and omens, and a record has come down to us of an eclipse of the moon, with details of the day of the month and the year of the king's reign when it occurred. It was considered a portent of the downfall of a rival ruler. With this astronomical information, modern scientists were able to suggest the probable date of the eclipse and of that king's rule. In early Egypt, priests observed the phenomena in the heavens to determine when festivals were to be held for astral gods, and their findings were used as the basis for their civil calendar. To this end, they noted the time of the appearance of each new moon. They also kept careful records of the time, day, month and the year of the

OPPOSITE An early sixth-century BC cuneiform document from the reign of Nebuchadnezzar, discovered in Babylon, which lists supplies of food delivered to notables who were prisoners or otherwise dependent upon the royal household. Among those mentioned is 'Jehoiachin king of Judah'.

king's reign when there was a special rising of Sirius, also known as the dog-star, the brightest star in the heavens. The Egyptians called it Sothis. This star was particularly favoured in Egypt because, after a long period of invisibility, it became visible forty-two minutes before dawn on the very day of the year that the waters of the Nile started to rise. They therefore inaugurated a festival to Sothis. The discovery of early records of two such festivals made it possible to determine their dates. One account reported that the special rising of Sothis took place on the first day of the eighth month in the seventh year of the reign of pharaoh Sesostris III. With this data, astronomers have calculated that the event took place some time between 1876 and 1864 BC. The other document recorded that the Sothic festival was celebrated on the ninth day of the eleventh month in the ninth year of the reign of Amenhotep I. Again, astronomical calculation puts the date at approximately 1540 BC.

The kings-list of the First Babylonian Dynasty together with another document containing astronomical observations enabled scholars to propose absolute dates for this dynastic period. The sixth king in the list was the great Hammurabi. The tenth king was his great-great-grandson, a certain Ammi-saduqa. It so happens that this king's name appears in a document which records that 'in the eighth year' of his reign, the royal astronomers witnessed a certain cyclical rising of the planet Venus which occurs once every fifty-six or sixty-four years. This served as the basis for the scholarly suggestion of probable dates for this monarch's reign, and, accordingly, the dates for the other kings in the list. Then came the discovery of the Assyrian kings-list, which contained the name of Shamshi-Adad I. He appears again in a further document suggesting a specific date for him. And yet another document shows him to have been a contemporary of Babylon's Hammurabi; it records that in the tenth year of Hammurabi's reign, witnesses in an economic transaction took an oath 'by the life of' Hammurabi and Shamshi-Adad. These dates were then combined with the probable dates suggested by the astronomical data to reach the most likely dates for the history of the region during the 2nd millennium BC.

Additional light was shed on this history – and the earlier dating corrected – by the discovery of what turned out to be the fourteenth century BC royal Egyptian archives at Tel el-Amarna. They contained the diplomatic letters written to the pharaoh Amenhotep III and his son, Amenhotep IV (better known as the individualist and heretic Ikhnaton), by the kings of Babylonia and Assyria, as well as by the vassal rulers in Syria and Palestine. Here, then, was a helpful aid to synchronized dating, for the signatures on the letters

A letter in cuneiform sent by a vassal city-chief in Canaan to the pharaoh, found in the fourteenth-century BC royal archives of Amenhotep III and his son Amenhotep IV (Ikhnaton) at Tel el-Amarna. Rulers of biblical towns who appear in these Amarna letters include 'Labayu prince of Shechem', 'Zatatna prince of Acco [Acre]', and 'Biridiya prince of Megiddo'.

OPPOSITE Sir Flinders Petrie, 'the Nestor of archaeologists'. A portrait by Philip Alexius Laszlo.

showed who were the contemporary rulers of the various countries in the region. Tel el-Amarna, 191 miles south of Cairo, is the modern name for the ruins of the city of Akhetaton, built by Amenhotep IV as his new capital, replacing Thebes. Actually, the first to investigate the site, in 1891–2, was the very Flinders Petrie who was to make the experimental excavation at Tel el-Hesi in Palestine eight years later; but it was not he who discovered the royal archives. These were found by chance by an Egyptian peasant woman in 1887, who was scrabbling around in the area and poked through into what was the records office of the ancient capital. In it was a collection of some 350 tablets of baked clay inscribed in the cuneiform script. These were the treasured documents. Incidentally, it was in an adjoining building that the archaeologists later found the celebrated sculpture of queen Nefertiti, the wife of Ikhnaton-Amenhotep IV.

Fathoming the secrets of ancient records with the aid of astronomical calculation has considerably advanced the archaeological efforts to recover the chronology of biblical times. Yet few subjects have occasioned sharper controversy among scholars. Those who had propounded beautiful theories which were now assailed by the new evidence argued that the material was too fragmentary. Copies of the writings may have been corrupted in transmission. The kings-lists may have been falsified for political reasons – a king may have pre-dated his accession in order to strengthen his legitimacy by eliminating all mention of his predecessor (like the successive deletion of 'non-persons' by new regimes from the Soviet encyclopaedia of our day). Astronomical records may not have been accurate; an error of minutes in the observed rising of a planet 3,500 years ago might throw out today's calculation of the date by several years.

Much of this is true. Certain ancient reports are now known to be misleading, and recent discoveries have led to the revision of former scholarly estimates. But whereas at the beginning of this century the gap between the conflicting proposals for dating were several hundred years, today it has been narrowed in some cases to decades. Up to fifty years ago, for example, the date for Hammurabi was variously held to be the twenty-second, twenty-first and twentieth centuries BC. All now agree that he reigned in the first half of the eighteenth century BC. It is also generally accepted that the ultimate proof of date is to be found only through an archaeological excavation. The Exodus of the Hebrews from Egypt, the trek led by Moses in the wilderness, and Joshua's conquest of Canaan, were long held to have occurred in the fourteenth century BC. Only by the discovery of a characteristic type of pottery at an Israeli excavation in the 1950s has it now been established that

OPPOSITE ABOVE The second to third-century AD synagogue of Capernaum on the northern shore of the Sea of Galilee.

OPPOSITE BELOW The ruins of Qumran at the Dead Sea.

these events took place in the thirteenth century BC. The Egyptian pharaoh who had so much trouble with Moses and Aaron was probably Rameses II.

We have spoken of ancient documents from Babylonia and Assyria and Egypt. But what was their language, how were they written, and on what? How were they found and deciphered? These ancient tongues had long fallen into oblivion, and no-one knew how they were spoken, or what signs were used to transcribe the words they used. One knew that the Egyptian script was hieroglyphic – picture-writing – for hieroglyphs appeared on many monuments. It was evident that each hieroglyph, the figure of an object, stood for some component of language, but whether it was a word, a syllable, a sound or a concept remained a mystery, and the capacity to read its meaning was forgotten by about the fourth century AD. As for Babylonian and Assyrian, no-one even knew what the script had looked like.

The first philological code-cracking of ancient writing was achieved with Egyptian hieroglyphs by a French genius, Jean François Champollion, who deciphered the script on a slab of black basalt, known as the Rosetta Stone, in 1821. The stone had been found by Bouchard, a French engineer, who was in Napoleon's expeditionary force which in 1798 had landed in Egypt, then a province of the Ottoman empire, fought a successful campaign and occupied the country. In July of the following year, the engineer was repairing an old fort near the town of Rashid (which the Europeans called Rosetta), at the mouth of the western branch of the Nile some thirty miles north-east of Alexandria, when he came across this unusual stone in the ruins. He brought it to the French scientific commission in Cairo, and this body of scholars, whom Napoleon had attached to his expedition, promptly recognized it as a unique antiquity. Napoleon's own deep interest was such that he ordered copies of the inscription made for distribution among the learned men of Europe. Two skilled lithographers were accordingly brought over from Paris to take impressions. They covered the surface with printer's ink, laid a sheet of paper upon it, and rolled it with india-rubber rollers. Several of these impressions were sent to Paris and to scholars of repute in other European countries. The stone itself was later transferred for safe-keeping from Cairo to the house of the French commander in Alexandria, General Menou, and it was there when the three-year French occupation was brought to an end in 1801 by the arrival of a strong British naval and military force.

Under the capitulation terms which followed the successful British siege of Alexandria, the French were to surrender the antiquities that had been collected by their experts. But in the negotiations over the fulfilment of this condition, the French stubbornly maintained that personal belongings were excluded, and the Rosetta stone was marked on the list submitted by the scientific commission as the personal property of their commanding general. The local British commander, however, was determined that this prize should go to Britain. He was Major General Sir Tomkyns Hilgrove Turner, a professional soldier with an interest in ancient history, and he realized, as he observed in an account of the transaction written in 1810, that here was 'a most valuable relick of antiquity, the feeble but only yet discovered link of the Egyptian to the known languages'. He accordingly cut the negotiations short and took 'a detachment of artillerymen, and an artillery-engine, called, from its powers, a devil cart, with which that evening I went to General Menou's house, and carried off the stone, without any injury, but with some difficulty, from the narrow streets, to my house, amid the sarcasms of numbers of French officers and men ... During the time the Stone remained at my house, some gentlemen attached to the corps of *scavans* [scholars from the French scientific commission] requested to have a cast, which I readily granted, providing the Stone should receive no injury; which cast they took to Paris, leaving the Stone well cleared from the printing ink which it had been covered with to take off several copies to send to France when it was first discovered.'

Turner himself brought the Rosetta stone with him when he sailed for England in February 1802, and it was subsequently handed to the British Museum. Thus, the stone itself has remained in Britain; but the glory remains with France, for it was Champollion who discovered the meaning of its inscription, working from the cast and the copies.

The Rosetta stone was a unique scholarly treasure not because it was particularly old – it was only second-century BC; nor for any special wisdom in the text – it was merely a record of the benefactions conferred on the priesthood by Ptolemy V Epiphanes (203–181) to mark the ninth anniversary of his accession to the throne. It was unique because the inscription appeared in two languages, one known and one unknown, and so it held its own key to the unknown writing. The known language was Greek; the other was Egyptian hieroglyphic. Thus, by comparing the two, the possibility arose for the first time of recovering the lost meaning of the elusive signs. If this could be accomplished, it would break the seal on many of the secrets of the numerous hieroglyphic inscriptions of more ancient times, and might illuminate certain episodes involving Egypt in the biblical narrative.

[Though the Rosetta inscription was in two languages, it appeared in three scripts, for the Egyptian was inscribed in two forms. The most important was the one in hieroglyphic characters, the old picture writing which was employed, from the earliest Egyptian dynasties, for almost all state and ceremonial 'documents' that were intended to be seen by the public. The second script was in the demotic (or popular) character, less ancient and formal, and less pictorial. It was an abbreviated, modified and cursive form of the hieroglyphic writing which was in use during the period of the Ptolemies.]

Several French scholars had begun the attempt to decipher the Rosetta hieroglyphs shortly after the discovery of the stone. Though unsuccessful, they came up with one important conjecture: that where a group of hieroglyphs were enclosed in an oval ring, known as a cartouche, they represented a proper name, probably that of a king. This was seized upon by a versatile English scientist named Thomas Young, an outstanding physicist and physician. He had no specialist knowledge of either Egyptology or ancient languages, but he was intrigued by the intellectual challenge of the Rosetta mystery. After spending the year of 1814 applying his powers of reasoning to its decipherment, he proposed the identification of nine symbols in a cartouche, and it was subsequently established that he had got five right. For this, his name has often been linked with that of Champollion as the unveiler of the Rosetta secret.

However, from the modest point where Young gave up, Champollion took off, rocketed by ingenuity, erudition and methodical professional research. He had started young. Taught Latin and Greek as a child, he had read Homer when he was nine, turned to the study of eastern languages, and at seventeen was already reading a paper to a learned society on abstruse aspects of the Coptic tongue. At nineteen he became an assistant professor of history, with ancient Egypt as his main subject, the perfect apprenticeship for the task of recovering the meaning of a lost language.

The task was indeed formidable, for he had first to establish what each hieroglyph stood for, whether it was a letter, a syllable or a concept. He found, in fact, that the symbols were largely ideograms, namely, they expressed the idea of a thing, without 'spelling out' the sequence of sounds in its name – rather like our use of numerals: we write '25' for the sounds of 'twenty-five'. This of course added to the complexity of decipherment, for an ideogram might represent several related notions with different names, such as a picture of the sun which might stand for sun, sunshine, day, light or warmth. However, Champollion noted that certain symbols took on phonetic values when used to record a proper name,

OPPOSITE Jean François Champollion, the French genius who cracked the code of Egyptian hieroglyphic writing. A painting by L. Cogniet.

particularly when it was a foreign name, which could be transcribed not by meaning but only by its sound. Such a name was Ptolemy, the only royal name in the Rosetta inscription. It was of Greek origin, as was Cleopatra and all the other royal names in Egypt after that country was conquered by Alexander the Great in 332 BC, and one of his outstanding generals, Ptolemy, became its ruler and founder of the dynasty.

Champollion had therefore worked out that the hieroglyphs within the cartouche on the Rosetta stone had to stand for the sounds of the letters of the corresponding name 'Ptolemy' in the counterpart Greek inscription. He was now convinced that he could recover the Egyptian alphabet if only he could test his theory with other royal names which contained some of the same letters, and by the same token extend the list. His theory was confirmed when he received a copy of another inscription, also written in Greek and hieroglyphs, which had been found on the pedestal of an obelisk, and which contained the names within cartouches of both Ptolemy and Cleopatra. The signs for the sounds, p, t, o, l, and e, which appear in both names, were identical (with slight variations in the signs for the letter t).

Continuing his investigations along these lines with copies of inscriptions from older periods, he was able to report in September 1822 that 'after ten years of dedicated study', he had

reached the point where I can put together an almost complete survey of the general structure of the two forms of writing [the hieratic and the demotic] the origin, nature, form, and number of their signs ... thus laying the first foundations for what might be termed the grammar and dictionary of these two scripts, which are found on the majority of monuments, and the interpretation of which will throw so much light on the general history of Egypt.

The secrets of the ancient Babylonian and Assyrian documents, which were to throw sidelights on the biblical narrative more important than the Egyptian, took longer to penetrate than those of the hieroglyphics. They were inscribed in a writing system known as cuneiform, a term of Latin origin meaning wedge-shaped, for the basic component of its signs was a slim triangle, looking like a narrow wedge. These 'wedges' were used in different combinations, positions and arrangements to form a symbol that might represent a letter, syllable, word or idea, like the hieroglyph. With writing required for the conduct of general affairs, such as diplomatic correspondence or state records, the signs were pressed into small tablets of moist clay by a reed stylus with a wedge-shaped end, and the tablets hardened by drying. In monumental inscriptions, symbols were chiselled out of the stone or rock.

Two major obstacles had to be hurdled before the deciphering of cuneiform could be attempted, difficulties of which Champollion had been free. The Rosetta stone was comparatively small and easy to transport; it could therefore be copied in comparative comfort. The equivalent for cuneiform was a text carved in a rock-face high above the ground, and the man who would decipher it was the English soldier and orientalist Henry Creswicke Rawlinson. He had to make his copy by standing on the top rung of a tall ladder placed at the highest climbable point of the mount, and awkwardly support himself with one shoulder against the rock while he transferred the signs to his notebook. (With characteristic understatement, he would write later of this hazardous exploit:

I will not speak of the difficulties or dangers of this enterprise. They are such as any person with ordinary nerves may successfully encounter; but they are such, at the same time, as have alone prevented the inscriptions from being long ago presented to the public by some of the numerous travellers who had wistfully contemplated them at a distance.

And in any case, he added, copying all the upper inscriptions 'in this position . . . the interest of the occupation entirely did away with any sense of danger'.)

The second obstacle was that while this cuneiform text, like the Rosetta stone, appeared in three scripts, each script in this one represented a different language, and, graver still, all three languages were unknown. Thus, where the known language in the Rosetta inscription, Greek, held the key to the corresponding hieroglyphs, the three cuneiform scripts contained no built-in key.

Eventual decipherment brought the discovery that this cuneiform system of writing was first employed by a people of unknown origin called Sumerians, who reached and inhabited southern Mesopotamia some 5,500 years ago. The land they occupied became known as Sumer (and one of its most important towns was 'Ur of the Chaldees', the birthplace of Abraham). The territory to the immediate north of Sumer was invaded by the Akkadians, a Semitic people, in the middle of the 3rd millennium BC, and was called Akkad. [Later, the joint lands of Sumer and Akkad became known as Babylonia, named after its principal city, Babylon. The area north of Babylonia, lying along the upper reaches of the river Tigris, was peopled by the Assyrians. The combined territories of Babylonia and Assyria were subsequently referred to by Greek geographers as Mesopotamia, 'the land between the two rivers' Euphrates and Tigris, though at times their boundaries were far more extensive; and Mesopotamia was the name by which this stretch of land was long known. It corresponds roughly to the Iraq of today.]

Shortly after their entry into the area, the Akkadians adopted the Sumerian cuneiform writing for their own quite different Semitic language, and Akkadian eventually displaced Sumerian as the popular language of Mesopotamia. It remained the language of both Babylonia and Assyria even after the fall of the Akkad dynasty. In the 2nd millennium, particularly after the eighteenth century BC, when king Hammurabi of Babylonia carved out his great empire, Akkadian became the lingua franca of the entire Near and Middle East. Nations living within the broad crescent of territory from Turkey in the north-west to the Persian Gulf in the south-east employed it for international correspondence, while using the cuneiform adapted to their individual languages for local affairs.

Many of these nations disappeared, their writings were lost; and even those who had survived began replacing cuneiform with the more efficient cursive form of writing in the opening centuries of the 1st millennium. By about 500 BC, cuneiform was abandoned – except, curiously enough, in Persia, which had been almost the last country to have adopted it, and which had just absorbed within its empire the very region where it had been created: Mesopotamia. Persia had always used cuneiform for its inscriptions on monuments, and the kings of the Achaemenid dynasty (sixth to fourth century BC), which included Cyrus the Great, founder of the Persian empire, and Darius I, continued this practice, using the Akkadian language alongside Old Persian and Elamite. (Elam lay between Persia and Mesopotamia.) In many cases these inscriptions were carved on a prominent mount that all could see; and so it was from Persia that the first cuneiform characters were brought to the attention of the countries of the west.

Several decades before Rawlinson worked on his huge key inscription at Behistun in the wild mountains of north-western Persia, a start had been made on cuneiform decoding with the shorter texts at Persepolis, an ancient Persian town near today's Shiraz in southern Iran. A few western travellers in the seventeenth century AD had reported on the strange writings they had seen here, amid the ruins of colossal buildings and royal tombs. Only in the following century, however, was an account accompanied by careful drawings of the bas-relief inscriptions. They were made by Carsten Niebuhr, an explorer who had joined a Danish scientific expedition to the east and was its sole survivor. He stayed in Persia in 1766 on his way home and visited Persepolis. His copies and report, which included the observation that the writings were in three scripts, formed the basis of studies made by the German scholar Georg Friedrich Grotefend at the end of that century.

A relief of the Persian emperor
Xerxes at the entrance to his
Throne Hall at Persepolis.
'Captions' to such reliefs,
carved on the walls in Persian
cuneiform, were copied by
travellers, and launched
European scholars on the task
of deciphering this ancient
writing.

Grotefend proceeded on the assumption that the three scripts carried the identical content in three languages; that they related and referred to Persian royalty – he reasoned from historical data that they were most likely to have been Achaemenid kings; and that the language of the main script was Old Persian. If later Persian records of the pattern of royal inscriptions were any guide, it was probable that the introductory lines of the cuneiform text contained the name and title and genealogy of the ruler, such as 'king so-and-so son of king so-and-so'. The repetition of a certain group of cuneiform characters suggested to him that they represented 'king', and another group stood for 'son'. Since the rulers of the Achaemenid dynasty were known from the writings of the fifth-century BC Greek historian and traveller Herodotus, Grotefend could test his theory.

He thought the likeliest candidates were the outstanding kings of this dynasty: Cyrus (550–530 BC) and his son Cambyses (530–522 BC), from one Achaemenid branch; and Darius (522–486 BC) and his son Xerxes (486–465 BC) from another. But Cyrus was quickly abandoned, for it would have meant that the inscription for his son would read 'king Cambyses son of king Cyrus', both names beginning with a character representing the sound of the letter 'C', and there was no common initial for a son and father in the text. Grotefend next considered Darius, and here came his ingenious deduction. He noticed that the name of the king in one inscription was the same as that of the father in the next. But whereas he appeared in both inscriptions with his title of king, his own father in the first inscription bore no title. Thus, the first inscription was 'king X son of Y', whereas the second inscription read 'king Z son of king X'. This fitted perfectly with 'king Darius son of Hystaspes' and 'king Xerxes son of king Darius', for the father of Darius had not been a king. In the year 522 BC, king Cambyses died while campaigning abroad, and the Persian throne was seized by Gaumata. But he was overthrown by Darius, who thus became king not through father–son succession but by armed force. Hence the absence of the royal title in the mention of Hystaspes.

Grotefend was able to proceed from this discovery to read several long proper names in Old Persian and ascribe sound values to a number of cuneiform characters in this language. He published his initial results in 1802, just about the time that the Rosetta stone was on its way in Turner's custody from Egypt to England. Thereafter, Grotefend made little further progress. Other scholars sought to refine and expand his findings; but the breakthrough into the entire world of cuneiform came only when Rawlinson, some forty years later, published his studies of the great Behistun inscription – which turned out also to be associated with Darius I.

LEFT A Persian cuneiform inscription by the emperor Xerxes commemorating the new royal structures he built at Persepolis.

BELOW German scholar Georg Friedrich Grotefend was the first to try his hand at the decipherment of Old Persian cuneiform, and these are notes of his early attempts. He worked from copies of inscriptions at Persepolis made and brought back by Danish explorer Carsten Niebuhr in 1766, and he published his results in 1802.

Alphabetum Zendicum Persepolitanum   Zu Beylage 1.

É.			*Sphalmata.*	M.		
S.		‏س‏	B.	O.		
E.			B.	K?		‏ک‏
V.		‏و‏	B.	Dj?		‏ج‏
R.		‏ر‏	N. *semper g. fere* B.	Tsch.		‏چ‏ B. N.
D.		‏د‏	N. B.	A.		B.
N.		‏ن‏	B.	Sch.		‏ش‏ N. B.
B/p.			N. B.	Z (ds.ts)		‏ژ ز‏ N.
G.			B.	U.		B.
Ô.			N. B.	Kh.		‏خ‏ B.
Gh.		‏غ‏	B.	N g.		‏گ‏
incerta.				H.		‏ه‏ B.
Ê.f.a.		‏ا‏	B.	I.		‏ی‏ N.
Th?				F.f.ph.		‏ف‏
T.			N.	(comp. lect.) rex.		

Inscriptio ap. Niebuhr Tom. II. Pl. XXIV. G.

KH·SCH·H·Ê·R·SCH·Ê : KH·SCH·Ê·H·I·Ô·H : E·GH·R·TCH·Â·O : D·Â·R·H·E·A·Û·SCH·KH·SCH·Ê·H·I·
Xer———xes : rex ... for ... um:(filius) : Da———ri———i———re

Ê : KH·SCH·Ê·H·I·Ô·H : KH·SCH·Ê·H·I·Ô·H · Ê ... ÔH·Â·H·Ê : B·U·N : A·KH·Ê·Ô·TCH·Ô·SCH·Ô·H
-us : rex ... reg ... -gis ... surps ... mun——di ... ree——to——ris

Darius had chosen well when he had ordered the tri-lingual inscription to be carved on the precipitous rock of Behistun. It was a dramatic site, lying along a strategic caravan route from Persia to Babylon at the foot of the Zagros range where the mountains rise to a height of 4,000 feet. When eventually transcribed, deciphered and interpreted by Rawlinson, it was found to be a boastful record of how Darius, following the death of Cambyses, had slain the usurper Gaumata, defeated the rebels, and gained the Persian throne. In order that this chronicle of his mighty deed should attract permanent attention yet be safeguarded against defacement or destruction, he arranged for it to be inscribed on the sheer rock-face some 500 feet above the valley floor. His foresight was well rewarded, thanks to the hazardous efforts and the sagacity of a singular Englishman more than 2,300 years later.

Rawlinson had started copying the inscription in 1835 when he was a twenty-four-year-old British army officer serving in Persia and stationed near Behistun. During the next twelve years, he completed the transcription and made several drafts of the translation. (His official duties during this period were military, political and consular respectively, in Persia, Afghanistan and Mesopotamia.) His final decipherment of the Old Persian inscription appeared in 1846. Like Grotefend – though at first unaware of his findings – Rawlinson had also discerned the first clues in the proper names and titles. With one of the tri-linguals now known, the identification and decipherment of the other two soon followed. They turned out to be Elamite and Babylonian (Akkadian). A particularly valuable contribution had been made with the Akkadian cuneiform by the Irish scholar-clergyman Edward Hincks; and the work of French scholar Félicien de Saulcy had also been helpful. Rawlinson's presentation of the Akkadian decipherment to the Royal Asiatic Society of Britain at the end of 1850 was a landmark event in Assyro–Babylonian studies, for with the key to Akkadian, the central language of cuneiform culture, the very core of the cuneiform system of writing lay revealed. All other languages in this script could now become intelligible.

However there were some who questioned the principles on which Rawlinson had based his conclusions, and if the principles were unsound, the proposed meanings given to the cuneiform characters would be wide of the mark. There seemed no way of proving the faithfulness of Rawlinson's interpretation, until one scholar came up with an unusual suggestion in 1857. Shortly before, archaeologists in Mesopotamia had found a clay cylinder inscribed with Akkadian cuneiform in the ruins of a temple at Asshur, the first Assyrian capital. It was brought to London, and a proposal was made to the Asiatic Society that copies be sent to four

Sir Henry Creswicke Rawlinson, British soldier and orientalist, who fathomed the secrets of cuneiform writing with his decipherment of the key tri-lingual inscription in Akkadian, Old Persian and Elamite of the emperor Darius, carved on the precipitous rock of Behistun in Persia – an inscription which he himself copied, at great risk.

outstanding Assyriologists; Rawlinson, Hincks, their friend Fox Talbot (who is credited with the invention of photography), and Jules Oppert, a German Jew who had moved to France, since Jews at the time were unable to pursue an academic career in Germany. Each scholar was to decipher the cuneiform text independently and send the sealed result to a distinguished committee appointed by the Society. The committee was to make a judgement not on the quality of the decipherment – they were less expert than the 'examinees' – but on the measure of agreement between the translations. The proposal was accepted, and the results were published two and a half months later. The inscription on the clay cylinder turned out to be a flamboyant account of the deeds of Tiglath-Pileser I, king of Assyria in the twelfth century BC.

The verdict of the committee was that 'the coincidence between the translations, both as to the general sense and verbal rendering, were very remarkable. . . .' It was now evident to all that Akkadian was no longer a cryptogram but an open language; and the numerous clay tablets and wall inscriptions which had just begun to be discovered at excavations in Mesopotamia could now be reliably translated, to shed authentic light on biblical times.

4 Discovery

THE FIRST OF the spectacular discoveries of ancient cuneiform writings which interlock with the biblical narrative was made in 1843 by a French consular official and antiquarian, Paul Emile Botta, among the remains of the fabulous palace of Sargon II, king of Assyria from 722 to 705 BC. The site of the excavation was Dur Sharrukin, 'Sargon's Castle', today's Khorsabad in Iraq, some twelve miles north of Mosul on the upper Tigris. Sargon built this fortified town and made it the third of the four cities he used as his successive capitals. (The others were biblical Asshur, Calah and Nineveh.)

Botta found and copied the cuneiform characters on Sargon's walls. Deciphered by Rawlinson and Hincks, they added vital details to the account of the Bible of one of the gravest events in Israelite history: the fall of the northern kingdom of Israel in 722 BC. It was precipitated by the successful Assyrian siege of its capital, Samaria. For almost 2,500 years, the only known chronicle of this episode was the one in the Bible. Suddenly, a contemporary record was discovered which paralleled the biblical report. (Equally suddenly, sceptics who had doubted the authenticity even of the historical parts of the Old Testament began to revise their views.)

The event is related in the Second Book of Kings (17:6): 'In the ninth year of Hoshea [king of Israel] the king of Assyria took Samaria, and carried Israel away into Assyria. . . .' Sargon's inscription found by Botta states: 'I besieged and conquered Samaria, led away as booty 27,290 inhabitants of it. . . .' Here, then, were two reports in the annals of the conqueror and the vanquished, one almost a mirror of the other. This kind of identical 'war reporting' from both sides was unusual in the Middle East of ancient times (and on occasion in modern times too). It occurred only when the countries in conflict were Israel and one of its neighbours, and only when Israel was defeated. When Israel won, no record of failure appeared in the chronicles of the enemy. Israel

OPPOSITE Assyrian king Sargon II, from his palace at Khorsabad which was discovered by French consular official and explorer Paul Emile Botta in 1843.

was the only country in the area which recorded in what became the narrative books of the Bible its defeats as well as its triumphs. The neighbouring nations recorded only their victories, and almost invariably in display inscriptions in the royal palace to exalt the emperor. This became evident as more and more Egyptian hieroglyphic and Babylonian and Assyrian inscriptions were discovered and deciphered. It was then also seen that, on occasion, defeat on the battlefield became a victory on the palace walls, with each of the rival monarchs emerging the winner from the same battle. More often, however, the vanquished ruler – if he survived – maintained silence, while the victor's inscription tended to exaggerate the extent of his conquests.

Modern historical research and archaeological excavations have shown that Sargon's palace inscriptions were singularly accurate. They are certainly more direct and pithy than the bombastic and flamboyant accounts of some of the other monarchs of the region. 'I besieged and conquered Samaria' is as terse and economical as a sentence in the Bible. Curiously enough, only with Botta's discovery was it realized that Sargon was the 'king of Assyria' referred to in the biblical account as the victor of Samaria. Until then, this king was thought to have been Shalmaneser v, Sargon's predecessor, for he is mentioned three verses earlier (in 2 Kings 17:3: 'Against him [Hoshea] came up Shalmaneser king of Assyria'), whereas the king who 'took Samaria' (17:6) is not named. Sargon appears in the Bible only once, in the Book of Isaiah, as the king who sent his commander-in-chief to capture another city of the Hebrews, this time in the southern kingdom of Judah: 'In the year that Tartan came unto Ashdod, when Sargon the king of Assyria sent him, and fought against Ashdod, and took it.' (20:1.)

[To avoid confusion about the two Israelite kingdoms, it may be recalled that the united Jewish kingdom, with its extensive borders, and Jerusalem its capital, was established by king David and consolidated by his son Solomon in the tenth century BC. After Solomon's death, it split in two. The northern kingdom was named Israel; it eventually built its capital at Samaria, and it lasted until 722 BC when it fell to Sargon. The southern kingdom was called Judah; its territory included Jerusalem, the capital, and it fell 135 years later, in 587 BC, to the Babylonian king Nebuchadnezzar, who carried off the Jews to exile in Babylon. Less than fifty years later, in 538 BC, the Babylonian empire was swept away by king Cyrus of Persia, who allowed the Jews to return to Jerusalem and Judah.]

OPPOSITE The Franciscan Church of St Catherine adjoining the Constantinian Church of the Nativity in Bethlehem.

The Sargon inscription found by Botta, and other cuneiform texts discovered later, filled gaps in the biblical account of the fateful events which led to Samaria's destruction. It had indeed

been Shalmaneser v who laid siege to Samaria, but the city withstood attack for more than two years, and was still resisting when, in 722 BC, Shalmaneser died. An Assyrian general promptly seized the throne, and to ease acceptance of his legitimacy assumed the name of Sargon, founder of the Akkad dynasty some 1,600 years earlier. His first action was to mount a more vigorous assault on Samaria, and it was to him that the city fell. He went on to carve out a huge empire, and to establish a new capital, with a strong citadel and a vast palace whose art and scriptural treasures would be dug up by a French diplomat-scholar 2,500 years later.

It was luck – and a peasant dyer from the village of Khorsabad – that brought Botta to the site of Sargon's glory. His intention had been to excavate ancient Nineveh, the seat of Sargon's son and successor, Sennacherib, and the last capital of Assyria. It had enjoyed a brief period of greatness under Sennacherib and his son, Esarhaddon, and grandson, Ashurbanipal, and was destroyed in 612 BC, never to rise again. It was preserved in western memory only through the biblical references to Sennacherib, and above all through the timeless story in the Book of Jonah. For this was the city which Jonah the prophet was divinely instructed to save from its wicked ways, but he took ship for Tarshish instead and ended up in the belly of 'a great fish' (popularly but inaccurately thought of as a whale): 'Arise, go to Nineveh, that great city, and cry against it; for their wickedness is come up before me.' (Jonah 1:2.)

When the explorer Botta was appointed French consul in Mesopotamia in 1842 and stationed in Mosul, the recovery of Nineveh became the focus of his expectations, for there was a local tradition that the ancient site lay beneath one of two conspicuous mounds across the river from Mosul. One of them was called by the local Arabs Nebi Yunus – the prophet Jonah, which says something for the length and strength of a tradition. (It will be recalled that Jonah, after emerging from the fish, did proceed to Nineveh and the people of the city repented and were saved.) The other mound was called Kuyunjik, and that is where Botta started excavating in December 1842, after encountering difficulties in digging up the preferred site of Nebi Yunus. He was disappointed with his first efforts, for although he turned up many fragments of bas-reliefs and cuneiform inscriptions, which showed that there were genuine Assyrian remains beneath the mound, 'nothing in a perfect state was obtained', as he wrote later, 'to reward the trouble and outlay' – he was conducting the dig at his own expense.

Nevertheless he persisted for a while longer, moving back and forth across the river from his post at Mosul to the Kuyunjik mound, examining every item his labourers brought out of the

OPPOSITE The saline deposits in the Dead Sea, known in ancient times as the Sea of Salt.

ground. He always found a group of villagers round the trenches whenever he arrived on the site, for it was a matter of local interest, amusement and possible profit, that this strange foreigner should be searching and paying a bonus for what he described as 'figures on stone' and 'bricks with markings on them', namely, sculptured slabs and cuneiform tablets. One day in December, he was approached by one of the bystanders who told him he was a dyer from the village of Khorsabad, twelve miles away, and the 'bricks' in which Botta seemed interested were the same kind as those he used to build his ovens. There were plenty, he said, in and around the mound on which his village stood, and he could bring Botta as many as he wished.

The Frenchman paid little heed to this news, believing, as he wrote later, that 'the Arab usually aimed to please' and eagerly reported what he thought his listener wished to hear. His interest was quickened when the dyer returned a few days later bringing two small inscribed tablets – but not enough to be diverted from his efforts at Kuyunjik. However, after more than three months of

Relief of a hunting scene on the wall of the seventh-century BC north-western palace of the Assyrian monarch Ashurbanipal, grandson of Sennacherib, discovered at Kuyunjik, the site of ancient Nineveh.

digging without any startling finds, he bethought himself of the dyer with his 'bricks' and the story of his village mound, and he decided to abandon his frustrating mound and move up river to Khorsabad. He arrived at the end of March 1843, and promptly began excavating its tel. Within days he realized that here was the greatest stroke of luck in his life, for as his workmen began cutting their first trenches they came across slabs of wall covered with large, albeit mutilated, pictorial bas-reliefs interspersed with cuneiform inscriptions. It was immediately clear to Botta that this site held tremendous riches of antiquity, for such wall decorations could belong only to a powerful monarch, and the remains of the hall which they had exposed were assuredly part of his palace. Only later, with the decipherment of the numerous additional writings that were unearthed, was it established that this was the palace of Sargon II. It was a formidable building indeed, consisting of several halls with wall reliefs and display inscriptions, numerous auxiliary chambers ranged round some thirty open courts, and a large number of 'very natural and admirably sculptured' human and animal figures. It was Botta's successor – both as French consul in Mosul and as archaeologist at Khorsabad – an architect named Victor Place, who discovered at the angle of the two palace walls a box containing seven inscribed tablets of different materials, from gold and silver to copper and lapis lazuli, all bearing identical cuneiform accounts of the history of Sargon's palace structures.

Botta had shone the first torch on a civilization that had vanished from human sight and memory, opened an exciting new field of biblical research, and brought treasures to the Louvre and glory to France. His reputation was firmly established. He could therefore respond with wry benevolence at the ironic hand of chance upon hearing the news that, four years after he had abandoned the frustrating mound of Kuyunjik and moved on to win renown at Khorsabad, the mound was yielding to an English explorer what it had denied to him. It appeared from preliminary reports that Kuyunjik was likely to offer the Englishman the success that had awaited Botta at Khorsabad.

The Englishman was Austen Henry Layard, and he was to achieve an even greater reputation than the Frenchman, and enable the British Museum to vie with the Louvre over Assyrian and Babylonian antiquities. Layard, a great traveller with a passionate interest in the Mesopotamian past, had come to the area in 1842. In that year, on the very site of Kuyunjik, he had actually met Botta, who had cut his first tentative trenches and was already beginning to be despondent over the meagre results. They became friends, and Layard, who was equally anxious to excavate but

Sir Austen Henry Layard, who discovered Nineveh and its royal palaces, and also excavated Nimrud and Babylon. A drawing by the celebrated English painter and sculptor, George Frederick Watts.

91

Scenes in bas-relief on the Black Obelisk of Shalmaneser III unearthed by Layard at Nimrud in Mesopotamia. The second panel from the top depicts the ninth-century BC Assyrian emperor receiving tribute from Jehu king of Israel.

lacked the funds, encouraged him to persist. When Botta finally decided to give up at Kuyunjik, Layard urged him to try the lofty tel of Nimrud, believed to be the site of ancient Calah, a few miles south of Mosul. Botta elected to go to Khorsabad instead.

Layard was in Turkey, performing unofficial diplomatic services for his friend the British ambassador to Constantinople, when he heard from Botta of his brilliant discovery, and he became even more determined to do some excavation of his own. In October 1845, with encouragement and financial assistance from the ambassador, he set forth in haste to dig up the past. He left the shores of the Bosphorus by ship for the Black Sea port of Samsun, and from there, taking only effects that would fill a pair of saddle-bags, he crossed the mountains of Kurdistan and galloped over the plains of Assyria, travelling day and night almost without rest, and reached Mosul, 600 miles away, twelve days later. His aim was the site he had recommended to Botta three years earlier – Nimrud. Mesopotamia was then part of the Ottoman empire, and the local Turkish governor was ill-disposed towards foreigners, and par-ticularly to the kind of venture this foreigner had in mind. Accord-ingly, Layard announced that he was off on an innocuous expedi-tion 'to hunt wild boars', and on 8 November he left Mosul on a small river raft, appropriately carrying on board 'guns, spears, and other formidable weapons'. He was accompanied by a local British merchant and two servants. They floated down the Tigris and reached Nimrud by nightfall. Layard sent a servant to hire a few local labourers, went to sleep, and by sunrise next morning was out surveying the mound to determine where were the most hopeful spots in which to sink his spades. Within the next few hours of that very first day, his workmen had come upon the remains of exten-sive buildings and had partly excavated two chambers with walls covered by slabs inscribed with cuneiform characters. These were clear signs to him, as those at Khorsabad had been to Botta, that here were the ruins of a royal Assyrian palace. In the months that followed, many more writings were found, together with pictorial bas-reliefs and monumental sculptures. It subsequently trans-pired, after decipherment, that Layard had found not one but two palaces, or rather one belonging to Shalmaneser III (859–824 BC) which had been completely rebuilt by the redoubtable Tiglath-Pileser III (745–727 BC). Both monarchs had left inscriptions directly relating to episodes in the Bible.

However, these writings of biblical interest were not discovered immediately. Layard was having difficulties with the Turkish authorities, and he had frequently to leave the Nimrud site to arrange matters in Mosul. While there during an early summer month in 1846, he crossed the river to try his luck at Kuyunjik. He soon found fragments of sculptures, cuneiform slabs, and structural remains which were very promising, and he resolved to tackle this mound again in the future. He then returned to Nimrud, and in December of that year, made a find with a biblical reference. Lying on its side was a seven-foot flat-topped obelisk of black marble, which Layard described soon after his discovery, not yet knowing its significance: 'It was sculptured on the four sides; there were in all twenty small bas-reliefs, and above, below, and between them was carved an inscription 210 lines in length. . . .' The text, deciphered later by Rawlinson, revealed that this was a victory stele containing the annals of king Shalmaneser III: Above one series of three reliefs depicting the emperor receiving tribute from a vassal was the caption: 'The tribute of Jehu. . . . I received from him silver, gold, a golden bowl, a golden vase with pointed bottom, golden tumblers, golden buckets, tin, a staff for a king. . . .' Jehu was the king of Israel, remembered chiefly for the laconic biblical description of the way he handled a chariot: 'he driveth furiously'. (2 Kings 9:20.)

Layard completed his work at Nimrud in May 1847, and then spent another month at Kuyunjik, which he had probed the previous year. This time he found enough inscriptions and royal artefacts to convince him that, as local tradition had long held, the Kuyunjik mound did indeed hold the remains of ancient Nineveh. Though this was not confirmed until four years later, Layard returned in 1849 to conduct concentrated operations, and over the following two years he brought to light a palace as magnificent as that of Sargon II which Botta had uncovered at Khorsabad, but with far more inscriptions of greater importance, and with pictorial wall reliefs more vividly portrayed on slabs of alabaster. The writings consisted not only of captions on the pictorial panels but also of texts on clay cylinders and cuneiform chronicles inscribed on the huge winged bulls with human heads which commanded the entrance to the palace. When Layard left for home in the spring of 1851, he realized that he had found a striking treasure; but since he was not proficient in cuneiform, he did not know what the writings said or which king it was who had ordered them written for display in his palace. Only in the summer of that year did Layard's friend Rawlinson, who had received copies of the texts for decipherment, announce the exciting news that the writings were from the palace of Sennacherib at Nineveh, and that they contained illuminating references to important episodes in the Bible. [The excavations of Layard and his successors also brought to light on this site of Nineveh the palace of Sennacherib's grandson, Ashurbanipal, together with his collection of more than 20,000 clay tablets with cuneiform texts.]

OVERLEAF Layard supervising the removal of winged bulls with human heads which guarded Sennacherib's palace at Nineveh, and which bore inscriptions recording the annals of the king. An 1848 lithograph.

An eighth-century BC relief from the palace of Tiglath-Pileser III at Nimrud showing the assault on a fortified town, with a mobile battering-ram covered by archers (right) and a storming party mounting the walls by scaling-ladder (left).

The gems of Sennacherib's palace for biblical scholars were a series of thirteen slabs of wall reliefs depicting Sennacherib seated upon a throne on a hill-slope before a besieged city amidst the landscape of what was evidently meant to be the land of Judah. The reliefs (which may be seen in the British Museum) are clearly recognizable as a dramatic thirteen-part story in pictures of Sennacherib's campaign in this southern Israelite kingdom. There sits the Assyrian monarch, richly attired, observing his army attacking a fortified city which is being stoutly defended. His battering rams are being pushed up towards the walls over ramps, and are covered by archers, sling-throwers and spearmen to keep the defenders at bay. In one panel prisoners are being impaled by Assyrian soldiers; in another they are being flayed. Moving out of the city under guard is a long procession of captives, and carts laden with booty. In a panel facing the king is a cuneiform caption: 'Sennacherib, king of the Universe, king of Assyria, sat upon a throne and passed in review the booty taken from the city of Lachish.' The text on one of the clay cylinders adds details of the campaign:

As to Hezekiah, the Jew [king Hezekiah, 715–687 BC], he did not submit to my yoke, I laid siege to forty-six of his strong cities, walled forts and to the countless small villages in their vicinity, and conquered them by means of well-stamped earth-ramps, and battering-rams brought thus near to the walls, combined with the attack by foot soldiers, using . . . breeches as well as sapper work. I drove out of them 200,150 people, young and old, male and female, horses, mules, donkeys, camels, big and small cattle beyond counting, and considered them booty. . . .

This was a stupendous discovery. Here, as with Sargon's conquest of Samaria, though far more extensive, was the story from 'the other side of the hill', the Assyrian counterpart of the reference in the Bible: 'Now in the fourteenth year of king Hezekiah did Sennacherib king of Assyria come up against all the fenced cities of Judah, and took them.' (2 Kings 18:13.) What made this find especially important was that for the first time a detailed text was accompanied by even more detailed bas-relief illustrations which evoke the very atmosphere of the biblical battlefield and capture the full drama of the action. Moreover, with their graphic portrayal of every military component in the attack on Lachish, they remain to this day the primary source for the study of the assault techniques and weaponry by powerful armies against walled cities in this period of the biblical age, the eighth and seventh centuries, as well as the defence patterns of the besieged.

Sennacherib and his gleaming cohorts did indeed come down on Judah 'like the wolf on the fold' in the year 701 BC, and destroyed many 'strong cities', though not perhaps forty-six, as he claimed. The one city he sought to subdue, but failed, was Jerusalem, the capital of Judah, where king Hezekiah's spirit of resistance was much strengthened by the tough advice of the prophet Isaiah. Doubtless he would have wished the centrepiece of his wall decorations to have depicted the fall of Jerusalem. Instead, judging by the prominence given to Lachish, this must have been the scene of the fiercest fighting, and he evidently regarded its capture against stubborn defence as his most outstanding victory in this land.

The magnitude of Layard's discovery was given an added dimension some eighty years later when excavations unearthed the very stratum of ancient Lachish that was stormed by Sennacherib's forces. Arrow-heads and sling-shots used by the Assyrians in that battle were among the finds, and from the remains of the shattered city it was possible to reconstruct the plan of its defensive fortifications. They virtually matched those depicted in the reliefs on Sennacherib's palace walls. Thus, Lachish is a superb example of archaeological discovery joining ancient records in word and picture to enrich the background of an episode in the Bible.

Small wonder that Flinders Petrie had been so anxious to find, dig

The Prism of Sennacherib, a clay cylinder with a fulsome account in cuneiform of the Assyrian king's military campaigns. Describing his siege of Jerusalem – which he failed to take – in 701 BC, he claims to have made king 'Hezekiah the Jew' a prisoner 'like a bird in a cage', and exacted tribute.

and test his pottery-dating theory at the mound of Lachish on his first archaeological assignment in Palestine in 1890 – and thought he was doing so when he probed Tel el-Hesi. If Lachish had put up so determined a defence as to gain a distinctive place in Sennacherib's battle report, it must have been a more important town than had been thought before Layard's discovery. Historians and explorers of the land of the Bible would therefore have wished to investigate the site itself, if only they knew its exact location, in order to examine its material remains both before and during the Assyrian destruction, as well as the ruins of its subsequent resettlement. For they knew from the later chapters of the Bible – and they now had a healthier respect for the authenticity of its narrative sections – that Lachish was soon rebuilt by the Jews of Judah and flourished long after Sennacherib had passed from the scene. An irony of history, it had even remained an important city after that emperor's capital, the great Nineveh, had been destroyed.

However, not knowing precisely beneath which of the tels in the Judean foothills Lachish lay buried, the few adventurous scholars who were setting out on this new path of biblical archaeology chose the known spots. Jerusalem accordingly became the principal centre of archaeological activity in the second half of the nineteenth century, and this was both understandable and justifiable. Petrie was the first to try Lachish; but it was his disciple, John Llewelyn Starkey, who found the authentic site; this ancient city lay buried within the mound of Tel ed-Duweir. The man who first proposed it was William Foxwell Albright, who was on his way to becoming the greatest biblical archaeologist of this century. Starkey was able to confirm his theory in the course of his six seasons of excavation, from 1932 to 1938. And it was he who discovered the ruins of the city that Sennacherib had found so tough to conquer.

But this was by no means Starkey's only outstanding discovery. His most exciting find was associated with another battle against another invader, also a Mesopotamian emperor, more than 100 years later, and is the subject of record and dramatic comment in several books of the Bible. The emperor was Nebuchadnezzar, the Chaldean who ruled Babylon from 604 to 562 BC. Some know him as the king who beautified his capital with the fabled 'hanging gardens', called by the Greeks one of the seven wonders of the world, and the monumental Ishtar Gate to his palace, decorated with lively animal figures executed in moulded and glazed bricks. He is best known however, certainly to those familiar with the Bible, as the ruler who, in the year 587 BC, destroyed Jerusalem, ravaged the sacred Jewish Temple which king Solomon had built 450 years earlier, and carried off most of the surviving Jews into Babylonian exile.

Animal figures in moulded and glazed bricks on the monumental Ishtar Gate to the palace of Nebuchadnezzar in Babylon.

This was the climax to months of grim fighting throughout the kingdom of Judah, with Nebuchadnezzar's armies storming several fortified cities in their drive towards the Judean capital. One of them was Lachish, and Starkey's remarkable discovery were twenty-one ostraca – pieces of pottery with writing upon them. The writing on these inscribed potsherds turned out to be biblical Hebrew, and the contents were letters written by a subordinate officer in one of the outposts to his commander in Lachish on the eve of the Babylonian attack. Taken together with the accounts in Kings and Chronicles, and particularly with the utterances of the prophet Jeremiah, they convey the poignant mood and temper in the land of the Bible during those calamitous days.

The wider historical background was the clash between Egypt and Babylon, with the Jewish kingdom in the middle. Nebuchadnezzar's father, Nabopolassar, had captured the mighty Nineveh in 612 BC and laid it waste, swept away the Assyrian empire three years later, and founded the new Babylonian empire (which in turn would be wiped out after a few decades). Egypt, traditional rival of the successive powers that rose in Mesopotamia, gathered her

A mythical dragon-figure with horns, forked tongue and claws, on the Ishtar Gate in Babylon.

99

Nebuchadnezzar's siege of Jerusalem, an illustration from the *Livre des Rois* (*The Book of Kings*).

forces against Nabopolassar, both to seize the Assyrian territories he had just acquired and to check his southern expansion. The two armies met in the year 605 BC at Carchemish, on the upper Euphrates, and the Babylonian forces, commanded by crown prince Nebuchadnezzar, were the decisive victors. Nebuchadnezzar chased the Egyptian army southwards and dealt them a further crushing blow *en route*. He was well on his way to Egypt when the pursuit was suddenly halted by news of the death of his father, and Nebuchadnezzar hastened back to Babylon to safeguard his accession. He had not abandoned his designs for a vengeful strike against Egypt, but during the next three years he limited himself to southward forays in force, which gained him footholds closer to the Egyptian border. One of those footholds was Judah, which became a vassal of Babylon.

100

Nebuchadnezzar made his move against Egypt in 601; but in the pitched battle fought near the Egyptian frontier, both sides suffered heavily, and the Babylonian emperor returned home without his hoped-for victory. Encouraged by this – and by Egypt, who promised support – several vassal states, including Judah, revolted against Babylon. Retribution came in 598 BC, when a Babylonian force re-entered Judah, partially destroyed its major cities and besieged Jerusalem. The Judean king Jehoiakim died at the start of the siege, was succeeded by his teenage son Jehoiachin, and within three months the city surrendered. Egypt had looked on, and sent no help. Jehoiachin, other members of the royal family '. . . all the princes, and all the mighty men of valour, even ten thousand captives' (2 Kings 24:14) were exiled to Babylon, and the boy-king's uncle, Zedekiah, was installed by Nebuchadnezzar as vassal in his place.

Unlike the prophet Isaiah, who a century earlier had stiffened the resolve of king Hezekiah to stand up to Sennacherib, the prophet Jeremiah had urged Jehoiakim to placate Nebuchadnezzar. He expressed his views in religious terms, railing against the moral laxity of the people, and warning the public that an iniquitous Jerusalem would be destroyed. Behind such castigation was his political appraisal of the rival imperial strengths. Babylon was on the rise, and would soon return, vanquish Egypt, and take revenge on all the rebellious tributary states. The blandishments of Egypt should be ignored. In any case, Egypt could not be trusted, and her promise of help was worthless. The time for revolt was not yet ripe. Babylon would eventually overreach herself, and then would be the time to strike. For the moment, Babylon was being used as an instrument of divine punishment against Judah, who had forsaken the path of righteousness; but eventually Babylon would in turn be broken. Nebuchadnezzar who 'has devoured . . . crushed . . . swallowed . . . filled his belly' would be forced to disgorge his imperial acquisitions, and 'wild beasts shall dwell with hyenas in Babylon'. (Jeremiah 50:39, 51:34.) Jehoiakim had rejected Jeremiah's counsel.

Now his brother was on the throne and found himself torn between the conflicting policies of revolt and submission. The public mood was all for resistance, and so, in 588 BC, 'in the ninth year of his reign . . . Zedekiah rebelled against the king of Babylon', and 'Nebuchadnezzar king of Babylon came, he, and all his host, against Jerusalem, and pitched against it. . . . And the city was besieged unto the eleventh year of king Zedekiah.' (2 Kings 24:20, 25:1,2.) With Jerusalem placed under blockade by a holding unit, the main Babylonian forces went after the other walled cities of Judah, and steadily reduced them one by one. The last to fall, before the enemy returned to Jerusalem to deliver the *coup de grâce*, were Lachish and Azekah, its neighbour to the north-east.

This was the military situation when Jeremiah issued his final appeal to king Zedekiah to submit to Babylon and halt the destruction:

> Then Jeremiah the prophet spoke all these words to Zedekiah of Judah, in Jerusalem, when the army of the king of Babylon was fighting against Jerusalem and against all the cities of Judah that were left, Lachish and Azekah; for these were the only fortified cities of Judah that remained. (Jeremiah 34:6, 7.)

It must have been only a few days later that one of the Lachish Letters found by Starkey had been written by the officer in the outpost, evidently sited between Lachish and Azekah, to his commander: 'We are watching for the signals of Lachish . . . for we cannot see Azekah.' Azekah must just have fallen, and with the consequent breakdown in communications, the outpost was reporting that it was now dependent for information on the signals from Lachish.

One of the twenty-one Lachish letters discovered by Starkey, written in early Hebrew script on potsherds by a Judean officer shortly before the Babylonian conquest of Judah in 587 BC.

Starkey came upon his discovery in the third year of his excavations when he was examining the early sixth-century BC stratum. He found eighteen of the ostraca amidst the burnt debris in the guardhouse of the city gate in 1935. Another three were found later elsewhere on the site, with the same biblical style and early Hebrew script, written on broken pottery vessels in black ink made from iron-carbon. The letters reflect the feelings of the soldiers in the field, the defenders of Judah in imminent danger of annihilation, as well as the critical cross-currents of opinion in the besieged capital. The account in the Bible shows that the militant faction were furious with Jeremiah for lowering morale with his publicly proclaimed prophecies of doom: 'for thus he weakeneth the hands of the men of war that remain in this city, and the hands of all the people, in speaking such words to them'. (Jeremiah 38:4.) One of the Lachish Letters is a perfect counterpart of this biblical verse, written by Hoshaiah, the officer in charge of the outpost, to Yaosh, his commander at Lachish. Yaosh had sent him reports he had received from Jerusalem, with the note: 'Pray read them.' Hoshaiah replies:

> And behold the words . . . are not good, but to weaken our hands and to slacken the hands of the men who are informed about them . . . truly since thy servant read the [reports] there hath been no peace for thy servant. . . .

There was neither peace nor much life left for this 'servant', the writer of the Lachish Letters. He was already dead, and his city stormed and destroyed, when the Babylonian army turned its full force on the remaining bastion in Judah: Jerusalem. It had been under tight siege for two years, and now, in the hot summer of 587 BC, the northern wall of the starved capital was breached by battering rams, and the besieging forces poured through. The city and Temple were sacked. The king of Judah was brought before Nebuchadnezzar and forced to watch the slaying of his sons. The victors then 'put out the eyes of Zedekiah, and bound him with fetters of brass, and carried him to Babylon', where he died. (2 Kings 25:7.) Some of the prominent citizens who had escaped the deportations at the time of king Jehoiachin were executed, and the rest were taken off to Babylonian exile.

Starkey found in his excavations that Jeremiah's prophecy about the fate of Babylon was soon fulfilled – probably sooner than even the prophet had foreseen. Less than fifty years after Nebuchadnezzar's conquest of Judah, the great Babylonian empire fell as suddenly as it had risen, wiped out by Cyrus the Great, founder of a new Persian empire. Babylon, the capital, was captured at the end of 539 BC, and by 538 the entire empire, right up to the frontier of Egypt, came under Persian control. Judah was thus brought within the benevolent rule of Cyrus, and one of his first steps was to allow the exiled Jews in Babylon to return to Jerusalem and Judah and rebuild their Temple and their homes. Starkey found the remains of this Jewish re-settlement in the strata of the Persian period.

The name and region of Lachish flourish again in today's Israel. Archaeologist Starkey did not live to witness its revival, nor to enjoy for long the success of his unique discovery. His six-year dig ended abruptly on 10 January 1938 when he left the Lachish site to attend the opening of the Palestine Archaeological Museum in Jerusalem. He had reached the outskirts of Hebron when he was murdered by Arab brigands.

5 The Pioneer Diggers

Starkey had dug up Lachish and made history. He would hardly have had such success if he had attempted to excavate the site coveted by every scholar anxious to sink his spade into the Scriptural past: Jerusalem, the pre-eminent city of the Bible. Had he done so, he would have encountered the same limiting circumstances and the very problems that had plagued two of his compatriots some seventy years earlier; significant advances beyond their discoveries would doubtless have proved elusive. The two pioneers were Charles William Wilson and Charles Warren, both of them young army officers in the Royal Engineers, and both archaeological beginners. Yet it was they who laid the foundations for the eventual recovery of Jerusalem's material history. Wilson arrived in Jerusalem in 1864. Warren followed him three years later.

It was the chance convergence of three unrelated factors that first brought Wilson to the Holy Land: the early American gold rush, the benevolence of an English lady, and the penury of a brother officer. Wilson was then a twenty-eight-year-old captain, and he had already proved himself a first-rate topographer, well able to handle unexpected situations under grim physical conditions in unknown territory. He had returned only eighteen months earlier from a four-year stint of gruelling survey work in the wild northwestern region of the American continent, marking on the ground the western section of the boundary between the United States and Canada. The three-thousand-mile frontier from the Atlantic to the Pacific had been settled on paper by the treaty of 1783, a treaty which brought to a formal close the war between Britain and her rebellious north American colonies. The populated eastern section, from the Atlantic to the Great Lakes, had been fixed within a few decades; but the sparse, largely uninhabited section, notably from the Rocky Mountains to the Pacific, remained a boundary on

OPPOSITE The vase-like outline which appears in this aerial view of Jerusalem to the south of the Temple Mount formed the original bounds of the city in the time of David.

paper – the line was to follow the 49th parallel. After the 1840s, however, the rush to the gold mines on the western slopes of the Rockies brought speculators and settlers to the region, and with them the danger of future conflict between the rising colony of British Columbia and the adjacent American territory of Oregon. (The part of Oregon bordering on Canada later, in 1853, became the State of Washington.)

A joint British–United States North American Boundary Commission was accordingly established to chart and mark this section of the frontier. The teams started operations in 1858, working eastwards in all weathers from the Pacific towards the Rockies, slashing their way through dense forests, crossing flat, swampy prairies, negotiating rugged mountains and swift rivers, marking the boundary in wooded regions by twenty-foot-wide cuttings, and elsewhere by cairns and pickets. Most of the British Commission members were army officers of the Royal Engineers experienced in ordnance surveys. Wilson, a promising junior subaltern and the youngest member of the group, gained his experience on the job, which was completed in 1862.

Sir Charles William Wilson, whose topographic survey of Jerusalem in 1864–6 laid the foundations for the recovery of its material history.

Back in England, he was engaged on military fortifications for the next eighteen months, promoted to captain, and was well set for a life of soldiering when he was suddenly projected into the totally different world of biblical scholarship, conducting a survey of Jerusalem and its remains of antiquity. Not until sixteen years later, at the age of forty-six, would he see combat for the first time, joining the expedition which landed in Egypt in the summer of 1882 to suppress what was known as the Arabi Pasha rebellion, and taking part in the decisive battle of Tel el-Kebir. He was in action again two years later as part of the rescue force rushing to relieve the beleaguered garrison of Khartoum in the Sudan, which was commanded by General Charles George Gordon, one of the most remarkable British soldiers of the nineteenth century. The rescuers were too late. Wilson himself, at the head of a small advance party on a frail river craft, was running the gauntlet of enemy fire in a desperate attempt to reach Gordon when Khartoum fell and the entire garrison was butchered. Wilson was lucky to escape when his boat was wrecked, but he managed to bring his party through the enemy lines to safety. He ended his army career with the rank of major-general; however he was proudest of his scholarly association with the land of the Bible. To his dying day this remained his principal interest, stirred by his first visit to Jerusalem to undertake the survey.

This had come about when a philanthropic English lady, Miss (later Baroness) Burdett-Coutts, sought the privilege of improving Jerusalem's water-supply and sanitary system. Told that an accurate plan of the city was required before any scheme could be carried out, she contributed £500. The Secretary of State for War was then requested to allow a party of Royal Engineers from the Army Ordnance Survey to be seconded for the task, and he agreed. He stipulated, however, that the team was to be headed by an officer, but that the government would be put to no expense on that account. The officer would receive no remuneration, and he would even have to pay his own travel and other personal expenses.

Wilson first heard of this when he happened to visit a brother officer who had just been invited by his commanding general to accept the job. He told Wilson he was turning it down because he simply could not afford the cost. Wilson thereupon asked him to notify his general that he himself would like it: he had the means, and as he wrote later, 'I had always had a strong wish to visit Jerusalem and Palestine'. The general, familiar with Wilson's distinguished service on the North American Boundary Commission, warmly approved so capable a candidate, and Wilson was *en route* to Jerusalem by October 1864. He spent the next nine months industriously gathering the necessary data, probing, measuring, mapping, meticulously recording details of the visible remains of past centuries. He returned to England in July 1865 with such successful results that he was back in Jerusalem in November under new sponsorship, with the directive to complete the survey, deepen his investigation by archaeological soundings and carry out a reconnaissance of the country to indicate sites for future exploration.

The sponsor of Wilson's second Jerusalem assignment was an august institution which had been established in Britain only a few months earlier. The surface exploration of Palestine by Robinson and Tobler, and the discoveries in the neighbouring countries by Botta and Layard, had generated a passionate desire in the western world to unearth the biblical remains in the land of the Bible itself. The first country to act on this impulse was Britain. On 22 June 1865 a distinguished group of statesmen, prelates and scholars met under the patronage of Queen Victoria and the chairmanship of the Archbishop of York and founded the Palestine Exploration Fund. Among the original members were an ex-prime minister, three former and future Cabinet ministers, three bishops, and the speaker of the House of Commons; Sir Henry Rawlinson – he had been knighted for his Persian and Mesopotamian discoveries and his cuneiform decipherment; Canon Tristram, who would soon go out to Palestine for the Fund and write his classic work on the flora and fauna of the land; and Dean Stanley of Westminster, outspoken theologian, intellectual and traveller, who had shortly before accompanied the Prince of Wales on a visit to Egypt and Palestine.

They were an enlightened body, concerned with expanding the prevailing knowledge of the land of the Bible in biblical times, and it was the Archbishop of York himself who made clear at the founders' meeting that while one of its objects was to help eluci- date some of the biblical problems, the Palestine Exploration Fund was not to be a religious society. The work it undertook was to be conducted in accordance with strictly scientific principles. It must be said that this code was respected in all the subsequent activities of the Fund.

Jerusalem was chosen as the first city of antiquity to be investi- gated because of its biblical importance. It was also considered to possess all but one of the virtues of the ideal archaeological site. Its identification posed no problem. It was not like other cities of the ancient world, such as Lachish, or even great capitals, like Nineveh and Babylon, which lay buried beneath anonymous mounds of rubble for millennia. Jerusalem was inhabited continuously for more than 3,000 years, and was always known by that name – except for a relatively brief period during Roman times when it was officially called Aelia Capitolina. (The emperor Hadrian had changed its name in AD 135 and banned Jews from the city, in order to wipe out all trace of its Jewish associations. The emperor Con- stantine changed it back to Jerusalem in AD 325.) Thus, there was never any uncertainty about the city's location, though there was about its boundaries and the course of the city walls at different periods, as well as the exact siting of its major structures referred to in the Bible. Moreover, the Old Testament gave Jerusalem a recorded history of almost 1,000 years preceding the Christian era, the most detailed ancient chronicle of any city in the world, and this made it a tempting site for an archaeologist.

However, its major drawback, as young Captain Wilson soon discovered, stemmed from its very virtues: its unbroken settlement meant there was hardly any unoccupied space, so how and where could one excavate? The scholar tackling a remote and abandoned tel could level the entire mound layer by layer to expose the remains of each successive settlement of early days. But Jerusalem was a living city; moreover, it had become sacred to two additional faiths, first Christianity and then Islam, so that religious institu- tions and monuments as well as ordinary dwellings now stood on the sites most likely to hold remains of biblical buildings. The most prominent of such sites, for example, and the one of deepest interest to the archaeologist, was Temple Mount, the hill upon which Solomon had constructed the Jewish Temple in the tenth century BC. It was now the Moslem Haram esh-Sharif ('Noble

The Temple Mount in Jerusalem, showing the recent archaeological excavations at the foot of the southern wall (bottom left).

Sanctuary'), with its golden Dome of the Rock and the silver-domed Mosque of El Aksa built some 1,800 years later, in the seventh and eighth centuries AD. To reach the Solomonic treasures, one would have to tear down this Moslem shrine, which was unthinkable – just as it was not possible elsewhere in Jerusalem to go about demolishing other mosques and churches and houses and shops, and hacking through streets and alleys, in order to find the ruins of the cities of David and Solomon, Hezekiah and Josiah, Isaiah and Jeremiah, Ezra and Nehemiah. Yet this was precisely what the archaeologists were after, in order to shed light on the Old Testament narrative. And this was what Wilson's sponsors had in mind when they hoped that his topographical assignment might be developed into an archaeological enterprise.

It was eventually to become such an enterprise, but not immediately, and not by Wilson. This did not surprise him. He already knew from the experience of his first visit what lay in store for the archaeologist. He had encountered difficulties without number in his surface work; how much more difficult it would be to start excavating. Apart from the physical constraints which limited the exploration of promising sites, there were irksome bureaucratic

109

The beautifully-preserved first-century BC arch built by Herod, adjoining the western wall of the Temple compound in Jerusalem, discovered and cleared by Wilson and named after him. A contemporary engraving published in the *Illustrated London News*.

obstacles. Permits were not easy to come by from the corrupt, dilatory and suspicious Turkish administration. Bribery of local civilian and Moslem religious officials was the accepted procedure to circumvent obstruction, but the results were never certain.

Nevertheless, there was much that Wilson could do, and did. He applied himself to determining the most fruitful spots for more comprehensive archaeological investigation as and when conditions eased, and at the same time continued with his survey. In the total time he spent there between 1864 and 1866, he produced the first accurate and detailed ordnance map of Jerusalem, thereby laying the groundwork for his successors. It was so impressive – it still serves as the basic topographic record of the Old City – that he was entrusted with the ordnance survey of the Sinai peninsula a few years later. And despite frequent harassment, he also managed to conduct a fair degree of archaeological probing. He even succeeded in doing some digging near the Western Wall of the Temple Mount, in the course of which he penetrated what was then a subterranean structure but which today is at ground level – an arch thought to have supported the bridge mentioned by the first-century AD historian Josephus as having connected the Upper City of Jerusalem with the sacred compound during the Second Temple period. The arch was accordingly named after Wilson, just as the springer to an arch about a hundred yards to the south found by Robinson some thirty years earlier was called Robinson's Arch. (One hundred years later, shortly after the 1967 Six Day war, Wilson's Arch was re-discovered during excavations. It had been filled with debris and built on since his time. The debris was now removed and the approaches cleared, as was the area in front of the Western Wall which it adjoins, and the arch was found to be in a perfect state of preservation. It had been built by Herod in the first century BC, and the huge stones characteristic of his structures were immaculately laid to form a flawless curve.)

Wilson left Jerusalem without having accomplished any grand archaeological design of unearthing the city's past. But he had provided a basic tool – the topographic map – and he had made the initial probes which could be followed up 'as and when' conditions permitted. Little did he know that a hundred years would pass before such circumstances would arise to make possible the thorough and comprehensive archaeological excavations he envisaged. He would have been even more surprised could he but have known that his one archaeological discovery, the result of a minor dig, linking his name with an arch that abutted the Temple Mount, would gain him immortality.

The Palestine Exploration Fund were impressed with this discovery and well satisfied with their opening project, and in 1867 sent out Lieutenant Charles Warren, also of the Royal Engineers, to carry on where Wilson had left off the year before and start excavating. Warren and three corporals arrived in the open roadstead of Jaffa on a stormy mid-February day, were ferried hazardously to the landing stage, and, like Wilson, promptly ran up against the local Ottoman bureaucracy. (They, too, were to plumb its frustrating depths during the course of their Jerusalem excavations.) The customs officials inspected their boxes of equipment, and offered no objection to the crowbars, drills, jacks, handspikes, block and tackle contained therein. But they pronounced their sextants and theodolites to be 'warlike stores', and refused them permission to leave. They were released only after the intervention of the British vice-consul, and his assurance, as Warren later reported, that the instruments were 'of a peaceful nature and not liable to go off'. After securing horses for themselves and a string of eight pack-mules for their cumbrous implements, they set off for Jerusalem and all went well until they reached the Judean foothills. There they struck freak weather – 'a most furious piercing cold wind,' wrote Warren, 'the strongest wind I have met with, and we crept along like snails; our mules on several occasions were blown over.' It took them thirteen hours to cover the last twenty-four miles. The

111

road was poor, and they were also 'delayed a great deal in picking up our fallen animals'. Nevertheless they reached Jerusalem in good heart, and 'immediately commenced work'.

The British Army had again been pleased to lend an outstanding officer and his aides to the Fund, being interested in securing detailed topographical data of the lands adjoining Britain's strategic routes to her eastern empire. This interest would deepen when the Suez canal, which was then under construction, opened two years later. The association of the army and the Fund was to prove mutually beneficial, and several of the officers attained eminence in both the exploration and military fields. Wilson, as we have seen, achieved the rank of major-general. Warren, who improved on Wilson's record as an archaeologist and was the first to carry out actual digs in Jerusalem, also held more responsible military commands, with longer spells of distinguished and colourful active service, and became a full general. The even more renowned Field Marshal Lord Kitchener started service life as a junior officer carrying out an extensive survey of Palestine and part of Sinai for the Fund. And three decades later, Lawrence of Arabia's early meetings with the Middle East would be marked by a stint of exploration on the Fund's survey of northern Sinai.

The Fund, for its part, welcomed the choice of Warren. At twenty-seven, he had already completed a seven-year term as an army engineer on the Rock of Gibraltar, and had shown ingenuity in designing and constructing improved fortifications and gun emplacements, work which entailed much blasting and tunnelling. Little was known of archaeological methods at this stage, but it was evident, particularly after Wilson's report, that proficiency in engineering was invaluable to the explorer of Jerusalem, since antiquity lay buried beneath occupied buildings and might be reached only through tunnelling.

It was, indeed, largely by tunnelling – sinking vertical shafts with horizontal galleries running off them to the archaeological objectives – that Warren carried out his three-year project. He directed his main effort to the area around the Haram esh-Sharif enclosure, the biblical Temple Mount. It was the hope of the Fund that in the course of his investigations Warren might also find the remains and exact position of the Jewish Temple built by Solomon, described in such detail in the Bible. (1 Kings 7.)

Warren was familiar with its recorded history, and his aim was to recover the material remains of that history. Erected in the tenth century BC; destroyed at the beginning of the sixth century BC; rebuilt on the same site and duplicating the original dimensions fifty years later, and known thereafter as the Second Temple; refurbished, given a handsome new façade, and provided with a

Sir Charles Warren, at forty-eight, a distinguished senior army officer. Twenty-one years earlier, in 1867, he had succeeded Wilson in Jerusalem and was the first to undertake archaeological excavations in that city.

The large stone in the foreground covered the shaft sunk by Warren in 1868 against the Herodian western wall of the Temple compound, which exposed fifteen additional courses of that wall. The shaft was found intact 100 years later when the debris was cleared during the recent excavations.

huge platform, supported and enclosed by massive retaining walls by Herod in the first century BC; and destroyed by Rome's Titus in AD 70. It was left in ruins, ignored and untouched throughout the Byzantine Christian era, buried beneath the steadily gathering mounds of dust and rubbish for the next six centuries until the Moslem conquest in the year AD 638. In the following century the site was cleared and resuscitated as an Islamic shrine, crowned by the two magnificent mosques. In later centuries religious study halls, fountains, minarets, arcades and small prayer chambers were added to the Harem esh-Sharif. Warren would have to burrow beneath the edges of these structures if he were to reach the antiquities of the 1st millennium BC.

It was an impossible undertaking, certainly for one man, but Warren approached it undismayed. Using his engineering skills to drive tunnels beneath several centuries' accumulation of debris, he discovered ancient water-courses and pools, determined rock-levels which would give the future archaeologist essential information on the city's contours, and systematically registered every object he unearthed – the first time this had been done so meticulously. But he found nothing which could be linked to any specific record in the Bible. He encountered the inevitable bits of pottery, but these were valueless and meaningless – Petrie had not yet appeared on the scene. Two pieces of pottery, however, caused a stir. They were jar-handles bearing the Hebrew inscription 'la melech', 'belonging to the king', the first to be discovered. (Large

113

numbers would be found very much later at several archaeological sites.) But since there were no means of dating them, they remained simply curios, not clues.

Perhaps Warren's most important discovery emerged from the intricate series of excavations he carried out close to the huge retaining walls of the Temple enclosure. These proved to be even more massive than they appeared, going down to a depth ranging from 80 to 125 feet below the present surface, with as many as fifteen additional courses. These lower courses were seen 100 years later when one of Warren's shafts was found intact during the 1968 clearance of the debris in Wilson's Arch. (Since then, much excavation has exposed larger stretches of the formidable walls.) Another shaft sunk by Warren in the ridge of the south-eastern corner of the Temple Mount revealed the archaeologically significant remains of a tower and a city wall. This was the area known as the Ophel, considered to have been the site of Jerusalem in David's time before it was extended northwards by Solomon. This particular discovery was to become the subject of sharp debate by later archaeologists over the exact boundaries of the city of David, and the history of its expansion to the north and north-west during the reigns of the subsequent Hebrew kings.

It is remarkable that Warren achieved as much as he did with all the harassment and obstruction to which he was subjected by the local Turkish officials. The imperial Ottoman government in Constantinople felt threatened by the growing influence of the European powers in the Middle East, and its representatives in Palestine were accordingly suspicious of an Englishman who came ferreting around Jerusalem, wanting to dig here and there. Their obvious duty was to curb his activities, though without causing a diplomatic incident between Britain and Turkey. Some did it amiably, like 'the civil old gentleman', as Warren called the military governor of Jerusalem, whom he had met on arrival, and accordingly he 'immediately commenced work' near the Haram esh-Sharif. 'But in four days,' wrote Warren, 'the work was stopped', as the governor feared 'that if we dug near the wall we should bring it down.' When Warren reassured him, he tried another tack, expressing 'much astonishment at my mission'. It was superfluous. There was nothing to learn about the Haram esh-Sharif. 'He could tell me what was under every stone!' Besides, he said that the sanctuary 'lay on the top leaves of a palm tree, from the roots of which spring all the rivers of the world, and that any attempt of a Frank [European] to explore them would only be attended by some dire calamity.' However, when Warren persisted and resumed work, no action was taken against him.

The governor retired shortly afterwards, and his successor was less civil. He first 'tried to stop the work on the pretext that we were digging in a cemetery'. This was quickly shown to be untrue. He then 'stopped our work near the Damascus Gate', and ordered that 'we were not to dig nearer than forty feet to any of the city walls or the Sanctuary'. But, 'I had a long list of places for excavating in, and as fast as he stopped us at one point we went off to another.' Warren then conceived a new idea for reaching the walls. The governor had prohibited their working closer to the walls than forty feet, 'but he was quite unaware of our powers of *mining....* My plan then was to commence at the required distance, mine up to the wall, and obtain the necessary information.' And that was what he did.

Warren had a simple solution to the problem of bribery: he refused to pay. His system was to employ as labourers the tenants of the ground he was excavating, cover any damage to their crops, and pay the landlords 'for the privilege of digging in their soil'. However, officials of the Turkish Government endeavoured 'to extort backsheesh by bringing pressure to bear against us, with a view to being bought off. Had I given way, it would have been as well to have closed the works at once: it would have been necessary to fee all the officials employed, who would again, after the custom of the country, have expected money from the land-owners, and these again would have recouped themselves at our expense. When they found that I would not give way, all kinds of difficulties were thrown in our path.' Eventually 'firmness carried the day', and the work progressed.

What of the scholarly quality of Warren's exploration? Well, with archaeology in its infancy, he had no means of identifying what it was he was discovering. With no criterion for putting a date to masonry or pottery, there was no way of determining to which period of biblical history a wall or an artefact belonged – whether it was one, two or three thousand years old. Thus, while Warren's systematic notes registering all he did and discovered proved extremely valuable to later scholars, many of the historical values he attached to his finds were shown to have been erroneous. For example, he thought he had indeed found the remains of the First Temple by ascribing the great retaining walls of the enclosure to Solomon. They were in fact built one thousand years later, by Herod. Conversely, when he excavated Tel el-Ful, the biblical site of Gibeah of Saul three miles north of Jerusalem, he ascribed the ruins of a citadel to the Crusaders of the twelfth century A.D. The great William Foxwell Albright, who excavated the site in 1922, found this ruin to be 1,400 years older. It was a second-century BC Maccabee fortress.

Apart from its interest in the Temple area, the Palestine Exploration Fund was also hopeful that Warren might clear up a problem associated with the New Testament. The iconoclastic Robinson had cast doubts on the authenticity of the siting of the Church of the Holy Sepulchre, and this had evoked a good deal of controversy, and genuine concern among the faithful. The conflict of views turned on the question of where Jerusalem's city walls had been at the time of Jesus. The church is located in the northwestern quarter of the Old City, inside the walls. It was argued by the sceptics that if the northern wall followed the same course in the first century, Calvary could not have been where the church is today, for no executions and no burials could have taken place inside the city walls. This was countered by the claim that the present walls, built by Suleiman the Great in the sixteenth century, enclosed a larger area, and that the northern wall in the time of Jesus excluded the site of the Crucifixion and the Sepulchre. It was one of Warren's purposes to try and solve this enigma by finding the ruined foundations of the first-century city wall. He did not succeed; nor did any other archaeologist. The scholarly controversy persists to this day, with differing interpretations given to various finds that have been unearthed in the last 100 years, none of them conclusive. Thus, each of the rivals holds to his own line of the northern wall, including or excluding the Church of the Holy Sepulchre to suit his theory.

The Palestine Exploration Fund had set Warren an ambitious goal which could have been reached only by a huge expedition mounted at vast expense and with the freedom to demolish whatever it wished. In the circumstances, Warren's lone assignment was more productive than any realist could have expected. His scientific approach, his careful records of what and how he was doing at all stages of each excavation, his accurate measurements, his topographic soundings, all proved extremely valuable to the development of this new branch of knowledge called biblical archaeology. So did his mistakes.

It was now evident, for example, that despite his imaginative engineering, tunnelling was a highly unsatisfactory archaeological excavation process. It was costly, laborious, lengthy; and it could destroy or damage vital historical clues which might never be recovered, or it might even miss them. Since it exposed only limited areas, and not necessarily the most fruitful ones, an important inscription, object, or part of a building might lie concealed an inch above the roof or below the base of a tunnelled gallery. And if part of a ruin were brought to light in the course of the quarrying, the small patch of exposed masonry could offer no accurate pointer to the plan and nature of the total structure.

OPPOSITE The ambulatory in the Church of the Holy Sepulchre in the Old City of Jerusalem. One of Warren's archaeological aims was to determine whether this traditional site of Calvary had been within or outside the city walls at the time of the Crucifixion.

Moreover, tunnelling provided no opportunity for the archaeologist to gain an overall view of the site, see the scattered finds in relation to each other, and read the historical story behind the mute remains.

Warren left Jerusalem in 1870, and went on to greater glory as a soldier. One of his exploits was a direct outcome of the experience he had gained during his three-year archaeological stay in Palestine. After spending most of the next decade in South Africa in responsible positions of military command, as well as settling conflicts over the boundary of the British possessions by skilful diplomacy, he was back in the Middle East in 1882. He was there to undertake a hazardous rescue mission in the Sinai peninsula. The task called for a knowledge of Arabic, experience in dealing with Arab sheikhs and Bedouin, and a topographic eye for desert terrain. Warren had acquired these qualifications partly on his Jerusalem excavations and partly on extended journeys in Transjordan and Sinai during the intervals between the digging seasons.

The background to his dangerous venture was the threat to the newly constructed Suez Canal by rebellious Bedouin tribes in Sinai; and Britain, with its new route to India at risk, considered sending in a military expedition. Before doing so, however, the authorities decided to consult the outstanding British orientalist at the time, Professor Edward Henry Palmer, who had carried out a survey of the Sinai desert at the very time when Warren was working in Jerusalem, and was reputed to have 'gained the confidence of the wild Bedouin tribes'. Palmer recommended that instead of quelling the rebels by force, he himself should visit the territory to try, as he put it, 'to arrange matters personally with the sheikhs'. This proposal was accepted, and he went into the desert early in August 1882 accompanied by two military aides together with their Syrian Christian dragoman, a Jewish cook, a reliable Bedouin Moslem guide, cameleers – and three bags of gold, each containing £1,000. They were never heard from again.

Anxiety mounted as days passed without authentic news of their fate. When this became known to Warren, who was in England at the time, he promptly volunteered to lead a search and rescue party; and, if the worst had indeed happened, he would carry out the Palmer assignment of pacifying the tribes – and he would do it without gold. His offer was welcomed, and he was on a ship to Suez two days later.

After several perilous weeks in the hostile desert of Sinai, with its equally hostile people, seeking Palmer's camel-tracks, using firmness and bluff to interrogate reluctant informants and sifting their stories for kernels of truth, Warren learned that Palmer and his party had been murdered and the gold stolen. Their 'reliable' Bedouin guide had betrayed them, leading them to a rendezvous with their Bedouin murderers. Warren and his group went in search of their bodies and found the gruesome remains at the bottom of a gully. Most of October and November was spent in tracking down the culprits – something which also became part of Warren's method of bringing the sheikhs to heel. One of the latter was even induced to cooperate, if he valued his future, by rounding up 'all the wanted men within thirty-one days', with the result that by 25 December, 'all the principal and many of their accomplices' were in custody. (The quotations are from Warren's account of his mission which was published in the Parliamentary Blue Book of 21 February 1883.) It transpired from their sworn confessions that five men had been involved in the actual killing. They had led Palmer and his four companions to the edge of a precipice, and promptly shot Palmer, 'finished him off with a sword, and then pushed him over' into the gully below. The two military aides, the dragoman and the cook had then been 'driven over the precipice and shot from above'. Two, who were still alive, 'were finished off. I saw all five dead.'

The five murderers were brought to trial, sentenced to death, and executed in the presence of a sheikh and two Bedouin from every tribe. One third of the plundered gold was recovered.

Two years later Warren was in command of the Bechuanaland expedition, which established Britain's claims to that disputed territory in South Africa. He was then appointed Governor of the Red Sea Littoral, but was soon recalled to England to become Chief Commissioner of the Metropolitan Police of London at a time when police morale was low and public confidence in them shaken. Warren's appointment was widely welcomed, even by the distinguished satirical weekly, *Punch*. He was back in the army in 1889 and spent the next five years in Singapore as commander of the troops in the Straits Settlements.

This man, one of the 'fathers of biblical archaeology', had come a long way since his Jerusalem explorations, and he was to go further. He reached the pinnacle of his military career as a divisional commander in the South African War (the Boer War, 1899–1902). A little-known episode of a battlefield encounter between the sixty-year-old General Warren and a twenty-six-year-old war correspondent and freelance subaltern named Winston Churchill sheds light on the character of both men. The Boers had put the key Natal town of Ladysmith under siege on 1 November 1899, and Warren's division was entrusted with the critical task of relieving it. This was accomplished on 28 February 1900, but only after a series of bitter engagements for possession of

PUNCH TO THE PEELERS.

ALL honour to your management, my WARREN
    All honour to the Force you featly led!
And that honour, *Punch* opines, should not be barren
    (May he hear hereafter more upon *that* head).
'Midst the Jubilee's joyous pageantry and pother,
    (Though 'tis common of our Bobbies to make fun)
"Taking one consideration with another,"
    The Policemen's work was excellently done.

Mr. Punch from post of vantage proudly viewed them;
    They combined unshrinking toil with ready tact,
Whilst the sultry summer sunshine broiled and stewed them,
    Showing judgment when to act or not to act.
Their thin blue line kept order; firm yet kindly,
    They stood with faces flushed, but pulses cool,
Whilst the multitude around them crowded blindly,
    True type of a free people's civic rule!

By Jingo, how they worked amidst the jostle
    With steady backs and ever ready hands!
When the whistle sounded, mellow as a throstle,
    How they helped the Ambulance's helpful hands!
Fainting woman, shrieking girl, or panting 'ARRY,
    All with equal care and courtesy they served,
With ready arm to cover or to carry
    From the press where the packed people swayed and swerved.

How many lives and limbs they saved, those Peelers,
    And the Ambulance with which they worked so well,
Unless the rescued all should turn revealers,
    No record will declare, no story tell.
But *Mr. Punch's* vigilant observation
    Marked their hard toil amidst the mob's wild fun,
And, filled with genuine pride and admiration,
    He publicly awards his warm "Well done!"

the peaks that dominated the route to Ladysmith. Churchill appeared at Warren's headquarters on 24 January 1900, when the toughest of those engagements, the battle for the strategic height of Spion Kop, had reached a desperate stage. Signals had broken down, and messengers had not reached their destination. Warren was thus without details of the situation on the summit, and the summit commander was unaware that Warren was sending reinforcements and water. A despatch covering these critical hours, which appears in Volume II of the official history of the campaign, contains the one message from Warren to the local commander that *did* get through: 'The General Officer Commanding Force would be glad to have your views of the situation and measures to be adopted, by Lt Winston Churchill, who takes this note.'

An unofficial account written some years later by Sir Cecil Levita, who had been on Warren's staff, gives the background: 'The difficulty was to get communication of any kind through to the top of Spion Kop. I sent up three or four messengers [who failed to arrive].... Not long afterwards I saw Winston Churchill approaching me; he was in a somewhat excited condition and he rushed up to me and said, "For God's sake, Levita, don't let this be a second Majuba." [This was a reference to the mountain in northern Natal where the Boers had routed the British nineteen years earlier.] I told him what I knew ... and I was very busy, and that if he had any information or suggestions he could give them direct to Sir Charles Warren, who was pacing up and down a little way apart from where I was working. Churchill immediately went over to Warren and began haranguing him. Warren stopped in his pacing ... glared at Churchill, and, after hearing some of his remarks, called out to me, "Who is this man? Put him under arrest." I replied, "This is Mr Winston Churchill ..." Sir Charles Warren was not to be pacified by Churchill's advice.' But instead of arresting him, Levita 'called Churchill over and told him I was anxious to get a message [from Warren] to the top of Spion Kop.... Churchill said he would take the message ... and he went off.... I believe that it was the only message that reached Thorneycroft [the summit commander] of the many that I despatched.'

Warren's life was indeed colourful and exciting, and 'wide and varied were his occupations', as the Palestine Exploration Fund Quarterly wrote when he died in 1927 at the age of eighty-seven. 'Yet we have ample evidence that the interest he acquired in Palestine and its biblical and archaeological problems during the early days when he worked there, remained with him throughout his life.'

The Fund learned sober lessons from the experience gained in its

OPPOSITE Between archaeology and soldiering, Warren had a brief spell as Head of London's Metropolitan Police. A *Punch* cartoon congratulated him on his handling of the crowds at Queen Victoria's Golden Jubilee procession with a complimentary parody of the then popular 'Policeman's Song' from the Gilbert and Sullivan opera *The Pirates of Penzance*.

first two assignments, undertaken by Wilson and Warren. Archaeology in Jerusalem would need to wait, and excavation at other sites required more knowledge and preparation. Warren had gained much from Wilson's topographical preliminary. Logic suggested, and these two young officers recommended, that the kind of surface exploration carried out in Jerusalem should be done for the whole country before proceeding with the actual digging up of the Bible. The Fund agreed, and resolved to halt archaeological assignments for a time. Instead, it would undertake a thorough topographical survey of the Holy Land, with special concern for ruins and any other signs of ancient settlement. Greater resources and more advanced surveying equipment, techniques and skills should produce results which went beyond the cartographic work of all earlier one-man explorations, and beyond the successes of Robinson, Tobler and Guérin in recovering the locations of biblical sites.

They did just, this, and from 1871 to 1878, as we have seen earlier, the Fund kept an expedition in the field preparing a detailed inch-to-a-mile survey, most of it carried out under the direction of Lieutenant Conder, and completed by Lieutenant Kitchener. The British Army had again given their help, more readily this time since this project suited their interests more directly than archaeological excavation, and had supplied the teams and the two young subalterns from the Royal Engineers. The great map appeared in 1880, and the prodigious seven-volume *Survey of Western Palestine*, to which other scholars also contributed, was published between 1880 and 1884. They were studied thereafter by every biblical archaeologist before he put his spade to a tel.

Conder had written of his work in Palestine that 'the Survey was no holiday task'. He was referring only partly to the rough living, which is the lot of any explorer or archaeologist; to long hours in the saddle, and even longer hours on foot; to the winter snow and heavy rains that went right through their rotting tents; to the mid-summer heat which burst thermometers; to the fever that was rife everywhere in the valleys and to which one of his assistants succumbed – to be replaced by Kitchener. He also had in mind the frequent harassment and danger of assault by an unfriendly population. 'They are all born with stones in their hands,' he noted in one of his field reports. Sometimes the weapons were more lethal. In a particularly grave attack by an Arab mob in the Galilee town of Safad, Kitchener saved Conder's life. He did the same thing again on a more peaceful occasion. They were swimming off the coast of Ashkelon, and 'the surf was breaking,' wrote Conder. Suddenly, 'a strong suck-back of the waves carried me out into the broken water, whence I was rescued by Lieutenant Kitchener.' (Kitchener would fail to save himself from drowning forty-one years later when the ship carrying him on a mission to Russia in 1916 went down with nearly all hands.)

Conder's reports spoke of his new assistant's 'tireless energy and exhaustive thoroughness' when they were working together in 1874–5, and with Kitchener on the team they were able to 'exceed their former rate of progress'. When the party left Palestine in October 1875, Conder's 'four years of splendid patient work', as the Fund reported, resulted in the survey and mapping of 4,700 square miles of the Holy Land. Kitchener, back in Palestine in 1877 in command of the team, completed the remaining 1,340 square miles, concentrating on a survey of Galilee. His progress reports make absorbing reading, the scientific record alternating with enchanting descriptions of the countryside. Thus, he notes in precise detail the visible relics of antiquity, the geographical features, the varied water-levels 'fixed to within a foot', and every habitation, road, track, water-course, cistern, well, spring, as well as the vineyards, orchards, tombs, and even the wine-presses which he would later mark on his map with special signs. But he could also give expression to his wonder at the colourful sight of Galilee in the spring, with its scarlet anemonies, pink and yellow flax, tulips, irises, gladioli, poppies, asphodel and oleanders.

Kitchener had been brought up on the Bible, but he was no specialized scholar when he joined Conder. However, by the time he returned to carry out his own survey, he had familiarized himself with the works of the early historians and geographers, as well as the texts of pilgrims and travellers throughout the centuries. He had made a particular study of the first-century AD historical narrative by Josephus, and the recovery of biblical locations by Eusebius in the fourth century AD. The recollection of these writings would merge with his topographical and military perceptions as he moved through the land of antiquity on his exploration. One notable case appears in his report of a reconnaissance ride along the shores of the Sea of Galilee when he saw what he thought must surely be 'the sire of Sennabris, mentioned by Josephus as the place where [the Roman general, later emperor] Vespasian pitched his camp when marching on the insurgents of Tiberias' during the War of the Jews against the Romans, AD 65–70. Remembering, and following, Robinson's practice, Kitchener sought to learn whether a local place-name might carry the hint of ancient nomenclature. He found that what he had spotted as Sennabris was indeed called 'Sin en-Nabra'. This name

... still exists, and is well known to the natives. It applies to a ruin situated on a spur from the hills that close the southern end of the Sea of Galilee. It formed, therefore, the defence against an invader from the Jordan plain, and blocked the great main road in the valley. Close beside it there is a large artificially-formed plateau, defended by a water ditch on the south ... and is, I have not the slightest doubt, the remains of Vespasian's camp described by Josephus. It is just like another Roman camp near [the Samarian town of] Jenin, where an army was camped. Thus we have an example still in the country of the military precision of those irresistible conquerors.

When he came to the ridge above Jezreel and looked upon the broad plain, the soldier clutching his Bible could hardly fail to observe that here was

... the greatest battlefield of the world, from the days of Joshua and the defeat of the mighty host of Sisera [in the time of Deborah the Judge], till, almost in our own day, Napoleon the Great.... Here also is the ancient Megiddo, where the last great battle of Armageddon is to be fought.

The battles which he himself was yet to fight would win him renown; yet for years after he had left Palestine in 1878 and resumed active service, he hankered after an occasional return to Holy Land exploration. An opportunity presented itself in October 1883 in Cairo, where he chanced to meet Professor Edward Hull, who was about to undertake a reconnaissance of southern Palestine and Sinai. Kitchener at the time was in command of the British forces in Cairo and also working with the Egyptian army, which was being reorganized under British officers; but he was intrigued by Hull's mission and anxious to take part, if only for a brief period. Hull for his part was eager to secure the services of so notable and experienced a topographer. The military authorities were approached and, as Hull wrote later:

Kitchener received permission to join our party in order to carry out the trigonometrical survey of the region of the Arabah Valley ... between the Gulf of Akaba and the Dead Sea.... He ascended Mount Sinai [the Mount of Moses], 7,373 feet above the sea, on Tuesday, 20 November, and planting his theodolite on the roof of the little mosque took a series of angles on all the conspicuous heights within sight of that celebrated Mount wherewith to connect their positions with his base in southern Palestine. This experiment was afterwards repeated on Mount Hor ... the tomb of Aaron.... During our wanderings in the Sinaitic desert his presence with our little party was a source of strength.... He was of exceptional service in negotiation with the Arabs owing to his knowledge of Arabic, which he spoke fluently, and to his acquaintance with the habits of the wild natives.... On Sunday morning, 16 December, we camped by the shore of the Dead Sea.... Here we were destined to remain for several days, including Christmas Day, awaiting the arrival of horses and mules from Jerusalem. Meanwhile, great events had occurred in Egypt during the six weeks we had been absent from Cairo and wandering along the Arabah Valley. Christmas Eve brought with it tidings from Cairo, the first we had received from the outer world up till this period: four Arabs of the Hawatat tribe, on swift camels, arrived in the afternoon in our camp bearing a letter addressed to me by Sir Evelyn Baring [British Consul-General for Egypt]. It informed us of the defeat of General Hicks's army in the Sudan . . .

That cut short Kitchener's stay. He left immediately for Cairo 'to organize a force to avenge the defeat of Hicks's army, as also to prepare for still further achievements'.

Those achievements were formidable. After fighting in the Sudan, he served as governor-general of its eastern territory. Then came his appointment as commander of the Egyptian army, and he spent three years completing the reorganization which his predecessor had begun. By 1898 he was in a position to lead into the Sudan a mixed Anglo-Egyptian expeditionary force to restore Anglo-Egyptian authority. Insurgents, known as Mahdists, had seized power fourteen years earlier, after capturing Khartoum, the capital, and massacring the garrison, including the commander, General Gordon. (It will be recalled that the advance party of the relief force sent – too late – to rescue Gordon and his men was led by archaeologist Wilson.) The Mahdists had abandoned Khartoum and established their capital, Omdurman, on the opposite bank of the Nile. It was Kitchener's decisive victory in the Battle of Omdurman in September 1898 that swept the Mahdists from power. Khartoum was promptly restored as the seat of government, and Kitchener was rewarded with a peerage. He took as his title, and was known thereafter as, Lord Kitchener of Khartoum. Incidentally, Britain's 21st Lancers made a memorable cavalry charge in the Battle of Omdurman. One of the subalterns taking part was Winston Churchill – almost two years before his encounter with archaeologist Warren at Spion Kop. A marble obelisk marks the spot where the charge took place.

Field Marshal Lord Kitchener, outstanding British soldier who, as a subaltern, made a valuable contribution to the Great Survey of Western Palestine. A portrait by Sir Hubert von Herkomer.

Kitchener was in South Africa less than a year later with the outbreak of the Boer War, and a year after that, in November 1900, he became Commander-in-Chief of the British forces. Though criticized for his method of dealing with guerrilla resistance, when war ended with the Boer submission in June 1902, it was Kitchener's influence that produced moderate peace terms.

Further positions of high responsibility followed: seven years in India as Commander-in-Chief of the East Indies, and the next two in a similar post in the Mediterranean. There were also high honours: promotion to field marshal; elevation from baron to viscount to earl. In 1911 he was appointed British agent and consul-general in Egypt. He had been picked for the job when Britain decided that a forceful personality was required to deal with the unrest in that country, and, indeed, he soon became the power behind the administration. A well-earned leave took him back to England in June 1914; but it was cut short at the end of July as the European crisis deepened, and all diplomatic heads of mission were ordered to return to their posts. Kitchener was actually aboard the Channel boat on 3 August when he received a message from Prime Minister Asquith requiring him to stay. Three days later he joined the Cabinet as war minister. He was in office only a week before the outbreak of the First World War; but in that week he issued an overall directive to plan immediately for a vast expansion of the army – the target was later set at seventy divisions – so that maximum strength would be reached in the crucial third year of the war. Despite the scepticism with which it was greeted at the time, the programme was fulfilled, as planned, in 1916. There had been an intensive recruiting campaign to encourage volunteering. Its central feature was a personal message from the war minister, with the consequence that Kitchener's face became part of the landscape of Britain. It stared out from huge posters on every billboard in town and village, with Kitchener's finger pointed directly at the viewer, and beneath it the peremptory appeal: 'YOUR COUNTRY NEEDS YOU!'

In May 1916 the Russian Tsar requested that Kitchener visit Moscow. The emperor was known to be greatly impressed by this outstanding British soldier, and his invitation held the prospect that Kitchener might be able to get the Russian military establishment to do what he had done for the British army. He set out from England on 5 June on his doomed voyage aboard the cruiser *Hampshire*, and went down with the ship when it struck a German mine, leaving behind a halted wake – and one of the great 'ifs' of history. If only the cruiser's route had been better planned; if bad weather had not forced the escorting destroyers to turn back; if the *Hampshire* had done the same instead of proceeding alone through an unswept channel; then – Kitchener would have reached Moscow, seen the Tsar, perhaps been able to strengthen the fighting capacity and morale of the Russian army, held off the mood of desperation that enveloped the Russian people – and there might have been no Lenin in a sealed train. Some historians to this day have found it entertaining, though idle, to speculate that the man who started his professional life as an explorer in Palestine might well have been instrumental in preventing the Russian revolution – at least from occurring in 1917 – if journey's end had been Moscow and not the watery deep.

The Fund sent out no archaeological expeditions from England throughout the 1870s and '80s while it was occupied with the expedition and subsequent publication of the Survey. But from time to time they used the services of a few foreign residents of Palestine. These were men who knew the country, the language, and the ways of the people, and who had undertaken some surface exploration and archaeological probes on their own. The most outstanding of these men was undoubtedly a young French consular official named Charles Clermont-Ganneau. His first junior post had been at the embassy in Constantinople, the control centre of Turkey's imperial provinces which included Palestine, and this stood him in good stead when he was soon transferred to the consulate in Jerusalem. As a student he had sat at the feet of orientalist and philosopher Ernest Renan, one of the foremost savants of the nineteenth century, who had also headed a French archaeological expedition to Syria. On his arrival in Palestine in 1867 at the age of twenty-one, he seems to have spent all his leisure time in the quest for biblical antiquities. He could hardly have dreamt that within a year his name would become a household word to all scholars engaged in biblical research.

Curiously enough, although he would later make some brilliant archaeological discoveries based on ingenious reasoning, he remains best known for his dramatic role in the recovery, not the actual find, of a priceless ancient text directly linked to the Bible. This was a ninth-century BC inscription on a stele, an upright slab of black basalt, written by Mesha, king of Moab, and is accordingly known as the Mesha or the Moabite Stone. Moab, lying east of the river Jordan and the Dead Sea, had been a subject state of the kingdom of Israel during the reigns of Omri and Ahab. Shortly after Ahab's death and upon the accession of his second son, Jehoram (849–842 BC), Mesha rebelled, and the Bible gives a detailed account of the military action that ensued:

A ninth-century BC inscription on the black basalt stele of Mesha, king of Moab, relating how he freed Moab from Israelite tutelage.

> And Mesha king of Moab was a sheepmaster, and rendered unto the king of Israel an hundred thousand lambs, and an hundred thousand rams, with the wool. But it came to pass, when Ahab was dead, that the king of Moab rebelled against the king of Israel. (2 Kings 3:4, 5.)

Jehoram mustered his army and together with the forces of two allies inflicted great damage on the vassal State; but he was apparently unable to bring the rebel to terms, for the biblical report makes no claim that Mesha was defeated. It concludes with a harrowing incident to explain why the Israelites departed without re-imposing their control over their tributary. 'And when the king of Moab saw that the battle was too sore for him, he took . . . his eldest son that should have' been his successor 'and offered him for a burnt offering upon the wall'. The Israelite troops were filled with

127

such consternation and loathing at the sight that 'they departed from him, and returned to their own land'. (2 Kings 3:26, 27.)

The Mesha inscription describes the result as a Moabite victory, which it was, despite the military stalemate; for thereafter Moab ceased to be under Israelite tutelage. It is written as a first-person account by the king:

> I am Mesha, son of Chemosh, king of Moab, the Dibonite. My father had reigned over Moab thirty years, and I reigned after my father.... As for Omri, king of Israel, he humbled Moab many years.... And his son [grandson] followed him and he also said 'I will humble Moab'. In my time he spoke thus, but I have triumphed over him and over his house...

This inscription caused a great stir in the world of biblical scholarship, for not only was it a direct contemporary reference to an episode narrated in the Bible, but it made specific mention of Israel and the Omri dynasty. The language and script bear so close a resemblance to the biblical Hebrew of the period as to suggest that Moabite was virtually a dialect of Hebrew, the result of prolonged Israelite influence over the vassal. The text was therefore comparatively easy to decipher, particularly as each letter is clear and well-shaped, and there are special signs to mark the end of a word and of a sentence.

Clermont-Ganneau played an adventurous part not in its discovery but in its rescue. It was a German pastor attached to the Anglican Church Missionary Society in Jerusalem, the Reverend F. A. Klein, who first came across it while travelling through Transjordan in August 1868. Reaching the village of Dhiban, the site of biblical Dibon, Mesha's capital, on the eastern side of the Dead Sea opposite En-gedi, he was apprised of an old stone bearing strange markings. It was almost completely buried in the sand when he saw it, but by scraping away the top part he could discern its opening lines, and he promptly recognized them as ancient writing. After clearing away all the sand and exposing the entire stele, he realized that whatever it was, it was certainly important. By then, however, he found himself surrounded by a crowd of armed Bedouin, who were puzzled by his odd behaviour, actions and obvious interest in the slab, and demanded an explanation. They were delighted by his reply. It appeared that this worthless old stone which had been there as long as they could remember was considered by this foreigner to be a great treasure. Yes, they told him, he could take it – for a price, way beyond his means. Since he had neither the money nor the vehicle to remove it, he promised to return with both. Before leaving, he made a quick sketch of the stele, with its flat base and rounded top; recorded its dimensions – just three feet high by two feet wide; copied some of the written characters, noting that there were thirty-four lines of text; marked the site on his map; and hastened to Jerusalem to try and raise the funds to secure this antiquity for the Berlin museum.

However, months passed and he had no success. The Dhiban Arabs, in the meantime, were weaving wondrous tales of the fortune promised them by this foreigner for their mysterious stone, and word of this soon spread to Jerusalem. This coincided with reports going around Jerusalem concerning the German missionary's efforts to acquire a rare antiquity. When both stories reached Clermont-Ganneau, he left for Dhiban without delay.

Despite his youth, he was a more learned orientalist than Klein, and when he saw the stele, it was clear to him that the writing was akin to ancient Hebrew. The Arabs allowed him to take a squeeze of the text (pressing a damp paper or wax against the surface to secure an impression), and named a price for the stone. Clermont-Ganneau, like Klein, said he would return later with the money. But unlike the missionary, he was resourceful and persistent, and as a consular official had more direct and responsible contact with his government. Back in Jerusalem, he sent the squeeze to Paris for expert appraisal, and soon received authorization to purchase. He again set out for Dhiban, equipped this time with a modest caravan and the funds.

On arrival at the site, however, he found to his horror that the stone was no longer there. He quickly learnt to his even greater horror that it had been hacked to pieces. It appeared that while waiting for the foreigners to return – if they ever did – the Arabs bemoaned the fact that the stone had been too heavy to carry away. Otherwise, they could have sold it on the spot and had their money long ago. It then occurred to them that if the stone was indeed precious, it would be more saleable and fetch more if it were broken up into portable bits and each one sold separately!

Clermont-Ganneau then began the long and laborious search for the missing pieces. He finally tracked down and haggled over twenty fragments in twenty different hands. Two were large chunks; the rest were small pieces. Matching them against a copy of the squeeze he had fortunately made, it was possible to reconstruct the Mesha Stele with only a few lines missing. And off it went to the Louvre, where it remains to this day.

Clermont-Ganneau's adventures with the Mesha stone had impressed many people, not least the directors of the Palestine Exploration Fund in London. They had not relished the decision they had felt compelled to take suspending archaeological expeditions from England while the great Survey was under way; and they had engaged a local expert to hold an archaeological watching brief over developments in the country. They now decided to play a more direct part at little cost by supporting this bright young French scholar-diplomat, who had just pulled off an exciting coup. They suggested that he request leave of absence from the Consulate, and undertake some archaeological probing and surface exploration for them. Clermont-Ganneau accepted their proposal, and this was the start of his long association with the Fund.

He did some work in and around Jerusalem, picking up where Wilson and Warren had left off. He exposed buried portions of the walls, examined certain ruins and tomb-chambers, inspected ancient cemeteries, and was given the rare privilege by the Moslem authorities of studying the Temple Mount, their Haram esh-Sharif. He also investigated the region between Jerusalem and Jaffa, and paid visits to biblical Samaria. The results were of professional value to later archaeologists. Two of his discoveries were spectacular. One was his identification of the site of biblical Gezer, which showed him as the scholarly detective. The other was his chance find of a first-century BC inscription on a tablet which had originally been set against a ritual barrier on the Temple Mount during the reign of Herod.

The Gezer identification was indeed ingenious. Clermont-Ganneau knew of the importance of this town in ancient times, as did all biblical scholars, only from the Bible. It was known that in Solomon's time it was one of this king's three great chariot cities; that it lay at the edge of the Judean foothills where they meet the Mediterranean coastal plain; and that it had commanded the strategic road-junction of the Way of the Sea (the Via Maris) and the branch road running off it through the valley of Aijalon (where Joshua bade the moon stand still), and up the hills to Jerusalem. Added evidence of its importance came only later, after Clermont-Ganneau's identification, at subsequent archaeological excavations, and in references to this city in Egyptian and Mesopotamian inscriptions. It was then found to have flourished, with intervals, from the middle of the 3rd millennium BC to the first century BC. Thereafter, its location had gradually been lost to memory. It had even eluded Robinson.

From time to time in the months following his arrangement with the Exploration Fund, Clermont-Ganneau had examined the general area in which he expected Gezer to be from his studies of the Bible and the works of early historians and geographers; but without result. One evening in Jerusalem, reading in his study, he was struck by an episode in a book by an Arabic writer named Mujir al-Din al Ulaymi which he sensed contained a clue to the whereabouts of Gezer. Mujir al-Din was born in Palestine in AD 1456 and lived there until his death in 1521. This was unusual, for

Remains of the gates to the city of Gezer built in the tenth century BC by Solomon.

gifted inhabitants during this period of Mameluke occupation rarely remained in the country; they tended to emigrate to Egypt or Syria. It was also rare at the time for Arabs to write about Palestine, since to them it was an insignificant, neglected backwater of the Middle East. It was precisely for this reason that Clermont-Ganneau had decided to read this uncommon author's history of Jerusalem and Hebron.

At one point in the book, Mujir al-Din was describing a clash between a unit of the Mameluke army and a band of Bedouin marauders, which had occurred in his lifetime. The incident had taken place in the region of Ramle, near Lod (and nowadays Israel's international airport). To convey in dramatic terms the fury of the skirmish, the writer noted that the battle-cries could be heard as far away as Tel Jazar and the village of Hulda. The sight of the

131

word Jazar on the Arabic page sent a tingling signal to the man who was searching for a biblical place with a similar name. It sounded so like an Arabic corruption of the Hebrew Gezer that he could hardly wait for dawn before rushing off to the Ramle area to investigate. However success was neither easy nor quick. It took a long time to examine the spots likely to hold the remains of an ancient city which also satisfied the strategic and geographical conditions given by the Bible. He finally hit on a large mound some seven miles south of Ramle which seemed to him to possess all the required qualities. (Hulda is a few miles further south, so the war-cries must have been loud indeed.) This, he was convinced, was the Tel Jazar of Mujir al-Din's chronicle and the authentic site of biblical Gezer, and he published his proposal in 1871.

It touched off a spate of controversial articles in learned journals, all written with confidence since there could be no proof one way or the other until the mound was excavated. Two years later, however, Clermont-Ganneau had the rare experience for an explorer of finding material evidence, without excavation, to confirm his theory. He kept visiting what had become his favourite site looking for signs of antiquity, and one day in 1873 he had the enormous thrill of finding boundary markers with the very name of the city marked thereon. Incised in the rock at the edges of the tel were several inscriptions with the Hebrew words for 'boundary of Gezer'. This was one of the few lost sites whose biblical identification was certified without having to dig it up, but of course it made a future dig even more tempting – and the Exploration Fund would finance such an archaeological expedition thirty years later.

In 1872 Clermont-Ganneau had made another discovery, this time in Jerusalem. Examining the tombstones and the ground between them as he walked one day in a deserted cemetery near the southern wall, he chanced to find a fragment of a tablet with a Greek inscription. It turned out to be one of the public notices which had originally been posted on the Temple compound refurbished by Herod in the first century BC. There had been several courts adjoining the Temple building, separate courts for the altar, the priests and the Israelites. Surrounding this inner complex was the Outer Court. It was also known as the Court of the Gentiles, for among the crowds who entered the Temple Mount were Gentile visitors from many lands. They, however, were not allowed beyond this enclosure. Inscriptions were therefore posted in languages they could understand, Latin and Greek, warning them on pain of death against passing through to the inner Temple. What Clermont-Ganneau had found was one of the Greek inscriptions. (A fragment of one of the Latin inscriptions was found in 1935 near the eastern wall.)

Seventy years later, the great Albright would write of Charles Clermont-Ganneau and his 'numerous brilliant discoveries' what could well be said of Professor Albright himself:

His career, like that of Robinson, illustrates the fact that a single man of genius may advance the sum of knowledge in a given field more than a whole generation of inferior investigators or a treasury full of money for a costly series of undertakings.

The Palestine Exploration Fund, having completed the work and publication of the Survey, resumed archaeological excavation with its own men in 1890. It could not have marked the end of the twenty-year non-operational interval with a happier choice – Flinders Petrie, who can be bracketed with Robinson and Clermont-Ganneau as the third genius of the nineteenth century in the area of biblical exploration. After Petrie's brief but momentous work at Tel el-Hesi, the full-scale excavation of the site was entrusted to the American scholar Frederick Jones Bliss. He completed this assignment in 1893, and then headed the Fund's next project, assisted by architect A. C. Dickie, in Jerusalem, working there from 1894 to 1897. Jerusalem had always been central to the Fund's interest, and despite the difficulties encountered by Wilson and Warren, it was felt that Bliss, with his Tel el-Hesi experience, might do better.

Frederick Jones Bliss, who was the first biblical archaeologist to recognize the importance of Petrie's pottery-dating theory, and to apply it to his Palestine digs.

Bliss quickly found that he was up against the same obstacles as his predecessors. 'Our field of actual excavation was indeed limited,' he wrote later, explaining why he was compelled to fall back on the same unsatisfactory devices of tunnelling and shaft-sinking that they had used. And each day 'fresh problems arose'. Nevertheless, he and Dickie were competent craftsmen, and they made some useful finds, though their interpretation was sometimes faulty. For example, they did well to unearth considerable sections of the city's southern wall from various periods near the Siloam pool, much further to the south than the present wall. They attributed one section to the First Temple period, which misled scholars into believing that the city at that time was larger than it was. A later excavation proved conclusively that the section was built several centuries later.

However, the report by Bliss shows that he could discern a clue by cogent reasoning. On one occasion he was tracing the remains of a wall when it suddenly disappeared, having been destroyed completely at that point. He went on quarrying, hoping to come upon another section further on – if indeed he was quarrying in the right direction and if there were additional remains. But all he came across was an ancient drainage ditch, which he ignored at first, being pre-occupied with the wall. Only days later did he realize that the drain could be a clue to finding the lost wall. This was how he reasoned:

The drain clearly ran under a paved street; the paved street was doubtless within the city; followed in the right direction, it must lead to a gate; to discover a gate would be to rediscover the wall. And so the matter turned out.

The next excavation sponsored by the Fund was that of the large mound which Clermont-Ganneau had identified as the site of Gezer. It was conducted almost single-handedly by a brilliant, thirty-two-year-old Irish archaeologist, Robert Alexander Stewart Macalister, from 1902 to 1905 and again from 1907 to 1909. Two years before tackling this site he had assisted Bliss in digging up four mounds in the low hill-country of Judah, and gained valuable experience. He was now carrying out a dig on his own. He made some rich finds. The outstanding structural remains he unearthed included those of four city-wall systems from various periods; a shaft linked to a tunnel dug through solid rock for some 220 feet that led to a hidden spring, to ensure the water supply in time of siege; and the ruins of a Canaanite pagan shrine, with a stone altar and ten pillars surrounded by a low stone wall.

Macalister also found some rare inscriptions. The earliest was a seventeenth or sixteenth-century BC piece of pottery inscribed with pictographic characters which is now known as the 'Gezer potsherd'. Then came three cuneiform tablets which Macalister ascribed to the seventh century BC; but Albright showed many years later that one of them belonged to the much earlier El-Amarna period – the fourteenth century BC. It contained an order to the prince of Gezer summoning him to the presence of the Egyptian commander. Macalister may have erred because the other two, which were legal contracts, did indeed belong to the seventh century Assyrian period. Also found on the site were eighth or seventh-century BC jar-handles bearing the royal stamp of one of the kings of Judah; and more boundary inscriptions which, like those discovered by Clermont-Ganneau, bore the Hebrew name 'Gezer'.

The most important inscription, however, was a Hebrew farming calendar, inscribed on a tablet of soft limestone. This, too, was dated by Macalister several centuries too late. It is now known to belong to the latter part of the tenth century BC, the time of Solomon, and is the earliest known Hebrew inscription, written in a very early spelling. It is called the Gezer Calendar, giving the annual cycle of agricultural activities in verse form, possibly intended as a mnemonic ditty for children. It begins with the month of Tishri in the Hebrew lunar calendar, corresponding to September or October, and recites what the farmer does throughout the year:

His two months [September–October] are olive harvest; His two months [November–December] are planting grain; His two months [January–February] are late planting; His month [March] is hoeing up the flax; His month [April] is harvest of barley; His month [May] is harvest and feasting; His two months [June–July] are vine-tending; His [last] month, [Elul, corresponding to August] is summer fruit.

(The translation is Albright's.)

Macalister's material finds were impressive, and they showed that Gezer had indeed been an important strategic town in biblical times, as the Bible recorded. But these discoveries served little to fill in the gaps and expand our knowledge of the biblical narrative by permitting the recovery of the consecutive history of the site. Methods of excavation were still primitive at the time, and Macalister had to work alone. With all his industry and brilliance, he was unable to supervise and survey and produce plans and drawings to the required standard, nor to assimilate and classify accurately the mass of excavated material. Moreover, with pottery dating still in its infancy – though he himself had contributed to the advancement of Petrie's theory and method – he was not always correct in attributing a chronological period to a particular stratum of settlement. In addition, by a mistaken interpretation of the evidence, he thought there had been a five-century gap in the occupation of Gezer. This led to his error in dating the pottery, and therefore the strata in which it was found, ascribing later periods to earlier levels of settlement. The most notable example of such error, apart from the misdating of certain inscriptions, was his labelling of a structure as a second-century BC Maccabean castle. Fifty years later, Israel's Professor Yigael Yadin ingeniously showed that it had been built by Solomon in the tenth century BC.

6 The New Pathfinders

MACALISTER WAS IN the final stage of his Gezer dig when in 1908 an American-sponsored expedition arrived in the country to enter the field of Palestinian archaeology – and make a lasting impact on the new scientific discipline. It was the Harvard exploration of Samaria, the ancient capital of the northern kingdom of Israel, directed by George Andrew Reisner, greatly aided by his assistant, Clarence Stanley Fisher. The three-year dig was the first systematic large-scale, well organized and well financed archaeological excavation undertaken in the country, and it was blessed both by the resources amply provided by the New York philanthropist Jacob Schiff, and the superb choice of director. Reisner had already established a reputation for outstanding archaeological work in Egypt, where he had spent ten years before coming to Palestine – just like Petrie, whose theory he absorbed and refined, and whom he resembled in intellectual stature.

Unlike the self-taught Petrie, however, Reisner's formal academic background was impeccable. Ancient Eastern tongues were his subjects at Harvard both as star student and lecturer, and he first came to scholarly notice not as an archaeologist but as linguist and philologist, in an esoteric doctoral thesis on an aspect of Akkadian entitled 'A Review of the Grammatical Development of the Noun Endings in Assyro-Babylonian'. He continued his researches in cuneiform, took time off to master Egyptian, taught both for several university terms, and in 1899, at the age of thirty-two, was entrusted with an expedition to Egypt on behalf of the University of California, with funds provided by Mrs Phoebe Apperson Hearst. (This project was taken over by Harvard University and the Boston Museum of Fine Arts six years later as their Joint Egyptian Expedition.) On this exploration assignment, his first, Reisner the scholar proved to be an excellent organizer and a superb field archaeologist, conceiving new archaeological

OPPOSITE The hilltop site of ancient Samaria, established in the ninth century BC by king Omri as the capital of the northern breakaway kingdom of Israel, and rebuilt and re-named Sebaste by Herod in the first century BC. These are the remains of a Roman basilica constructed on the ruins of a Herodian building.

techniques that he would later apply to the Samaria excavation, and that would be known thereafter as the Reisner-Fisher method.

With the requisite funds, Reisner was able to employ on the Samaria project a trained staff for surveying, architectural analysis and photography, draughtsmen for the plans, drawings and sketches, experienced foremen for the teams of diggers, and competent camp managers. Each find was photographed and a record made not only of its exact location but the nature of the debris in which it had lain and its relation to the other ancient remains in the immediate vicinity. It was indeed the most meticulously organized and recorded excavation that had ever been carried out in Palestine.

The results matched the effort, discovery giving tangibility to the biblical story. In the ninth century BC, king Omri of Israel 'bought the hill of Samaria of Shemer for two talents of silver, and built on the hill, and called the name of the city ... Samaria'. (1 Kings 16:24.) He did so for reasons of State. The family ties between his northern kingdom and the southern kingdom of Judah were still bitterly strained when he reached the throne in 876 BC. Yet Jerusalem, the capital of Judah, as it had been of David and Solomon's united kingdom, was above all the site of the Temple, and it continued to exercise a unique religious influence upon all Jews, including his own citizens. Omri sought to diminish this influence by creating an impressive capital of his own which might vie, at least temporally, with the capital of the southern kingdom.

The archaeologists found the remains of that city, discovering that Omri had started, and his son Ahab had continued, a formidable construction programme on this magnificent location, set amidst the Samarian hills and commanding routes northwards to Galilee and Damascus and westwards to the Mediterranean. Omri had built a rectangular acropolis or citadel on the summit, enclosed by a wall of square-hewn stones. Sections of this wall were well preserved. The enclosure had been extended and a second wall built in Ahab's time; and there had been additional later construction by Jeroboam II. The town itself was constructed on the lower slopes. Within the acropolis was the palace of Omri and Ahab and other buildings. One of them was a storehouse, and in it Reisner found scores of ostraca, which appear to have been invoices for the dispatch of oil and wine from the lessees of royal lands in the neighbourhood of Samaria. The inscriptions on these potsherds are in ancient Hebrew. Reisner ascribed them to the time of Ahab in the ninth century, but later finds by other archaeologists, including further ostraca, suggest that they belong to the following century, probably during the reign of Jeroboam II. Also found within the citadel enclosure was a large well-plastered reservoir, prompting

George Andrew Reisner, who conceived new archaeological techniques which he applied to the excavation of Samaria in 1908, the first American-sponsored, systematic and large-scale exploration undertaken in the country.

the suggestion that this may have been 'the pool of Samaria' in which was 'washed the chariot' of Ahab after he was killed in the battle against Aram-Damascus at Ramoth-gilead. (1 Kings 22:38.)

Palestinian archaeology reached its highest level under Reisner, and did much to advance his purpose, which was to develop and improve, as he put it, 'methods of excavation and recording with the idea of making archaeological field-work a scientific method of historical research'. Nevertheless, although his pottery dating was more advanced than that of any of his predecessors, the subsequent progress made in this field showed him to have been occasionally in error. He also missed a few objects of some importance. One of the most interesting was a group of carved ivory plaques found in the ruins of the palace building. They were discovered twenty years later by a joint American (Harvard University), British (Palestine Exploration Fund) and Jerusalem's Hebrew University expedition, which continued the work of Reisner and Fisher in 1931–5. It was headed by British orientalist John Winter Crowfoot, director of the British School of Archaeology at the time, assisted by his wife Grace, who was a specialist in ancient pottery and textiles, and by Kathleen Kenyon, who already showed the gifts which would make her one of the finest British archaeologists of the century. The Hebrew University was represented by its first field archaeologist who would soon hold the university chair in archaeology, Eliezer Lipa Sukenik (father of a later archaeology professor at the Hebrew University, Yigael Yadin). It was Crowfoot and Sukenik who unearthed the ivories in 1932. They are similar to those found at Calah (Nimrud), first excavated by Layard, and at Arslan Tash, also in Mesopotamia, which belong to the ninth and eighth centuries BC – the reigns of Ahab and Jeroboam II respectively. Like them, the Samarian ivories are Phoenician in style, with motifs of pagan gods, sphinxes and animals, notably the lion and bull, as well as floral designs, carved in low and high relief. Some seem to have been fashioned in Phoenician workshops, others in Samaria by imported or itinerant foreign craftsmen. These ivory panels were used as inlays for expensive wooden furniture such as couches, thrones and stools. The excavated ivories immediately evoked, and gave meaning to, the words of the Hebrew prophets who railed against the royal hankering after idolatry and opulence rather than justice. They were particularly pained by the submission of Ahab to the pagan influence of his Phoenician wife Jezebel, and the ivories of Phoenician workmanship must have symbolized that influence, which continued long after Ahab. Thus, the prophet Amos cried out against those 'that lie upon beds of ivory', and predicted their doom when he thundered that the Lord 'will smite the [royal]

An ivory carving found at Nimrud, similar to the ivory plaques found in king Ahab's 'house of ivory' at Samaria.

winter house with the summer house; and the houses of ivory shall perish'. (Amos 3:15, 6:4.) The ruined building in which the archaeologists found the Samaria ivories was probably the 'house of ivory' built by Ahab for Jezebel. Also found were the grim signs of prophetic fulfilment – a thick layer of ashes at the chronological level of the latter part of the eighth century BC. Samaria was destroyed and the northern kingdom fell in 722 BC.

While Reisner and Fisher were engaged at Samaria, two German scholars were excavating at Tel es-Sultan, the site of Jericho. They were the first to do so since Captain Warren had probed the mound in the late 1860s during his Jerusalem investigations – he would go there on winter days when rain interrupted work in Jerusalem. Like Robinson before him, though convinced that this was indeed the authentic location of the biblical city, Warren found the tel unrewarding. The German archaeologists, forty years later, were more hopeful. They were Ernst Sellin, who a few years earlier had made extensive soundings at the mound of Ta'anach, near Megiddo, and Carl Watzinger, noted for his recovery, with Heinrich Kohl, of the ancient synagogues in Galilee.

Though not in Reisner's class, and operating on a far more modest scale than the Samarian expedition, they worked quite systematically at Jericho from 1907 to 1909, and published their results in 1913. Such speed was, and is, uncommon for archaeologists. Reisner's two massive volumes on his Samarian dig were not published until 1924, thereby greatly delaying the influence of his innovations on his successors, though some of it filtered through in the work of his assistant, Fisher. It may well be that Sellin and Watzinger were to regret that they had rushed into print so quickly.

Their Jericho excavation was carried out very competently. The stratigraphy – determining the order and relative positions of the strata of the site – was capably handled. The results were well presented. The finds were clearly described and illustrated with good plans, maps, drawings and photographs. There was only one thing wrong – the chronology of the key biblical periods! Thus, in a way, it might be said that this Jericho dig was an archaeological failure, for while Sellin and Watzinger had successfully recovered the site, they failed to recover its history; and that, after all, is the principal purpose of archaeology. They failed through the faulty interpretation of their finds. They were a little like the general with a good army at his command, and with excellent intelligence information before him, who fails to assess it correctly and loses the battle. On the other hand, Sellin and Watzinger might have argued that while they became casualties when their judgement was later

shown to be in error, their detailed publication enabled subsequent scholars to follow each stage of their work, gain all the necessary 'intelligence information', and apply their own interpretation. So ultimately archaeology was not the loser.

Sellin was led astray only partly because he ignored the lessons on pottery dating provided by Petrie and developed by Bliss and Macalister. This was due primarily to an obsessive determination to unearth the 'walls of Jericho' that had collapsed before Joshua's army, as well as a later wall built in Ahab's time as suggested in the Bible: 'In his days did Hiel the Bethelite build Jericho.' (1 Kings 16:34.) Sellin therefore seems to have seen what was not there. The wall he ascribed to the ninth century BC builder, Hiel of Bethel, turned out to belong to the seventeenth century BC, so that much else which he found in that stratum and in the related levels was also inaccurate by eight centuries.

Where then was the Jericho wall of Joshua's time? British archaeologist John Garstang, who resumed excavations at Jericho from 1930 to 1936, found many things, but not that. The most sensational discovery at Jericho was made in our own generation, by Kathleen Kenyon, in her comprehensive dig from 1952 to 1958. But what she found was not the wall that came tumbling down at Joshua's onslaught, but a far older rampart. She brought to light the remains of a huge stone wall, and an impressive circular tower attached to it built of stone and mud. A flight of steps enclosed within a shaft running through the tower enabled the defenders in time of danger to reach the top of the wall without being seen by an enemy. Miss Kenyon realized that what she had found was very ancient, probably Neolithic; but only when organic material found with it was subjected to the radioactive Carbon 14 test was the date determined. It was 6850 BC, plus or minus some 200 years, which makes the structures about 9,000 years old, and Jericho the oldest city in the world.

Joshua and the Israelite army marching round the walls of Jericho, a panel in bronze relief from the 'Gate of Paradise' in Florence.

141

As for the wall of Joshua fame, Miss Kenyon stated that she had found no remains which could be attributed to the fortifications of the Canaanite city he had captured. She already knew when that had occurred, for while she was digging up Jericho, Yigael Yadin was excavating Hazor, and made a remarkable discovery which established the period of the Joshua conquest as the thirteenth century BC. The Kenyon report continues to excite controversy among scholars, for there are many who hold that there is such overwhelming archaeological evidence from other excavations substantiating the biblical reports of Joshua's battles that there is no reason to doubt Joshua's destruction of Jericho. With a less experienced archaeologist than Kenyon, they would say that finding nothing is no proof that nothing existed. Many scholars have made

One of the early town walls of Jericho unearthed at the Kenyon excavation.

discoveries missed by predecessors. In this case, however, they suggest that the mud-brick wall which fortified the city in the thirteenth century BC was eroded by rain and wind over the long period that the town stood in ruins, and was simply washed away and disappeared.

The end of the First World War brought great hopes for archaeology in Palestine. With Turkey defeated and Britain in control and about to become the Mandatory authority in the country, a Department of Antiquities was established in 1920 with a more helpful policy towards both British and foreign scholars anxious to dig up the Bible. We have seen that major expeditions resumed work in Samaria and Jericho, and successfully unearthed Lachish. The first large-scale postwar excavation was American, sponsored by the University of Pennsylvania Museum and headed by Clarence Fisher, who by now, a decade after his Samarian work with Reisner, had established his own reputation as an outstanding archaeologist. The site chosen was biblical Beth-shan, the subtropical meeting-place of the Jordan valley with the valley of Jezreel. Fisher started the dig in 1921, but left in 1925 to become Professor of Archaeology at the American School of Oriental Research in Jerusalem. Excavations continued until 1933 under the successive direction of Fisher's trainees, Alan Rowe and G. M. FitzGerald.

Kathleen Kenyon, outstanding British archaeologist, who dug up Jericho.

The main area of the well-planned dig was Tel el-Hosn, 'mound of the fortress', one of the most prominent tels in the country, its very name suggesting that buried within it were the citadels and principal buildings of the successive cities of Beth-shan. They had selected this site because of its high promise, since they knew of its importance in olden times both from the Bible and from ancient writings which had come to light in neighbouring lands during the previous few decades. Among the more interesting of such 'documents' are the Egyptian Execration Texts. These may well be the oldest examples of psychological warfare, belonging to the nineteenth and eighteenth centuries BC when Egypt was at the height of its early imperial power. The texts were a pharaonic device to exercise political witchcraft, aimed at weakening the morale of active enemies and deterring potential foes. In the nineteenth-century group of texts, the names of such enemies and imprecations against them were inscribed on pottery bowls; in the next century, they were written on crude human figurines in clay representing bound captives. Ceremoniously smashing the bowl or figurine was held to make the curse effective. In a superstitious world, a potential foe or vassal might think twice before attacking or rebelling if he knew that it was within the power of the pharaoh to do him harm by violent execration – or so the pharaoh must have expected. (In our own day, the practice of sticking pins in a cloth doll representing a hated victim is not unknown.) At all events, it is only from these texts that biblical scholars now have detailed geographic lists of neighbouring Egyptian lands including the names of vassal rulers and cities in these early times. Beth-shan appears on a fragment of a bowl, showing that it was a city of importance in the eyes of the Egyptian rulers in the nineteenth century BC. It also reveals the extent of Egypt's sphere of influence in that period. Appearing on the same lists are Jerusalem and Ashkelon 'and all the retainers who are with them'; and the curse applies to all 'who may rebel, who may plot, who may fight, who may talk of fighting, or who may talk of rebelling'.

Beth-shan is also mentioned in the victory lists of pharaoh Thutmose III among the Canaanite cities he subdued after crushing the focus of their resistance at Megiddo in 1468 BC. In one of the fourteenth-century BC letters in the royal el-Amarna archives, there is one from Abdu-Heba, prince of Jerusalem, who is feuding with a certain Tagu, prince of Gath; and he writes to the pharaoh to take action against him by charging that Tagu's 'men of Gath' have spurned Egyptian authority and are themselves maintaining 'a garrison in Beth-shan'. Three thirteenth-century BC inscriptions

The mound of biblical Beth-shan, top left, which held the remains of temples and of the wall to which the Philistines 'fastened the body' of the defeated king Saul. In the foreground, the recently-excavated Roman theatre.

show that Beth-shan was being used at the time by the Egyptians as a military base.

Not that Fisher and his archaeological team required these supplementary records to persuade them that the Beth-shan tel should hold interesting remains. The biblical narrative was enough, though they were pleased to find their excavation of the pre-biblical strata confirming the Egyptian writings. Altogether they uncovered eighteen levels of occupation, from the 4th millennium BC to about the seventh century AD. The most moving discovery related to the dramatic biblical account of the death of king Saul at the very end of the eleventh century BC. By then, Egyptian imperial rule had declined, and the threat to the Israelites now came from the Philistines, who sought control of the country.

It was against them that Saul had gone out to do battle, and suffered defeat. The decisive engagement was fought on mount Gilboa, a short distance from Beth-shan. With his army in disarray, his sons killed, himself wounded by enemy archers, Saul fell on his sword to avoid being taken alive. On the morrow,

> When the Philistines came to strip the slain . . . they found Saul and his three sons fallen. . . . And they cut off his head, and stripped off his armour. . . . And they put his armour in the house of Ashtaroth; and they fastened his body to the wall of Beth-shan. (1 Samuel 31: 8–10.)

The account in the Book of Chronicles states that the Philistines 'put his armour in the house of their gods, and fastened his head in the temple of Dagon'. (1 Chronicles 10:10.) The main discovery at the excavations were the remains of a series of temples built by the Egyptians in honour of local deities. Two of them continued in use till about the year 1000 BC, one dedicated to a god, the other to a goddess. They are believed to have been the very 'house of Ashtoreth' – the goddess Astarte – and 'temple of Dagon' where Saul's armour and head were put on exhibition. The archaeological evidence of the destruction of these temples shortly afterwards suggests that it was the work of David, the king who followed Saul and finally stifled the Philistine threat. He avenged the Israelite defeat on mount Gilboa, took Beth-shan, and wiped out the structures where his slain predecessor had been so ignominiously displayed.

Fisher had left the Beth-shan dig to his capable successors in 1925, after four intriguing years at the site, because he received the kind of offer archaeologists believe is made only in never-never-land – virtually limitless funds and all the time he required to carry out a thorough excavation of Megiddo. Sponsored by the Oriental Institute of the University of Chicago, and financed by the Rockefeller family, the campaign lasted until 1939 – and ended then only because of the outbreak of the Second World War. But Fisher unfortunately did not survive it. Ill-health compelled him to withdraw after two years, and the work was directed thereafter successively by Philip L. O. Guy and Gordon Loud.

Fisher was primarily attracted by the challenge of Megiddo, and its rich biblical history. Joshua encountered the 'king of Megiddo' during his conquest of Canaan. (Josh. 12:21.) Deborah the Judge proclaims in her Song: 'The kings came and fought ... by the waters of Megiddo.' (Judges 5:19.) Solomon rebuilt and fortified it, imposing a special tax to do so: 'And this is the reason of the levy which king Solomon raised for to build ... Hazor, and Megiddo, and Gezer.' (1 Kings 9:15.) In the next century, 'Ahaziah, king of Judah, fled to Megiddo, and died there'. (2 Kings 9:27.) Another king of Judah, Josiah, fell there in battle in 609 BC: 'And his servants carried him in a chariot dead from Megiddo, and brought him to Jerusalem.' (2 Kings 23:30.)

Lying at the head of a mountain pass at the entrance to the valley of Jezreel, this strategic site dominated the intersection of two ancient trade and military routes. It commanded a vital link on the great trunk road between Egypt and Mesopotamia; and it guarded the lateral road from the Mediterranean to the Jordan valley and Jerusalem. It was thus an object of fortification by its occupiers and of attack by contending empires through the ages, from Thutmose III in the fifteenth century BC right down to General Allenby in the First World War. (Elevated to the peerage, the British commander took as his title Viscount Allenby of Megiddo.) Small wonder that this frequent battleground made it symbolic of warfare, envisioned in the New Testament Book of Revelation as the site of the last great battle to be fought at the end of time – 'a place called in the Hebrew tongue Armageddon'. (Rev. 16:16.) (Armageddon is a corruption of Har Megiddon, Hebrew for 'the hill of Megiddo'.)

The archaeologists unearthed material evidence of all this, and much else, as they exposed more than twenty superimposed cities, the first, at the lowest stratum, dating to the 4th millennium BC, and the last to the fourth century BC. Flint tools at the bedrock level gave way to mud-brick houses and primitive shrines in the next millennium. Later strata held the remains of the eighteenth to sixteenth centuries BC, the period ascribed to the Hebrew patriarchs and the Hyksos invasion and domination of Egypt and Canaan. Many archaeological sites in the country held remains of the fortifications built by the Hyksos, a northern people who thundered south with powerful new weapons – the horse-drawn chariot and the composite bow – to carve out a considerable western Asiatic empire before they vanished from history. The Hyksos traces left at Megiddo included parts of their characteristic protective embankments of beaten earth, and one of their earliest city gates. The sixteenth- to twelfth-century levels yielded remains of the palaces of the Canaanite kings, each built on the foundations of its predecessor. It was in the latest of these structures that the archaeologists in 1937 found inscriptions of Rameses III and Rameses IV, who reigned in the twelfth century BC, and a treasure of some 200 carved ivory tablets, 300 years older than the Samarian Ivories discovered by Crowfoot and Sukenik five years earlier.

The most exciting – and confusing – remains were those of the tenth- and ninth-century cities of Solomon and Ahab respectively. The expedition teams unearthed parts of city walls, a heavy gate with a tower at each side of the entrance and a gatehouse for the guards, and stables with stalls and stone pillars to which the horses were tethered. They ascribed them all to Solomon. The ingenious reasoning of an Israeli archaeologist twenty years later showed, as we shall see in a later chapter, that while most of these remains were Solomonic, some had been built in the following century, most probably by king Ahab.

This is also true of the Megiddo water system, a spectacular example of engineering skill in ancient days, which the archaeologists brought to light and attributed to the twelfth century BC. It was shown in 1960 to belong to the ninth century BC. To ensure the water supply from the spring outside the city walls in time of siege, the engineers sunk a wide shaft to a depth of 120 feet, and from the bottom of the shaft cut a tunnel through the rock for a distance of 213 feet to the water source. This outside spring was then hidden by a wall camouflaged by a covering of earth to prevent its being spotted, and used by a besieging force. Like the Hezekiah Tunnel in Jerusalem quarried a century later, this too showed signs of having been bored by two teams working from each end and meeting in the middle. This Megiddo site has recently been restored, with a staircase installed in the shaft and lighting in the tunnel so that the whole underground system may be explored with ease.

The most fortunate event that happened to Palestinian archaeology in the years between the two world wars was the arrival in Palestine in 1919 of a twenty-eight-year-old scholar who was to become the foremost biblical archaeologist of our times. He was William Foxwell Albright, an American of prodigious and wide-ranging scholarship. Philologist, historian and topographer, a master of Bible texts and the languages of the ancient Middle East, he was as imaginative as Robinson in surface exploration and as

ABOVE The ruins of Megiddo from the Solomonic period.

LEFT The structural finds at the excavations of Megiddo in a reconstructed scale-model.

Petrie in scientific excavation. His grasp of every aspect of the biblical world was all-embracing. He could glance at, and decipher, a squiggle on a piece of pottery, recall the stratum in which it was found, and instantly conjure up the living context in which it was written. He could read a Babylonian text and link it to a corresponding episode in the Bible. He could at once detect in the shape of a pottery vessel he had just dug up a similarity with one found in a dated stratum of someone else's excavation. He could, with equal facility, discern from the differences in language style the different periods when the Books of the Bible were written; and applying this knowledge to his archaeological finds could help him recover the history of a biblical site.

Small wonder that most of today's prominent American and Israeli biblical archaeologists were students of his. Unforgettable is the memory of Albright at the age of sixty, his build matching his intellectual stature, towering over the rostrum in Beersheba a few years after Israel's War of Independence and addressing an archaeological convention. He spoke for an hour, without notes, in impeccable Hebrew, on the current state of biblical discovery, gathering together all the threads of the sundry branches that constitute the overall discipline of biblical archaeology. As a scientific exposition it was a tour de force. No less so, to the surprise of those who had never met him, was his Hebrew. Enunciated with fluency and precision, it outshone the language of many others at the conference, Israeli scholars whose mother tongue was Hebrew.

Albright came to Jerusalem as director of the American School of Oriental Research, a post he held from 1920 to 1929, and again from 1933 to 1936 when he was already professor of Semitic languages at Johns Hopkins University. During those years he firmly set his stamp on archaeology in the country, showing that he was not only an able administrator and counsellor but also a first class field man. It was he who dug up in 1922–3, and again in 1933, the mound of Tel el-Ful, on the northern outskirts of today's Jerusalem, and identified it as Gibeah, the birthplace of king Saul. It was at that excavation that he began working out in detail the pottery chronology of the Old Testament period, taking a giant leap from the springboard fashioned by Flinders Petrie. At the start of his Gibeah dig, as he wrote later, 'the archaeological chronology of Palestine was in a state of indescribable confusion', and biblical scholars understandably found the archaeological work that had been carried out until then 'comparatively useless'. Thus, it was scarcely surprising that 'most biblical historians of the generation before us gave up any attempt to utilize archaeological data, except in the case of inscriptions or outstanding architectural monuments or museum objects'.

The water tunnel at Megiddo, leading to the spring outside the city, which gave the inhabitants access to their water source in time of siege. (The wooden platform and electric lighting were recently installed for the benefit of visitors.)

150

Albright was to change all that with his next excavation, undertaken from 1926 to 1932 at Tel Beit Mirsim, situated in the Judean hills as they drop towards the coastal plain. Located ten miles south-west of Hebron and sixteen miles north of Beersheba, this mound was held by Albright to be the site of biblical Debir, referred to in the Bible also as Kirjath-sepher. (Joshua 15:15, Judges 1:11.) He unearthed ten levels of settlement, from the late 3rd millennium to the sixth century BC, determining the chronology by the application of all he knew of the pottery that had come to light at excavations in the region. He was able to date the earliest stratum to the twenty-second century BC, for example, because he found pottery at that level which had been imported from Egypt during the period of the sixth Egyptian dynasty: 2345–2181 BC. (One of the eight kings in this dynasty was a certain Pepi II Nefetkare who is said to have reigned more than ninety years, the longest reign in history.) He found the typical Hyksos embankments of beaten earth in the eighteenth- to sixteenth-century levels, and concluded from the remains of handsome buildings and other finds that the cities during the Hyksos occupation flourished from about 1700 to 1540 BC. Sixth-century pottery, in particular two jar handles stamped in Hebrew with the seal of 'Elyakim the servant of Yochan', found amidst ashes in the latest stratum, point to the destruction of the last city of Debir during the Babylonian campaign of 589–587 BC.

Albright's excavation methods were punctilious. The remains he unearthed were notable. However the prime importance of his Tel Beit Mirsim dig was its establishment of pottery sequences on a firm basis. For the first time, the pottery was examined with scrupulous care, special attention being paid to its shape, texture, decoration and method of manufacture, and to the archaeological context in which it was found. By the precise differentiation between the pottery types, and each type related to a settlement level, it was possible to prepare a chronological sequence which could become a standard of comparison for the finds at all archaeological sites in the country. And this was done. Thereafter, Albright's ceramic typology system, with continued refinements of his own and others, became the archaeological key to the chronology, and therefore to the history, of every excavated biblical site. As it was put professionally by American scholar George Ernest Wright, himself an eminent archaeologist, Albright

American scholar William Foxwell Albright (1891–1971), the most distinguished biblical archaeologist of the century.

. . . presented the first detailed and controlled stratigraphic and ceramic yardstick for the whole country, one which is still basic. By employing the twin principles of stratigraphy and typology, together with wide-ranging comparative and historical data, he for the first time created a firm archaeological chronology and was able by critical judgement to set the archaeology of Palestine firmly within the historical framework of the ancient Near East. He is quite simply the creator of the disciplines of biblical and historical archaeology as we now know and follow them in Palestine.

What Albright called 'the most remarkable undertaking of all' by the American School of Oriental Research 'was not launched until 1933, when Nelson Glueck began a systematic archaeological survey of Transjordan, resumed year after year until 1946'. Wright described it as, next to Albright's, the most important individual contribution to the field of Palestinian archaeology in our generation. Glueck was an unusual American scholar who lived a double academic life – which he himself thought, however, was a single integrated life: he was a teaching rabbi and a biblical archaeologist. He rose to the top in both fields. Trained for the rabbinate at the Hebrew Union College in Cincinnati, he eventually became its president. Arriving in Jerusalem in 1928 at the age of twenty-eight to study archaeology at the American School, he became its director, serving from 1932 to 1933, 1936 to 1940, and again from 1942 to 1947.

In his exhaustive survey of eastern Palestine – a monumental work – he examined the entire stretch of territory from the Syrian border in the north to the Gulf of Akaba in the south, and found, recorded and dated literally hundreds of long-forgotten sites. Throughout his search, his main clues were the potsherds strewn on the surface of most sites. From these he succeeded in recovering the broad history of the country. He found that, apart from the lush Jordan valley and the extreme north, where settlement was fairly continuous throughout the 2nd and 1st millennia BC, most of this land maintained a settled population only from the thirteenth to the sixth century BC. This coincided with the biblical period from Joshua down to the destruction of the First Temple and the end of the kingdom of Judah. Following these eight centuries, the land was inhabited only by semi-nomads, until the arrival of the Nabateans in the second century BC. They re-established sedentary settlement in Transjordan (and the Negev) until the second century AD, rising to heights of wealth and power during the first centuries BC and AD. It was Glueck, beginning with his excavation of the Nabatean hilltop temple at Khirbet Tannur in central Transjordan, who revealed the culture of this extraordinary people who knew how 'to wrest a hard livelihood from an inhospitable environment'.

Glueck also carried out several intensive investigations in western Palestine, and excavated what was thought to have been the biblical site of Ezion-geber, near Eilat, where Solomon 'made a navy of ships'. (1 Kings 9:26.) Glueck found what he described as an industrial city, with smelters and workshops which produced the copper ingots and tools Solomon needed both for his considerable building programme and for his export trade. The copper was not found at this spot, but the Bible states that this area at the southern tip of the Negev was 'a land whose stones are iron, and out of whose hills thou mayest dig brass [copper]' (1 Kings 8:9), so Glueck went a few miles inland to look for it. He found a large mining site at Timna, where the ore was dug out of open mines, partly smelted in small stone furnaces and then transported to the coast, where it was further refined and turned into ingots. Some archaeologists today have suggested a reconsideration of the exact date and character of the excavated ruins, but none can dispute that his finds evoke the vibrancy of Negev life in ancient times.

After the establishment of the State of Israel, Glueck spent the early 1950s surveying the rest of the little-explored Negev, and found and probed its sites of antiquity. He then turned to an imaginative project and carried it to fulfilment. He created a Jerusalem campus of the American Hebrew Union College and attached to it a school of archaeology, so that rabbinical students, among others, could be introduced to Palestinian archaeology as part of their curriculum. He followed it up in 1964 by initiating and serving as adviser to the comprehensive College-sponsored dig at biblical Gezer, the first after Macalister's excavation at the beginning of the century. After Glueck's death in 1971, the school was named the Nelson Glueck School of Biblical Archaeology.

Excavations in Palestine before the 1920s were carried out exclusively by foreign expeditions, British, American, French, German. No dig had local sponsorship or local direction. The early Zionist pioneers lacked the archaeological skills and training. In any case they were busy building their cities and kibbutzim, and trying, as they put it, 'to make the desert bloom again'. But the interest was there, a passionate interest in their land and their history, and in 1914 they formed the Jewish Palestine Exploration Society. War broke out a few months later, and the Society remained an exploration body in name only. It was revived in 1920 with some amateur probings, but not until a few years later did it participate in professional archaeological projects.

This occurred after 1925, the founding year of the Hebrew University of Jerusalem, which also marked the beginning of systematic local excavation. Some of the digs were undertaken jointly by the University's department of archaeology and the Exploration Society, and several of the young scholars engaged in these small-

The second to fourth-century AD catacombs at Beth She'arim in Lower Galilee, the most favoured central burial place for the Jews of Palestine and the Diaspora after the Romans barred Jerusalem to Jewry in AD 135.

scale projects were to gain international reputations in their fields. There was Moshe Stekelis, for example, who specialized in prehistoric archaeology, and directed a number of important expeditions to such early sites. There were Egyptologist Shmuel Yeivin, and classicist Michael Avi-Yonah, an expert on the Roman period – later both would do much to develop Israel's Department of Antiquities. Another was Binyamin Mazar, whose notable excavation before the Second World War was an extraordinary second-century Galilean catacomb. It belonged to Beth She'arim, city of learning and seat of the Sanhedrin after the Romans banned Jews from Jerusalem, and the centre of Jewish national and religious life shifted from Judea to Galilee. And there was Nahman Avigad, who would take over direction of the Beth She'arim dig some fifteen years later, but who now carried out his significant investigation of ancient monuments in Jerusalem's valley of Kidron. During these years he also participated in several excavations directed by Sukenik, the leading figure among the early Palestinian archaeologists.

Sukenik, as we have seen earlier, was to share the credit with Crowfoot for the discovery of the Samaria Ivories in the early 1930s. But he made a sensational archaeological find as soon as the Hebrew University opened its doors. In 1925, together with the orientalist Leo Ary Mayer, his academic colleague, he excavated what was considered to be the first-century north wall of Jerusalem which Agrippa, king of Judea and last of the Hasmonean line, started to build during his brief reign from AD 41–4. This city wall, known to archaeologists as the Third Wall, ran considerably to the north of the one built by the emperor Hadrian in the following century. It was described, with details of its location, by the first-century historian, Josephus, but it had remained undetected until the arrival of Robinson eighteen centuries later. He recognized 'foundations consisting of large hewn blocks of stone' which he said were 'of a character corresponding to the works of those times' – he was writing of the period of Agrippa. It has been suggested that failure to detect it in the intervening centuries may have been prompted by a reluctance to face the implications it would hold for the authenticity of the site of the Holy Sepulchre, namely, whether it would put it within or outside the walled city. At all events, Robinson's words also went unnoticed by subsequent explorers until Sukenik and Mayer started excavating in 1925. In a more recent dig in the area, Kathleen Kenyon held to the conclusion that the course of Agrippa's wall roughly followed the line of today's northern wall. This, however, is disputed by other modern archaeologists, who support Sukenik's findings that Agrippa's wall lay much farther north, having been specially built to enclose and give protection to the new northern suburb of Bethesda, and that the only ancient wall matching the line of today's wall was the one constructed by Hadrian in the second century.

Sukenik went on to make significant discoveries at the sites of ancient synagogues and Jewish tombs, and he soon became the leading authority on these subjects. He also contributed much to the study of early tomb inscriptions which shed light on Jewish life towards the end of the Second Temple period. Of all his successes, however, he was proudest of a 'find' that was not the product of an archaeological excavation: he was the first to recognize the Dead Sea Scrolls as authentic ancient copies of Hebrew biblical texts, and original commentaries and cognate writings, and he acquired three of the seven complete scrolls for the Hebrew University. This was towards the end of 1947, when Palestine was in violent turmoil, and he spent the rest of his life on their study. He was never to know, for he died six years later, that shortly after his death his son would manage to secure the remaining four.

This son, Yigael Yadin, was to become a leading figure among the new generation of local biblical archaeologists, as his father had been among the first generation. This did not happen quickly, nor was the development conventional. There was nothing of the smooth uninterrupted progression from school to university to field training to expedition director, which was the common pattern in normal times. The times, in Palestine, were far from normal. Between 1936 and 1939 the country was torn by Arab–Jewish strife. For the next six years the world was at war. But when that war ended, with the world at peace, the violence in Palestine became more extreme as events moved towards their climax in May 1948 – the establishment of Israel and the invasion within hours of its birth by the regular armies of five neighbouring Arab countries. Israel had to fight a bitter war of independence to survive. It ended the following year with armistice agreements, the Arabs pushed back behind their own borders, and Israel still on the map.

Thus, from 1936 to the early 1950s, while archaeology had been much thought of, it could hardly have been actively pursued. For students like Yadin and his friends, the excavator's trowel had to give way to the soldier's rifle, though in the pre-State years, service in the Jewish underground defence forces allowed attendance at university lectures during the intervals of relative quiet. With mounting dangers in 1947 and full-scale war in 1948, soldiering became a full-time job. As for the veteran archaeologists, they were engaged in developing the university faculties to train the new generation of excavators after so long a gap.

It may seem surprising, with such handicaps, and so much leeway to make up, that, in less than a decade, Israeli scholars would be numbered among the foremost biblical archaeologists in the world. But to anyone who follows the Israeli scene, the reasons are apparent. It is not that Israelis are more brilliant than other people. It is simply that as Jews living in Israel, they can identify more readily than any non-Israeli scholar with the biblical past, and this is what the archaeologist seeks to recover. After all, they are as familiar with the land as were their forebears who lived there throughout the thirteen centuries before the Christian era. They behold the same landscape, till the same soil, follow the same farming pattern, build their cities and villages on the same sites, fight on the same battlefields, face similar threats from similar neighbours. They also speak the same language, Hebrew. And they are brought up on the Bible, which they read in the original tongue, and which is their basic school text book for language, history and geography. Thus, an Israeli archaeologist approaches an excavation site with a kind of sixth sense, which can give him spontaneous insights others might reach only after laborious effort and study. It is the sense of living with the Bible. This gives him unique perception when he stands on the tel of an ancient city whose remains he is about to excavate. He surveys the surrounding area to determine where to start digging, and it is a little as though he were standing with his antecedents as they consider where to construct their citadel, their homes, their defensive ramparts. He knows the terrain as they did, timeless, unchanging, having started his topographic encounters on the field-trips taken time and again by every Israeli schoolboy, and pursued during army service. And he knows its history from the biblical narrative, which he reads as if it all happened in his own lifetime.

The surprise, therefore, is not that Israeli archaeologists have caught up so quickly and done so well, but that their counterparts from other lands have had such distinguished records. What the biblical scholar from overseas has had to acquire at secondhand, learning history and topography, like Hebrew, as foreign subjects, the average Israeli has absorbed on the Bible's 'home ground' in the normal process of growing up. Several major excavations in the last twenty years have shown that when this Israeli background is coupled with imaginative reasoning, the results can be spectacular. This is what happened at Hazor in Galilee, the city referred to in the Bible as 'the head of all those kingdoms'.

7 Seven Scrolls and Three Royal Cities

THE HAZOR EXPEDITION, which started its first season of digging in the summer of 1955, was the first to be headed by Yigael Yadin, and it made his name as Israel's outstanding archaeologist. But he had already come to the attention of the scholarly world with the completion in the previous year of his highly original commentary on one of the Dead Sea Scrolls which his father had acquired. He gained wider attention in that year – world headlines in fact – for the part he played in securing the remaining four complete scrolls for Israel. Indeed, the entire story of the acquisition of all seven by father and son is as strange and exciting as that of the most precious discovery yielded by an archaeological dig.

It began on Sunday, 23 November 1947, when Professor Sukenik arrived for his lectures at the Hebrew University in Jerusalem to find an urgent message from an Armenian friend, a dealer in antiquities. He needed to see the professor on a matter too sensitive for the telephone, and he requested an early meeting. This was not easy: the country was in turmoil, and an eruption of violence seemed certain. The United Nations General Assembly was in the midst of deliberations which were leading up to a resolution ending the British Mandate and recommending the establishment of a Jewish State. Arab leaders had declared, and intelligence sources had confirmed the intention behind their pronouncements, that Arab attacks on Jewish cities and villages throughout the country would follow the passage of this resolution. The vote was expected any day – it took place, in fact, at the end of that week, on 29 November – and tension mounted as that day drew near. In the mixed city of Jerusalem, the British army had erected barriers between the Jewish and Arab sections, and a military pass was required to go from one zone to another. Sukenik was on the Jewish side of the line, the Armenian on the Arab side; neither could get a pass quickly. They accordingly met the next morning at

OPPOSITE Part of the Thanksgiving Scroll before it was unrolled, one of the seven complete Dead Sea scrolls acquired for Israel by the father-and-son archaeologists, Eliezer Lipa Sukenik and Yigael Yadin.

159

the barrier between their two sectors, and talked to each other across the barbed wire.

The Armenian told an unusual tale. An Arab antiquities dealer in Bethlehem had come to him the previous day bringing some 'leathers'. He had got them, he said, from Bedouin who claimed to have found them in a Dead Sea cave. The Bethlehemite had gone to the Armenian for his appraisal, and the Armenian had come to Sukenik to check their authenticity. If they were indeed ancient documents, would he be prepared to buy them for the Hebrew University? He then held up a scrap of parchment for Sukenik to see, and the professor gazed at it through the loops of barbed wire in an effort to make out the writing on it. The letters looked familiar. He had discovered similar writing on coffins and ossuaries in ancient tombs round Jerusalem. He had seen letters scratched, carved and painted on stone, but this was the first time he had seen this kind of Hebrew lettering written with a pen on leather. As he continued to peer, he had the strong hunch that, as he recorded in his diary, this was 'the real thing'. (Quotations from the diary appear in Yadin's book *The Message of the Scrolls*.) However, he had to have the parchment in his hand and study it before he could definitely rule out the possibility that it was merely a clever forgery. He accordingly asked his friend to go quickly to Bethlehem and bring back further samples of the scroll. Meanwhile he would try to get a military pass so that he could visit the Armenian at his store and examine the parchments closely.

His friend telephoned on Thursday 27 November to say that he had some additional 'leathers', and Sukenik, now in possession of a pass, hurried over to see them. Careful study convinced him that 'these were fragments of genuine scrolls', and he arranged to go with the Armenian to Bethlehem on the morrow and negotiate with the Arab dealer for the purchase of the complete manuscripts. Unfortunately, as he explained to his son the next day, he had been so excited by his meeting with the Armenian that when he returned home he was 'silly enough' to tell his wife that he was going to Bethlehem in the morning, and, he said to Yadin, 'you should have heard her reaction. She said I was crazy even to think of making such a dangerous journey entirely through Arab territory at a time of high tension.... So I had to put him off for the moment, but I cannot sit here doing nothing. What shall I do? Shall I go to Bethlehem?'

Yigael Yadin at that time was Chief of Operations of the Haganah underground defence force. (It was in the Haganah that Yigael Sukenik was given the code-name Yadin, and he kept it when the underground rose to the surface as the Army of Israel upon the establishment of the Jewish State.) On 28 November, the day his

OPPOSITE ABOVE Joshua at the close of the battle of Jericho, one of the bronze reliefs of scenes from the Old Testament on the 'Gate of Paradise', in Florence.

OPPOSITE BELOW The great stone Neolithic tower at Jericho, dating back to about 7000 BC, excavated by Kathleen Kenyon.

father had expected to visit Bethlehem, Yadin had come to Jerusalem in his military capacity to ensure that the Jewish defence arrangements were satisfactory. Before returning to headquarters, he had gone to visit his father, was thrilled by his story – and now found himself in a dilemma over his father's question, torn by his archaeological interest in the priceless documents, and his military judgement of the danger for a Jew to travel to Arab Bethlehem. He finally urged his father not to go.

But Sukenik went after all. Listening to the late-night radio news after his son had left, he learned that the UN decision had been postponed to the following day. Recalling that Yadin had told him that Arab attacks were likely to begin only after the UN vote, he decided that his one chance of securing the scrolls would be to get to Bethlehem and back to Jerusalem before the vote, namely, during the morning hours of 29 November. And that is what he did. He slipped out of the house shortly after dawn, crossed the British barrier with his pass, picked up the Armenian, boarded an Arab bus for the mile-long ride and the two of them reached Bethlehem without incident. They made straight for the house of the Arab antiquities dealer.

From him they heard the story of the Bedouin who had brought him the 'leathers'. They belonged to the Ta'amira tribe, and they had been moving with their goats along the north-western shore of the Dead Sea when one of the herd strayed. Clambering after it, they noticed a cave-opening in the rocks overlooking the sea, and idly cast stones into the dark recess. The answering sound was that of stone hitting pottery. Crawling into the cave, they found eight earthenware jars on the floor, and inside them were bundles of leather, some wrapped in linen. They had wandered for weeks with the bundles, and then decided to go to Bethlehem to see whether they could get money for their find.

At this point the dealer brought out two jars and carefully extracted the scrolls. Sukenik gently took one of them and began to unroll it. He glanced at the opening sentences and was moved beyond words by what he was able to read. They were written in beautiful biblical Hebrew, the style of language similar to that of the Psalms. It gave him the feeling, as he recorded in his journal, that he 'was privileged by destiny to gaze upon a Hebrew scroll which had not been read for more than two thousand years'.

After examining the other two scrolls, he told the Arab dealer that he would probably buy them, but wished to take them home for further scrutiny. He would give a definite reply to their mutual Armenian friend within forty-eight hours. The dealer agreed, and wrapped the leathers in paper. Sukenik and his friend made their way to the Bethlehem market place – the package under his arm

PREVIOUS PAGES Remains of ancient copper mines at Timna in the southern Negev.

OPPOSITE The Herodian ruins on the summit of Masada overlooking the Dead Sea, unearthed by Yigael Yadin.

165

looking like a bundle of market produce – to join the passengers waiting to board the Jerusalem bus. There were tense moments when a sullen Arab group began gesticulating wildly at their approach, but they were allowed to enter the bus without being molested, and they reached Jerusalem safely, much to the Armenian's relief. He confessed, as they parted at Jaffa Gate, that never in his life had he felt so apprehensive.

Sukenik hurried home to his study, unrolled the leathers and began reading, becoming more convinced than ever that his hunch had been right and that these were ancient writings of tremendous importance. While he was examining the precious documents, his youngest son, Mati, was in an adjoining room glued to the radio. He was tuned in to the session of the United Nations Assembly

Sukenik, one of the founders of archaeological studies in Israel, examines the scrolls.

listening to the final speeches before the historic vote, which was due to be taken that night (Israel time). Sukenik later wrote that he was 'engrossed in a particularly absorbing passage in one of the scrolls when my son rushed in with the shout that the vote on the Jewish State had been carried. This great event in Jewish history was thus combined in my home in Jerusalem with another event, no less historic, the one political, the other cultural.' A day later, he telephoned the Armenian to say that he was buying the three scrolls. It was subsequently confirmed that they were written not later than the first century AD by a Jewish sect who lived a communal life in Qumran, on the north-western shore of the Dead Sea. Its adherents continued to dwell there right up to AD 70, at the end of the five-year war of the Jews against the Romans. Shortly before Qumran fell, the Dead Sea sect hid their sacred scrolls in the caves of the nearby cliffs to avoid their desecration by the vanquishing Romans. Sealed in long pottery jars and well preserved in the dry atmosphere of the below-sea level rift, they remained untouched for some 2,000 years until their dramatic discovery – and recognition – in 1947.

The first column of the Isaiah scroll, dating back to the first century BC to first century AD, the oldest copy of a complete biblical Book discovered so far.

The sacred scrolls of the sect consisted of copies of texts which were eventually included in the canon of the Old Testament, familiar to us as the Books of the Bible, as well as original works, hitherto unknown, probably written by a member of the sect. This is evident not only from the few complete scrolls secured by Sukenik and later by Yadin, but also from the thousands of fragments discovered since 1947 which also come within the loose collective designation of Dead Sea Scrolls. Of the three complete ones acquired by Sukenik, two turned out to be non-biblical works. The one on which Yadin later wrote his learned commentary is called the 'The War of the Sons of Light against the Sons of Darkness'. It tells of divine salvation coming at a time of mighty trouble – which was the very time they were living through – and bringing victory to the sons of light, namely those who kept all the rules of the Bible as understood by the sect. It is of great value to scholars, for it prescribes how the sons of light should fight, gives details of tactics, weapons and army organization, and lays down principles for the conduct of war. The second scroll, known as the 'Thanksgiving Scroll', is a collection of hymns written in the form of psalms, but combining the author's religious views with autobiographical episodes. It is considered by scholars to have been written by the leader of the sect, who became an object of persecution because of his struggles to teach, and seek, the path of truth.

Most significant for those engaged in biblical research was Sukenik's third scroll: the biblical 'Book of the prophet Isaiah'. Before its discovery, the earliest known copy of the Hebrew Bible was the one that had been preserved in the synagogue of the Sephardi Jews of Aleppo, Syria, written in about the year AD 930. The importance of the Isaiah scroll is not simply that it is almost 1,000 years earlier than any previously known copy, but that it was written in a period before the Scriptural texts were 'frozen'. Yet the astonishing fact emerged after careful scrutiny that the text of this scroll was virtually identical with that in the Hebrew Bible of today. The words of Isaiah as recited in modern synagogues and studied in Jewish schools everywhere are the very words, with only minor differences, uttered by the Jews in those ancient times. The order and structure of sentences and chapters are the same.

This may not seem odd to us now, for we live in a world of books and printing and tape-recorders. But in those days, with oral transmission followed by hand-transcription and hand-copying, the possibilities for error and distortion were wide indeed. Moreover, there was no punctuation at that time, and Hebrew has no vowels. It says much for the faithfulness of the tradition of Judaism that despite the huge gap in time, the Hebrew biblical texts of then and now are the same. The Scriptures and the way of reading them were handed down from father to son, from rabbi to student, from scribe to scribe, with painstaking accuracy throughout the centuries.

The Dead Sea Scrolls have had a revolutionary impact on biblical, historical and linguistic scholarship. The biblical books shed light on the original texts, and on the development of the Hebrew and Aramaic languages. The non-biblical works reveal the views and beliefs of a particular Jewish sect during a critical period in the history of the Jewish people, and on the eve of the birth of Christianity. As Yadin writes:

> We now have a new basis for the clarification and elucidation of some of the facts concerning the foundation of Christianity, and especially of the influence of Judaism on the Christian faith. In each of these fields [textual, religious, linguistic] the commonplaces of scholarship are up for re-examination in the light of the new material offered by the scrolls.

Violence flared up in Jerusalem and throughout the country a day after Sukenik's trip to Bethlehem, and it grew in scope, scale and intensity throughout December and the first five months of 1948; but it was not yet all-out war. That would start in mid-May when the UN resolution would be put into effect, with the termination of the British Mandate, the establishment of Israel, and the invasion of the new-born State by the neighbouring Arab countries.

In December 1947, however, meetings were still possible – though dangerous – between the Arab and Jewish sectors of

Jerusalem, and Sukenik managed to see the Armenian and pay him for the scrolls. A few days later, he was surprised to receive a telephone call from another friend in the Arab quarter, a member of the Syrian Orthodox Christian community, telling him he had some 'ancient Hebrew scrolls' which might interest the professor. When they finally met, after complicated arrangements, the Syrian produced four scrolls which Sukenik soon saw were just like the three he had already acquired. And, indeed, his friend said he had bought them from another Bedouin of the Ta'amira tribe, and explained that they were now the joint property of himself and the head of his Church, the Syrian Metropolitan, Mar Athanasius Samuel, of the Monastery of St Mark in the Old City of Jerusalem. Sukenik said he would almost certainly wish to buy them for the Hebrew University, but needed to study them further and would like to take them home for a few days. His friend agreed.

When they met shortly after, Sukenik arrived with the scrolls and the decision to buy. He asked the price. The Syrian hedged. He would not name a figure, said he had to think about it, and proposed that they meet the following week to conclude the sale. Sukenik sadly parted with the scrolls, but looked forward to retrieving them at their next meeting. It never took place. And never again did Sukenik set eyes on those scrolls. He died in 1953.

The reason for the Syrian's failure to keep the crucial appointment with Sukenik became known later. He was really the emissary of the Syrian Metropolitan, and it was the Metropolitan himself who claimed to have bought the scrolls some months before they were offered to Sukenik. He had immediately sought the opinion of scholarly orientalists in the Arab sector, and most of them considered the scrolls to be not very old – some put their age at not more than 300 years. This was probably because they were more familiar with ancient Syriac than with ancient Hebrew. When the Metropolitan heard that Sukenik, a professor with a more expert knowledge, had thought three similar scrolls sufficiently significant to have risked his life to acquire them, he sent a member of his community to get his appraisal. That was the purpose of the first meeting between Sukenik and the Syrian. It seemed from that encounter, and became very clear from the second, that the professor judged the four scrolls to be both ancient and valuable, and important enough for him to wish to buy. With that encouraging judgement, the Metropolitan consulted American friends who assured him that he would get a far higher price in the United States than he would in Jerusalem. Thus, no further contact with Sukenik was thought either necessary or desirable.

In January 1949 the Metropolitan arrived in America with the four scrolls, wishing to sell them. He was told that publication would enhance their value and excite the interest of potential buyers, apart from providing important source material to biblical scholars. He accordingly allowed facsimiles of three of them to be published by the American School of Oriental Research, edited by Professor Millar Burrows of the Yale Divinity School. One of them proved to be another copy of Isaiah, better preserved than the one acquired by Sukenik, and containing all sixty-six chapters, whereas fragments were missing from Sukenik's scroll. The second was the Habakkuk Commentary, an interpretation of the words of the prophet and their application to contemporary events. The third was the Manual of Discipline, a detailed code of rules for the Qumran sect. The fourth, unpublished, scroll was later found to be the Genesis Apocryphon, an imaginative literary work embroidering the dramatic episodes in the Book of Genesis. Unlike the other scrolls, it was not in Hebrew but in Aramaic.

Meanwhile, the Metropolitan was busy trying to sell the scrolls himself, and finding the task not as easy as he had been led to believe – possibly because it was rumoured that his asking price was several million dollars. They were still unsold five years later when Yigael Yadin, in May 1954, arrived in the United States to lecture at Johns Hopkins University on the scrolls his father had secured and on which he himself had been working. After the lecture there was informal talk about the unsold scrolls. It appeared that the last one had not been published because the Metropolitan felt he had been misled. Publication had diminished the value of the first three, and he was therefore withholding permission to publish the fourth, hoping to sell all four as a package. The expected price was not millions but more like half-a-million; and apparently American academic institutions had not considered even that sum worth spending on the scrolls.

It may have been chance, or it may have been sparked by the press reports of Yadin's lecture, but five days later an advertisement appeared in the Wall Street journal under the bold heading: 'The Four Dead Sea Scrolls.' It announced that: 'Biblical manuscripts dating back to at least 200 BC are for sale . . . ideal gift to an educational or religious institution.' A box number was added for replies.

Yadin moved rapidly, acting through an American friend in case Arab agents might try to prevent the sale to an Israeli. A reply to the box number elicited a response from the Metropolitan's representative, and after speedy negotiations the deal was concluded for $250,000. Yadin now had to find the money. Securing a gift would take time. A loan was quicker, but it needed collateral – or a government guarantee. Yadin cabled Jerusalem, and received a prompt reply: 'The Prime Minister and Minister of Finance are

Yigael Yadin, the outstanding biblical archaeologist of his generation (and currently Deputy Prime Minister of Israel).

delighted with wonderful opportunity. Order for suitable guarantee has been despatched. Mazal-tov.'

A month after the advertisement appeared, Mar Athanasius Samuel, the Syrian Metropolitan, accompanied by his aides, arrived at the Waldorf-Astoria hotel to complete the final wording in the contract of sale with Yadin's representative. The scrolls were checked, removed from the hotel vault, and taken to Israel. New York industrialist and benefactor Samuel Gottesman later contributed the major part of the cost. When he died, his family established in his memory the Shrine of the Book in Jerusalem as a centre of biblical and scroll research. On display are ancient documents discovered at Israeli archaeological excavations; but pride of place is taken by the seven priceless Dead Sea Scrolls.

They may soon be joined by an eighth. As this book goes to press, Yadin is completing work on a scroll which was discovered in a Qumran cave and reached an Arab antiquities dealer in Jerusalem in 1956, when that city was divided between Jordan and Israel. The 1967 Six Day War swept away the division border, and with contact re-established between the two sectors, Yadin was able to acquire the manuscript. He calls it the Temple Scroll, and after working on its decipherment and commentary for more than ten years, he thinks it may prove to be perhaps the most important of all the Dead Sea Scrolls.

Though Yigael Yadin started his scroll adventures by buying them, he was to find it more adventurous and satisfying to discover them at archaeological excavations. And, indeed, he found ancient writings at almost all his digs. His greatest treasure of documents was brought to light on a daring exploration of what are now known as the caves of Bar Kochba, in the slopes of the wadis running off the Dead Sea near the biblical Judean site of En-gedi. Bar Kochba was the Jewish leader who raised the banner of revolt against the Romans in AD 132, sixty-two years after the fall of Jerusalem, and for the following three years the Jews again enjoyed independence in their land, with Jerusalem as their capital and religious centre. Then came Rome's emperor Hadrian himself, together with his legions and his outstanding commander, Julius Severus, whom he had recalled from Britain for the specific task of crushing this rebellion. Severus proceeded systematically, with the overwhelming weight of numbers and weaponry, to reduce the Jewish outposts one by one. In the closing weeks of the bitter campaign, Bar Kochba's resistance fighters sought refuge with their families in the Judean caves, which could also serve as bases for guerrilla sorties against the enemy legions.

It occurred to Israeli archaeologists, who in 1948 had themselves fought in the latest Jewish war of independence, that when Bar Kochba's men realized the end was near, they may well have hidden their treasured documents beneath the floors or in the walls of the caves, and they were worth looking for. The prospects seemed hopeful, since the Dead Sea Scrolls of the Qumran sect had been found in caves only a few miles north of En-gedi, just inside the territory of Jordan, from which Israelis at that time were barred. Perhaps a well-directed exploration of the caves on the Israeli side of the border might yield similar success. Two modest reconnaissance surveys were accordingly undertaken by archaeologist Yohanan Aharoni in the early and mid-1950s. He found that even those caves which he and his party could reach only with ropes and ladders showed signs of ferreting by Bedouin. World interest in the scrolls, and the huge sums they could fetch, had sent them scurrying among the Dead Sea cliffs on treasure hunts. But in one of the caves where the Bedouin had preceded him, Aharoni came upon gruesome remains from the Bar Kochba period – many skeletons of men, women and children. They were clearly all that was left of the second-century fighters and their kin, and where they had found refuge there they would have hidden their sacred works, which the Bedouin had probably removed. He therefore reported that it would prove rewarding to investigate caves which were definitely inaccessible to the ordinary climber. He added that it would take a large-scale expedition, with appropriate manpower and equipment, to reach, enter and excavate caves which in Bar Kochba's time had eluded the Romans, and in our own time the Bedouin.

Such an expedition was mounted in 1960 (and repeated in 1961) with the help of the Israel Defence Forces. The rugged region was divided into four sectors and each was assigned to a separate team, headed by an experienced archaeologist. The team leaders were Yohanan Aharoni, Nahman Avigad, Pesach Bar-Adon and Yigael Yadin. They were to explore the caves in the sheer slopes of the narrow canyons running off the north-western shore of the Dead Sea, which score the eastern escarpment of the Judean wilderness between En-gedi and Masada.

The preliminary reconnaissance to select the most hopeful caves was carried out by army helicopter. Each archaeologist, sitting with the pilot and an air force photographer, was flown through the canyon in his particular sector so that he could survey the cave-openings and crevices in the craggy walls at eye-level. All were on the lookout for traces of old trails, now impassable, which may have led to caves in the distant past. It was reasoned that the Bar Kochba fighters would assuredly have chosen hideouts to which the approach must have been possible, though difficult, such as narrow goat paths which had been obliterated over the centuries, or eroded down to perilous ledges. Such trails and caves were marked for investigation. Several of the most tempting caves were as much as 300 feet below the lip of the summit and 1,000 feet above the floor of the gorge. The archaeologists examined the photographs and planned the approaches to their targets; and the army established the base camps for the teams, linked them by field telephone, assembled their equipment – most of it great lengths of stout rope, and generators to provide light in the caves – and prepared the tracks on the summit to the 'jump-off' points.

One cave which had aroused high expectations seemed reasonably accessible, and the captain of the reconnaissance unit of a crack infantry brigade attached to the teams, made a trial descent at the end of a safety rope. After cautiously scrambling down some 80

Yadin and Pesach Bar Adon (on his left), two of the four team leaders of the archaeological expedition to the Dead Sea caves of Bar Kochba, consult on their exploration moves together with Major-General Avraham Yoffe (on Yadin's right). The Israel army gave considerable assistance to the expedition.

173

feet, he found that the rest of the slope fell away in a vertical drop to the bottom of a canyon. He climbed back, brought a jeep to the edge of the cliff, fastened a rope to its axle, and another army volunteer, equipped with a paratrooper harness and a walkie-talkie, was linked to the other end and gently lowered over the side. Guiding him was a soldier with a portable transmitter stationed on the bed of the canyon below. The volunteer soon found himself dangling above the gorge opposite the cave-opening but unable to reach it. The rock-face at this point proved to be not vertical but concave. However, by swinging, and choosing the right moment, he leapt into the cave and carried out a preliminary search. He found no scrolls and no pottery, only fallen rock. It had apparently been inaccessible even in the second century AD. He returned, made his report, and further exploration of the cave was abandoned. The team moved on to the next one.

This was the characteristic pattern of the opening days of the expedition. But when trial descents and spot searches offered fruitful prospects, the army widened the approach tracks where possible, put up rope guard rails along narrow ledges, and prepared rope ladders picketed to stakes in the plateau above, so that the archaeologists could reach the caves without too much hazard and start excavating inside. There, however, they faced the danger of rock falls and collapsing roofs, and the discomfort of working in a foetid atmosphere. Some caves contained additional chambers which could be entered only through constricted openings by crawling on all fours. Work within was possible only for brief periods at a time, with frequent intervals to replenish lungs. But the effort, the discomfort and the danger were well rewarded. The discoveries by two of the teams were spectacular; and all four made finds of considerable historical interest.

Aharoni, who reconnoitred the entire valley in his sector in addition to searching the caves, found remains belonging to the Chalcolithic, Israelite and Bar Kochba periods. One cave yielded a bronze coin struck by Bar Kochba during the second year (AD 133) of briefly-regained Jewish independence. An arsenal of arrows was found in another. His chief prize, discovered in a third cave, were fragments of parchments bearing parts of Chapter 13 of Exodus, and portions of phylactery prayers with minute Hebrew writing.

Avigad also found Chalcolithic and Israelite remains. One of his Bar Kochba finds was a cistern for the supply of water to the refugee rebels. Part of it was hewn out of the rock near the mouth of the cave, and the other part was built up. It was fed by rainwater channeled through a gulley just above it. An iron arrow-head, evidently fired by the Roman pursuers in the canyon, was found lodged in the roof of the cave close to the entrance.

OPPOSITE The team under Yohanan Aharoni at the mouth of the cave where they found skeletons of the Bar Kochba resistance fighters who battled to the end against the Roman legions.

The Bar Kochba cave excavated by Bar-Adon which yielded treasures from the Chalcolithic period.

Bar-Adon had little success in the 1960 season, but he made an astonishing discovery in the spring of 1961, though it was associated not with Bar Kochba but with the Chalcolithic period. He uncovered a cache of 420 copper artefacts from the 4th millennium BC, the largest archaeological treasure of that period ever unearthed. The objects were wrapped in a mat and had been secreted in the wall of a cave. They consisted of tools, mace-heads, sceptres, crowns, staves and standards of delicate artistry. They are thought to have belonged to a temple or a palace, and were buried in the cave when war threatened. The owners no doubt hoped to return. They never did; but they had hidden their treasure well. It defied disclosure for more than 5,000 years.

The most fortunate discovery – Bar Kochba documents – fell to Yadin's team when they began searching and excavating a large cave which has since been called the 'Cave of Letters'. Hopes were raised at the start of their exploration when they found a coin just outside the entrance which bore on one side the design of a palm tree and the inscription 'Shimon', Bar Kochba's first name. The obverse side showed a cluster of grapes and the Hebrew words 'Leherut Yerushalayim', 'For the Freedom of Jerusalem'. The first finds inside the cave were Roman ritual vessels of bronze, bearing reliefs of pagan images which had been deliberately defaced. They had almost certainly belonged to a unit of Roman occupation troops who had been defeated in the opening months of the revolt by Bar Kochba's men. The victors, devoutly religious, had scratched out the pagan ornamentation before putting the vessels to use.

Then came the amazing find of the manuscripts. One was a parchment fragment containing parts of the Hebrew text of Psalms 15 and 16. The rest were fifteen letters or battle despatches, most of them in Hebrew and Aramaic, from Bar Kochba at his field head-quarters to two of his officers, Yehonatan and Masabala, who appear to have been the military commander and the civil adminis-trator at En-gedi. The letters were excavated from a cavity in a corner of one of the chambers running off the large cave. They were wrapped in a kerchief which had been placed inside a leather water-skin. All except one were written on papyrus. The exception was a letter written on wood, which had been 'folded' into four slats, and inscribed with two columns of Aramaic. It opened with the words: 'Shimon bar Kosiba, Prince over Israel, to Yehonatan and Masabala, peace.' Bar Kosiba or Kosba is how he appears in rabbinic literature; but his followers during the revolt gave the name messianic overtones by changing the letter 's' for 'ch', rendering it Bar Kochba, Hebrew for 'Son of a Star', and evoking

Yadin handling the bundle of papyrus documents unearthed in one of the caves.

'there shall come a Star out of Jacob' in Numbers 24:17. It is by the popular name Bar Kochba that he has been known ever since. The Yadin discovery, however, shows that his original name was retained in his own letters and in official documents.

These battlefield letters from Bar Kochba to his rear base at En-gedi deal largely with the despatch of supplies and instructions on mobilization. They were written in AD 134 or 135. How did they reach the caves? They are thought to have been brought there by Yehonatan or Masabala or their wives or some other surviving member of their families who fled from En-gedi in the closing stage of the war.

Of special interest is a letter in which Bar Kochba demands that 'palm branches and citrons . . . and myrtles and willows' be sent to his camp so that he and his men could celebrate the Festival of Succot (tabernacles, or booths). This festival recalls the improvised shelters put up by the Israelites when they wandered through the wilderness after the Exodus on their way to the Promised Land. The four kinds of plants requested by Bar Kochba are to this day the ritual requirements for the observance of Succot, as set forth in Leviticus 23:39. The urgency of his message reveals that even amidst the harsh affliction of that bitter war, when he was being crushed by the might of Rome's legions, Bar Kochba sought scrupulously to fulfil the biblical injunctions. He was even careful enough to add the reminder before sending the plants, 'see that they are tithed'.

Yadin was rewarded with another documentary treasure when the teams returned the following year for a second season of exploration, and he decided on a thorough excavation of the entire 'Cave of Letters', with all its ancillary chambers. The result was the discovery of many manuscripts in Hebrew, Aramaic, Nabatean and Greek which shed light on the prevailing patterns of contemporary society in Judea, and contribute greatly to the studies of the Talmud, philology, history and geography. The Hebrew and some of the Aramaic documents deal with the leasing of land in and around En-gedi that had been 'crown property' during the Roman occupation. When the Jews liberated the area at the start of the revolt, the 'crown lands' reverted to Jewish control and were administered by Bar Kochba's local representatives. Thus, names familiar from the letters found the previous year appear once again. Yehonatan is down on some of the documents as 'the administrator of Shimom ben Kosiba, President of Israel, at En-gedi'. His colleague, Masabala, signs one of the deeds as a witness. The information that is so valuable to scholars is contained in the detailed specifications of the leased plots, their boundaries, agricultural produce, water rights, and terms of payment. What

A Hebrew land-lease found in the caves.

emerges from these writings is that, behind the battle zone, the civil administration tried to preserve the norms of daily living, while keeping supplies flowing to the troops in the field.

Facets of civilian life at the beginning of the second century AD are also reflected in the Yadin find of thirty-five papyrus documents in Nabatean, Aramaic and Greek, which turned out to be the complete family archive belonging to a lady of means named Babata. Here, too, are title deeds, as well as legal papers relating to mortgages, land leases and loans. The gems in the collection, for the philologists, are the Nabatean papyri, the first discovery of Nabatean writing other than brief rock inscriptions above their tombs. The Nabatean kingdom, with its capital at Petra in Transjordan, fell to the Romans in AD 106 and became a province of Rome, Provincia Arabia. Of special importance to archaeologists and historians is the record in the Babata documents of names and titles of known rulers, and dates. This is the rare information which makes it possible to fix with certainty the precise period of an archaeological stratum. The legal papers go further, for they use three systems of dating. In one, the year is given by reference to the reigning Roman emperor, so that 'the third year of Hadrian' would be AD 120, since he is known to have reached power in AD 117. The reference in the second system is to the founding of Provincia Arabia; thus, 'the fifteenth year of Provincia Arabia' would be AD 121. The third gives the date by reference to the consul in Rome. These documents thus offer a complete synchronization of all three systems, a rarity indeed.

A clue in one of the Babata letters suggests how her archive came to be in this Dead Sea cave. It reveals that she was a distant relative of Yehonatan, who together with Masabala led the Jewish contingent of En-gedi during the revolt. When they or their families fled to

179

the caves, Babata must have been with them, carrying her precious documents.

Yadin's exploration of the Bar Kochba caves and his scholarly work on the documents he discovered confirmed his reputation as an archaeologist of uncommon gift and flair. He gained that reputation with his first dig, the excavation of Hazor, which widened the horizons of biblical archaeology. The project was followed with keen interest by scholars throughout its four seasons. And the very announcement in the summer of 1955 that Yadin was on his way to Galilee to start the dig stirred no little excitement among the general public in Israel. It was the first major excavation undertaken in the seven-year-old State since its establishment. It was the largest ever to be directed by an Israeli archaeologist; and that archaeologist only three years earlier had been chief of the general staff of the Israel Army, and before that chief of operations during Israel's War of Independence.

It was no surprise that Yadin's choice of a civilian career upon leaving the army should be biblical archaeology. After all, he had grown up with it. As a boy he would visit his father's excavations whenever he could, and the table talk at home would turn on these digs and on the artefacts his father brought home to study. While still in his teens Yadin showed all the signs of a prodigy, reading the Bible as an archaeological text-book and a military manual, and conceiving novel theories about the tactics used in biblical battles. Some of these ideas subsequently appeared in print in learned journals when Yadin was dividing his years between university life and service with the Haganah underground. He was lucky to graduate before the outbreak of the 1948 war, so he could proceed to his doctorate upon his military retirement, and start excavating soon after.

It was also fortunate for the army that archaeology was the principal outside interest of the officer in charge of operations during that war. With his scientific background, Yadin knew the importance of primary source material. He would always scrutinize the detailed report of an excavation before accepting the archaeologist's interpretation of his finds. He adopted the same critical attitude towards battle intelligence and the assessment of his intelligence officers. On crucial occasions he insisted on studying the raw intelligence material himself, giving it his own interpretation and making his own judgement.

This was the case with the capture of Beersheba from the Egyptian army in October 1948. Five months earlier, in the fighting that followed their invasion in May, the Egyptians had advanced to a point only twenty-two miles from Tel Aviv. They were pushed

OPPOSITE ABOVE Archaeological excavations at the foot of the southern wall of the Temple Mount in Jerusalem.

OPPOSITE BELOW The Ark of the Covenant being brought into Jerusalem, preceded by David with harp (top), and placed in the Tabernacle (below). An illustration from *A Book of Old Testament Miniatures of the Thirteenth Century* which originated in Paris about 1250.

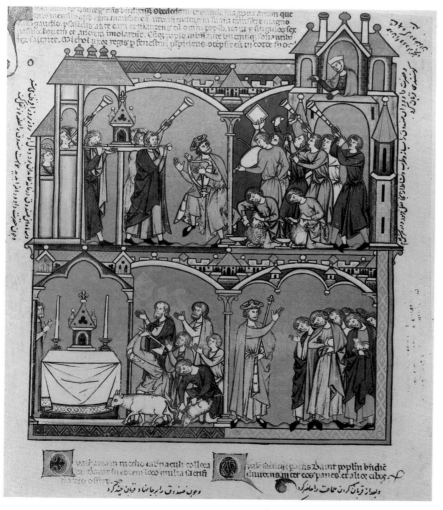

steadily back in the months that followed, when brief spells of combat alternated with a shaky truce. Hostilities broke out again in mid-October, and in the first six days of battle the Egyptians were driven further south, almost to Beersheba. The UN Security Council was about to call for a renewed truce within the following twenty-four hours. Israel army intelligence officers held that the Egyptians entrenched in Beersheba could not be overcome in that time. But in studying the intelligence material himself, notably the intercepts of Egyptian radio exchanges between the front-line troops and headquarters behind the lines, Yadin concluded that enemy morale was low and resistance likely to be light. He ordered an immediate attack, which Yigal Alon, the outstanding field commander, promptly launched. A few hours before the ceasefire deadline, Beersheba was restored to Israeli hands.

Archaeology played a more direct part in the planning of a decisive military action that occurred two months later. This was Israel's final thrust in the War of Independence, which drove the last Egyptian soldier from Israeli soil and ended the fighting on the southern front. Though they had lost Beersheba, the Egyptians were still inside Israeli territory. During the truce they had fortified two bases south of Beersheba, astride the only road to the Negev–Sinai frontier which could take wheeled traffic. The land on either side was desert, and the Egyptians knew that Israel possessed virtually no tanks or other tracked vehicles. Thus, expected Israeli action could only be a frontal assault from the direction of Beersheba.

That was the situation when fighting again erupted in the last week of December. Yadin's archaeological knowledge now contributed the crucial element to the Israeli operational plan. He recalled that in Roman times there had been a road which passed through the northern Negev desert and emerged precisely at the midway point between the two sites where the Egyptians were now based. He accordingly dispatched a four-man reconnaissance patrol in a jeep to see if there were still signs of this ancient route, and if so to test whether it could carry modern vehicles. The patrol found the road, and returned with a two-word report: 'Difficult. Possible.' And it was along this old route that the Israeli forces went into action. They split when they were between the two enemy bases, and attacked both simultaneously.

Surprise was complete. The guns at the first Egyptian base were still pointing the wrong way; and the Egyptians at the second were too astonished to fight effectively, wondering how on earth the Israelis had managed to get past the first barrier without their knowledge. The two Egyptian units, thoroughly confounded, were soon overwhelmed, and within hours the Israelis were across

PREVIOUS PAGES The city wall of Hazor in Galilee, the 'head of all those kingdoms' conquered by Joshua, excavated by Yigael Yadin.

OPPOSITE The Moslem Dome of the Rock in Jerusalem, built at the end of the seventh century AD on the mount where Solomon erected the Jewish Temple in the tenth century BC.

the frontier, engaging Egyptian forces inside Sinai and chasing them right up to the outskirts of Rafah. Only American and British ultimatums forced the Israelis to halt and withdraw.

Six weeks later, the Israel–Egypt Armistice Agreement was signed on the neutral Mediterranean island of Rhodes. Heading the military section of the Israeli delegation that negotiated the armistice was Yigael Yadin.

The sense of historical continuity was very much with him when he stood, some six years later, on the mound of Hazor at the start of his campaign, seeking to unlock the secrets of its biblical and pre-biblical past. The land was at peace, for a time; but Yadin felt, in a sense, that he was re-fighting, with pick and trowel and archaeologist's eye, one of the key battles of his forebear, Joshua, 3,300 years before. The biblical record shows that Joshua faced a formidable array of enemy forces:

> And it came to pass, when Jabin king of Hazor had heard those things [Joshua's victories in the territories to the south of Galilee], that he sent to Jobab king of Madon, and to the king of Shimron, and to the king of Achshaph, And to the kings that were on the north of the mountains, and of the plains south of Chinneroth, and in the valley, and in the borders of Dor on the west, And to the Canaanite on the east and on the west, and to the Amorite, and the Hittite, and the Perizzite, and the Jebusite in the mountains, and to the Hivite under Hermon in the land of Mizpeh. And they went out, they and all their hosts with them, much people, even as the sand that is upon the sea shore in multitude, with horses and chariots very many. And when all these kings were met together, they came and pitched together at the waters of Merom, to fight against Israel. (Joshua 11:1–5.)

It was this chapter in the Bible that first excited Yadin's interest in Hazor, particularly when it went on to record that after conquering 'all the cities of those kings' who had joined the alliance against the Israelites, 'Joshua at that time turned back, and took Hazor, and smote the king thereof with the sword: for Hazor beforetime was the head of all those kingdoms . . . and he burnt Hazor with fire.' If that were not enough to indicate what a powerful city Hazor was, the Bible goes on to stress that this was the only one in the region which suffered utter destruction. 'But as for the cities that stood still in their strength' – the original Hebrew makes it explicit that the reference is to fortified cities that 'stood on their mounds' – 'Israel burned none of them, save Hazor only; that did Joshua burn.' (Joshua 11:10–13.)

This biblical passage alone, with its repetitive emphasis on Hazor at the time of the Joshua conquest, had long planted the thought in Yadin's mind that it would be an exciting site to excavate. The idea was strengthened when, as a soldier on army manoeuvres, he had recognized its strategic value. Ideally, if he dug up a level of destruction belonging roughly to the period of Joshua, he might find pottery or even an inscription which would give the definitive date. The controversy as to whether it was the fifteenth, fourteenth or thirteenth century BC had been at its height when Yadin had been a student. Being able to establish the date of Joshua would help towards the absolute dating of other historical events, such as the Exodus, where the chronology was still obscure.

There was, however, more to Hazor than Joshua's battle and chronology. The next major biblical mention of this city occurs in the narrative on Solomon. Brief though it is, it was enough to stir the imagination of many archaeologists: 'And this is the reason of the levy which king Solomon raised: for to build the house of the Lord . . . and Hazor, and Megiddo, and Gezer.' (1 Kings 9:15.) To excavate the site of the 'house of the Lord', Solomon's Temple in Jerusalem, was simply not possible, for reasons given in an earlier chapter. But digging up the three major Solomonic fortress cities offered the rich prospect of finding remains of the majestic building projects the Bible indicates were carried out during that remarkable reign. It was perhaps the principal reason that had prompted Macalister to undertake his excavation at Gezer at the beginning of the century, and Fisher and his colleagues to dig up Megiddo in the 1920s. Hazor, alone of the three, was left, and Yadin was determined to tackle it. In addition to illuminating the history of Hazor, Yadin also hoped to clear up what appeared to him to be incongruities in the reports of the Gezer and Megiddo digs.

There was the further expectation of unearthing the tangible evidence of the destruction of Hazor by the Assyrians in the eighth century BC. The record of this event contains the last major reference to Hazor in the biblical narrative of the Israelite reigns. Assyria's Tiglath-pileser invaded the country in the year 732 BC, a date already established by the time Yadin came to excavate, so that any artefact found in that level of destruction – if indeed such a level were to be discovered – could most likely be given an absolute date, and in turn become a dating key.

Where exactly was this ancient city? From the biblical accounts it was situated in the eastern region of the Upper Galilee hills. The post-biblical Jewish historian Josephus, writing in the first century AD, notes the detail that Hazor lay 'over the Lake Semechonitis', identified with today's Huleh Lake, due north of the Sea of Galilee. In all the centuries since Josephus, its precise location was unknown, remaining unidentified by the surface explorers, including the ingenious Robinson. Even the great Albright in our own

187

century searched for it without success. It was John Garstang who found it in 1928. He was head of the Antiquities Department of the British Mandatory Administration in Palestine at the time, and he spent a few weeks on a trial dig at a large mound called Tel el-Qedah, nine miles north of the Sea of Galilee. He found enough to establish that this was undoubtedly the site of biblical Hazor.

Writing about it a few years later, Albright gave him credit in his characteristic way: 'Garstang discovered the ancient Galileean town of Hazor at Tel el-Qedah . . . after several scholars, including the writer, had been hunting for it in vain for years.' Curiously enough however, Yadin, in his preparatory research before starting to excavate, came across a certain J. L. Porter, a surface explorer, who in 1875 published his suggestion that Tel el-Qedah was the archaeological mound of Hazor. Describing his visit the previous year, Porter wrote that after viewing the mound from a distance, he mounted his horse, followed a broad path, 'and soon came upon the ruins of an ancient city. . . . I thought at the time that these might be the ruins of Hazor, and I have since become more and more confirmed in the belief.' His hunch was right, and it was endorsed by Garstang.

This, then, was the site of Yadin's four-season dig, his first, and it yielded remarkable discoveries. Beginner's luck? That was what some of his colleagues thought, but when he went on to reap similar rewards at all his subsequent excavations, they readily acknowledged that this phenomenon could not be ascribed to luck alone. Someone *did* have a stroke of luck at Hazor – finding a written inscription which helped to confirm Tel el-Qedah as the site of Hazor. But this was the good fortune neither of Yadin nor of any member of his team. It was a visiting tourist who chanced to stumble upon a fragment of a clay tablet bearing cuneiform writing. This turned out to be part of the record of a judicial hearing before the king concerning a dispute over property in Hazor. Luck of this kind, however, is rare. Behind most major archaeological discoveries lies careful reasoning. A good example is one of Yadin's early Hazor discoveries which Garstang missed in his 1928 soundings and, as a consequence, misled scholars for the next thirty years. This was the find of a certain type of pottery which had eluded Garstang's spade.

It is known as Mycenaean pottery, which was exported from Greece to the countries of the eastern Mediterranean, notably to Egypt and her dominions. It is easy to recognize because of its special shape, colour, texture, and the design and location of the handles on its jars. Much of this pottery was discovered at archaeological excavations in Egypt in the late nineteenth century,

ABOVE The humble Mycenaean pottery vessel found at Hazor which disclosed the secret of the date of the Joshua conquest and, indirectly, of the Exodus from Egypt.

OPPOSITE The remains of biblical Hazor, unearthed by Yadin in his first large-scale archaeological excavation.

and with Petrie's pottery-dating guidelines it was possible to trace its development, and to classify and date its variants with the passage of each generation. It was further learned from other archaeological and also historical sources that the import of this pottery into Egypt and the lands she controlled started in about the year 1400 BC and ended in 1230 BC.

In his trial excavation at Hazor in 1928, Garstang found a lot of potsherds; but none was Mycenaean. Since the evidence showed that the last settlement on the site, namely the one Joshua destroyed, had been 'brought to a close by a general conflagration', he naturally concluded that this had occurred before the appearance of Mycenaean pottery in the country. He accordingly suggested the date of the Joshua conquest, at the very latest, as 1400 BC.

Yadin, at first, shared Garstang's experience with the pottery. After a survey of the terrain and some preliminary probes, he noted that there were in fact two adjoining sites of Hazor. One, which he called the lower city, was a large rectangular enclosure. The other, to its immediate south, was on the mound. He began digging in the enclosure, which was bounded by huge, ancient earthen walls, by cutting an excavation trench that ran from the top of these ramparts towards the centre of this lower site, not far from where Garstang had dug. In the opening days he felt much as Garstang must have felt. They 'were rather disappointing,' he wrote later. Close to the ramp, 'where the slope began, we seemed to be digging in sterile soil – so much so that some members of our staff began to doubt the expediency of exploring any further.' But he persisted, and soon found the reason: the area near the foot of the earthen walls was 'covered with disintegrated mud bricks and clay material washed down from the top of the ramparts in past millennia. No wonder the soil was sterile: it sealed the last level of occupation!' Soon afterwards, only a few feet below the surface and not many yards from Garstang's dig, he made the major discovery of ruined buildings with cobblestone floors – and an abundance of Mycenaean pottery of the thirteenth-century type. Thus, as he wrote, 'the evidence in hand, contrary to Garstang's conclusions, shows that the city was destroyed around 1230 BC at the latest'; and in the course of the excavations he found indications that it occurred some time between 1250 and 1230 BC. This evidence, he says, 'is, indeed, among the most important and decisive archaeological testimonies ever uncovered in excavations concerning the date of the conquest by Joshua and, indirectly, of the Exodus itself'.

The four-season dig was thorough, going down to bedrock in the entire area, so that while the biblical period was Yadin's principal interest, recapturing the pre-biblical history of the site was also a fascinating experience, and of importance to the general historian. Yadin found that the first city of Hazor was built on the mound in the first half of the 3rd millennium BC, and only in the eighteenth century BC was the lower city founded. He already knew of Hazor's importance in pre-Israelite times before he started excavating, not only from the Bible but also from his reading of the ancient documents discovered by foreign explorers and archaeologists in Egypt and Mesopotamia. Its first mention appears in the nineteenth-century BC Execration Texts, listing the potential enemies of the Egyptian empire among her vassal provinces. Far more important and interesting, however, are the references to Hazor in eighteenth-century BC letters found in the royal archives of Mari, the ancient city on the middle Euphrates, where in 1935–8 the French archaeologist André Parrot unearthed the palace of king Zimri-Lim. Among some 20,000 Akkadian cuneiform inscriptions on clay tablets are several of which Hazor is the subject, and the king of Mari to whom the messages were sent was a contemporary of Hammurabi of Babylon. In one of the messages, the royal chamberlain informs the king that: 'Two messengers from Babylon who have long since resided at Hazor, with one man from Hazor as escort, are crossing to Babylon.' If king Hammurabi saw fit to maintain ambassadors in Hazor, it must certainly have been a city of note.

Hazor is next mentioned in Egyptian documents from the fifteenth to the thirteenth century BC among the Canaanite cities conquered or controlled by the pharaohs Thutmose III and Amenhotep II (fifteenth century), and Seti I (fourteenth–thirteenth centuries). It also appears in a thirteenth-century manuscript known as the Papyrus Anastasi I. The most important early references, however, are those in four letters written to the pharaoh by his vassals which were found in the fourteenth-century BC archives of el-Amarna. One is from the king of Tyre and one from the ruler of Ashtaroth. Both complain that 'Abdi-Tirshi, king of Hazor' has rebelled against the pharaoh and captured several of their cities. The other two letters are from the king of Hazor, denying the charges, reaffirming his loyalty to the Egyptian monarch, and bringing counter-charges against his irate neighbours.

Yadin recovered the early history of Hazor in his excavations – including what was probably the palace of Abdi-Tirshi – and found that the city had indeed merited attention in those times. He discovered that the rectangular enclosure was in fact a city covering 175 acres, large for those days and the largest in the country at its high point of settlement, which was shortly after it was founded in the eighteenth century BC. As with most large strategic cities at the time, it was the target of frequent assault. Destroyed and rebuilt, it flourished again in the fourteenth century, when it was ruled by Abdi-Tirshi. But not for long. It was destroyed again at the end of that century and re-settled at the beginning of the next. But its fortifications were now less formidable. This was the city that Joshua destroyed. The lower part, on the rectangular plateau, was never restored. Only the upper city on the mound was rebuilt, notably by Solomon.

The excavations unearthed the first of the lower cities, and revealed that it had been founded during the period of the Hyksos. It was they who fortified it with the huge earth walls which bounded the rectangular enclosure. The remains of buildings and the artefacts found by Yadin on this lower site and belonging to the various periods of its existence, from the eighteenth to the thirteenth centuries, included palaces, pagan temples, gates and towers, well-paved plazas, houses with a canalization system, exquisite stone reliefs, pottery from each period ending with Mycenaean ware, a fifteenth-century pottery model of a cow's liver used by priests to divine the future with a cuneiform inscription listing the events they foretold, and a bronze tablet of the same date with a magnificent portrait relief of, presumably, the city governor. Of special archaeological interest were the remains of the city gates from all the periods of settlement. This made it possible to trace the development of their design through five centuries, as the defen-

Cleaning the pottery finds at the excavation site enables the archaeologist to make an immediate on-the-spot evaluation of the strata in which they are discovered.

ders sought to keep pace with the constant invention of new weapons of assault. The earliest gate was a simple entrance protected by two towers. The last was a broad corridor flanked by garrison chambers and more powerful towers, and in front was a broad terrace and an approach road for chariots.

Similar finds from this pre-Joshua period were made on the mound, though here the remains of its first settlement established several centuries earlier were naturally more primitive. The prize discovery on this site of the upper city was unearthed in the Solomonic stratum. It was the casemate wall and gate of the city built by Solomon in the tenth century BC, one of the three for which he had levied a special tax. By inspired reasoning, Yadin was led by this remarkable find to further Solomonic discoveries which the earlier excavators had missed at the archaeological sites of Hazor's two sister cities, Gezer and Megiddo. Together, they constitute the material counterpart matching the biblical narrative of Solomon's reign. Archaeology in the Holy Land, Yadin once said, should be conducted with a spade in one hand and the Bible in the other. This dig, his first, is an example of the value of this principle. It also offers a glimpse into the working of an archaeologist's mind.

The Books of the Bible which recount the historical narrative are of course the prime source for valuable archaeological clues. But many are also offered by the Prophetic works. Albright had spotted one such clue in the Book of Ezekiel, and this had excited Yadin long before he came to dig at Hazor. It was to prove of direct help in the interpretation of a major find. Ezekiel had a vision when he was in Babylonian captivity fourteen years after the destruction of Jerusalem. In this vision the prophet saw himself brought back to the land of Israel and shown round the Temple by a messenger of the Lord, who enjoined him to 'declare all that thou seest to the house of Israel'. He did so, in great detail. Describing the eastern wall of the Temple, for example, Ezekiel wrote: 'Then came he [the messenger] unto the gate which looketh toward the east, and went up the stairs thereof, and measured the threshold of the gate. . . . And the little chambers of the gate eastward were three on this side, and three on that side.' (Ezekiel 40:4, 6, 16.) The prophet was clearly recalling the actual Temple, with which he was familiar from his residence in Jerusalem before his exile. Yadin was therefore not surprised when, as an archaeology student, he visited the pre-war Megiddo excavations and read the report by the archaeologists of their having found the remains of the foundations of the Solomonic city gate. It had a tower at each side of the entrance, and the gatehouse for the guards had six chambers, three on each side of the entrance, just like the Temple gate described by Ezekiel. The next step in his thinking was that Solomon had no doubt used his top architect and engineer for all his major building projects, and they had almost certainly used the same basic design for the standard parts of similar structures – the Temple gate and the city gate of Megiddo.

These thoughts were much in his mind when, at the Hazor excavation, his teams were approaching the Solomonic level. They had found the citadels erected during the Hellenistic period (332–363 BC) and below them the remains of the Persian period (538–332 BC). Digging through the two earlier centuries they discovered that at the beginning of this period Hazor had been a small unwalled settlement which had later been abandoned. They could already guess from the Bible why it had no fortified city walls; and when they reached the next level, the latter part of the eighth century, they found the evidence: those walls and the entire city had been destroyed by Assyria's Tiglath-pileser III, as recorded in 2 Kings 15:29. It occurred, says the biblical verses: 'In the days of Pekah king of Israel.' One of the wine jars found in this level bears the Hebrew inscription: 'Belonging to Pekah.' Those were grim decades for the Israelites, for when they were not being attacked by powerful imperial armies, they were being visited by natural catastrophe. Only a few years before the Assyrian destruction, an earthquake did much damage to the city. The earthquake is mentioned in the opening verse of the Book of the prophet Amos as having happened during the reign of Jeroboam II, in the middle of

Assyrian king Tiglath-pileser III portrayed in his war chariot, a wall panel discovered in his palace at Nimrud. The results of his attack on Hazor in the eighth century BC were found during the excavations.

the eighth century BC. Yadin found evidence of the damage, and also that the inhabitants had been quick to rebuild Hazor, only to be overwhelmed shortly afterwards by Tiglath-pileser.

The next stratum reached by the archaeologists belonged to the ninth century, and the remains of the buildings they unearthed are attributed to the reign of Ahab. They found a structure with pillars looking like hitching posts, which misled Garstang into thinking it was a huge stable. It had in fact been a large Israelite storehouse. The most important find in this stratum, however, were parts of the city wall, which showed that in this century the fortification techniques had much advanced to meet the challenge of a more effective device against walled cities. Yadin had been the first to point out that the casemate wall was characteristic of the tenth century BC – namely the time of Solomon – and that it had been strengthened in the ninth century. The casemate wall was a double wall, each comparatively thin, and the space between them was partitioned off into a series of chambers. This type of fortification was weaker than a single, very thick wall, but it was considered adequate defence against the wall-breaching weapon of the tenth century, and its rooms could be used for the troops or for stores. In the early part of the ninth century, however, a more powerful battering ram made its appearance, and the thin casemate type gave way to a solid wall. This is held to have developed during the reigns of Omri and his son Ahab. Yadin realized he would soon be reaching the Solomonic stratum.

Almost the first ruins found by his teams at several places in this upper city were sections of a thin casemate wall, and excitement was high. It rose as they continued excavating along the line of one section and came up against what appeared to be the beginnings of a large structure, which Yadin reasoned must be the city gate. Recalling Ezekiel's description, as well as the plan of the Solomonic gate discovered at the Megiddo excavations some thirty years earlier, and following his assumption that Solomon would have employed the same architect, Yadin halted the dig for a while. He then traced out on the ground the outline plan of the Megiddo gate, using the same dimensions, and told the diggers to excavate according to his markings. He also forecast, as he reported in his book *Hazor*, what they would unearth: 'Here you will find a wall; there, a chamber.' The labourers took up their spades and resumed digging, wonderment in their eyes as they found, beneath the markings, the very gate construction he had envisaged. They thought him a prophet – until he read them the relevant biblical passages. They were all devoutly religious Jews, and since the facts were all there in the Bible, it was understandable that he would have known what there was to find!

What he found was an almost perfect replica of the Megiddo gate. The gatehouse had six chambers, three on either side of the corridor, with a tower on each side of the entrance. The length of the gate, the width of the entrance passage, and the thickness of the walls were exactly the same measurements as their counterparts at Megiddo. There were only slight differences elsewhere, no doubt to suit the differences in topography.

Another example of neat archaeological reasoning, both by Yadin and a local farmer, lay behind the decision where to start digging. Yadin was accompanied on a reconnaissance visit by the Jewish farmer who owned the site and who noticed that the archaeologist was intrigued by the ruins of a structure on the western tip of the mound. It had in fact been partially unearthed by Garstang during his brief trial dig, and he had reported that: 'On the west end of the tel stood a palatial building or temple, the origin of which could not be determined.' Yadin, with his military experience, had already decided that it was worth a thorough excavation because of its commanding strategic location, dominating the entire area to the west. But when the farmer asked him what he was looking for, he simply said he would like to find, among other things, the fort or palace of the ancient city. Yadin writes that he then asked his companion where he would have built his palace if he had been Hazor's ruler. 'Right here,' said the farmer, pointing to the western tip of the mound. Asked why, the farmer surprised him by making no mention of the strategic reason. 'Having lived here for many years,' he replied, 'I know that this is the only spot where there is a pleasant breeze from the west even on a scorching summer day. I would definitely have built my palace here.' Whether or not that was also the reason prompting the governors of ancient Hazor, the Yadin expedition found that this was the location of palatial buildings, or large citadels, which had been built and rebuilt from Ahab's time in the ninth century BC right down to the second century BC. [Incidentally, the area supervisor on this excavation site was Ruth Amiran, who found valuable evidence of the material culture of Hazor throughout those eight centuries. She is today one of Israel's leading archaeologists. Other area supervisors who were at the beginning of their archaeological careers when they joined Yadin's professional staff and who went on to establish international reputations in the world of biblical archaeology were Yohanan Aharoni, Trude Dothan, Moshe Dothan, Jean Perrot and Claire Epstein. Hazor was also the training ground for students who worked with Yadin and who today direct their own digs. Among them were Magen Broshi, David Ussishkin, Moshe Kochavi, Avraham Eytan, Amnon Ben-Tor, and Ephraim Stern.]

Part of the Solomonic city gate of Hazor.

196

The Hazor dig is an excellent example of how the reasoning behind discovery at one excavation can lead to cognate discoveries at other archaeological sites. We have seen that the tenth-century gates of Solomon at Hazor and Megiddo were identical. But whereas the gate at Hazor was linked to a tenth-century casemate wall, the Megiddo gate appeared in the report of the archaeologists to have been attached to a wall of the kind which Yadin had long maintained belonged to the ninth century. This was not the only anomaly which bothered him. The third city, Gezer, had been the site of one of the first major excavations in Palestine, conducted, as we have seen, by Macalister in the first decade of this century. Yet in his voluminous and detailed report, Macalister had made no mention of a Solomonic gate.

Yadin thought this was distinctly odd. The Bible recorded that Solomon had built the three cities. In the three digs, Hazor had yielded both a Solomonic gate and wall, Megiddo only a gate, and Gezer neither. As for the latter, could it be that Macalister's report – or his excavation – was at fault? After all, archaeology at the beginning of the century was still in its infancy, and there was hardly any comparative archaeological data to help in the interpretation of finds. Moreover, Macalister had worked without a senior staff, performing all the professional functions himself. Was it not conceivable that he had indeed dug up the remains of these Solomonic structures but had not known what they were and had mis-dated them?

To find out, Yadin decided to 'excavate' not the *site* of Gezer – he was still busy with his own dig at Hazor – but the report that Macalister had issued in 1912. He made a fresh examination of the description and plans of Macalister's finds, and soon spotted the layout of structures which Macalister had ascribed to the second century BC and entitled 'Plan of the Maccabean Castle of Gezer'. Yadin needed no more than a glance to detect in this plan a casemate wall, and what looked to him like the western half of a Solomonic gate, with three chambers. Its eastern, three-chambered counterpart was missing. Macalister had not known what to make of this gate-section (Hazor and Megiddo had yet to be excavated) and he called it simply, though obscurely, 'stall-like spaces'. He had mis-dated it by eight centuries largely because he had found Hellenistic pottery and a Greek inscription in the area, and erroneously concluded that the original structure was of this late date.

Yadin published the conclusions of his archaeological detective work in a 1958 article entitled 'Solomon's City Wall and Gate at Gezer'. In it he suggested that the 'Maccabean Castle' was in fact the remains of Solomon's fortifications and gatehouse, and he showed that both the design and dimensions were similar to those of Hazor and Megiddo, and the masonry-dressing and building patterns were identical.

The theory was widely accepted; but it could be confirmed only by a re-investigation of the site itself. This was done in the late 1960s during the comprehensive and systematic excavation (and re-excavation) of Gezer. A huge ten-season archaeological project, it was sponsored by the Jerusalem branch of the Hebrew Union College, and aided by the Smithsonian Institution in Washington and the Harvard Semitic Museum. It was initiated in 1964 by the outstanding American scholar and Albright disciple George Ernest Wright, who was its first director, and by the remarkable Nelson Glueck, who served as adviser from the beginning until his death in 1971. Their Gezer dig is regarded as a model archaeological excavation. Wright himself, his pupils William G. Dever and H. Darrell Lance, who took over the direction from 1966 to 1971, and Joe Dick Seger, who was director for the final seasons in 1972 and 1973, employed the most modern methods and techniques, exercising careful judgement in the dating and interpretation of their finds. Also associated with the dig, and later, Director of the Gezer Publications Project, was a young rabbi, Sy Gitin, a graduate of Hebrew Union College, who, like Glueck in his time, went on to become professor of archaeology at the American School of Oriental Research in Jerusalem.

Yadin's theory was confirmed – Kathleen Kenyon wrote 'triumphantly confirmed' – during a season under Dever. He and his expert staff discovered the other half of the gate, found it almost identical with the gates at Hazor and Megiddo, conclusively established its date by the stratigraphy and pottery, and were able to add details of its plan and construction. The casemate wall connected to the gate was also investigated and also found to be Solomonic. Dever's excitement over his finds comes through in his report: 'The sealed pottery ... was characteristic red-burned ware of the late tenth century BC. Solomon did indeed re-build Gezer!'

So the Gezer anomaly was cleared up. But what of Megiddo, where the report of the dig showed the Solomonic gate linked to a solid wall? It simply did not seem feasible to Yadin. The gates at both Hazor and Gezer were now shown to have been part of a casemate wall system, and definitely established as belonging to the tenth century BC. Why would Solomon have called for a different type of wall at Megiddo when its function was the defence against the same type of battering ram with which potential enemies could threaten his other cities? Moreover, Yadin was convinced that only in the following century was the casemate

OPPOSITE Remains of the Solomonic gate at Gezer, found to be identical in design and dimension to the gate built by Solomon at Hazor.

198

rendered inadequate, and replaced by a solid wall. However, unlike his experience with the early Gezer excavation report, where he spotted an erroneous attribution to an actual find, a careful re-reading of the report of the Megiddo archaeologists showed nothing which suggested that they had indeed found a casemate wall but had failed to recognize it. Only a re-excavation could settle the matter.

Yadin was anxious to undertake this, but his own digs after Hazor, notably the investigation of the Bar Kochba caves and the large-scale dig at Masada, left him little time. He did, however, manage to spend a few days in 1960, 1967 and 1971 on what he called a post-mortem excavation at Megiddo, which brought impressive confirmation of his theory and set straight the material history of Megiddo.

Yadin saw the remains of the structures which the original Megiddo archaeologists had found and which they had ascribed to Solomon. The most notable ones were two sets of stables, the solid wall and the six-roomed gate. Yadin found, when he examined the site, that the stables and solid wall were indeed contemporary. This was evident from the stratigraphy. What he hoped to find was that they were not contemporary with the gate, but had been built some time after Solomon's reign, probably by Ahab in the ninth century BC.

He met with success on the opening day of his first post-mortem dig. While looking at a section of the solid wall before marking a trench for excavation, he noticed that the bottom part of its foundations were surfaced differently, and its stones were not the smaller type used in the rest of the solid wall but large well-dressed stones exactly like those in the Solomonic gate. Tracing the continuation of these lower foundations, Yadin's diggers found they ran beneath one of the two sets of stables. So the stables, like the solid wall – which we saw earlier were contemporary – were built later than the structures with the characteristic tenth-century stones.

The next find clinched the matter. Selecting another section of the solid wall, Yadin's men peeled off its foundations layer by layer, then dug through the fill of earth and field stones – and there, exposed, lay the remains of a casemate wall! Another dig near the city gate exposed further sections of a casemate wall. At a later dig, he discovered additional evidence showing that the casemate wall was an integral part of the known Solomonic fortification system, and that Megiddo in Solomon's time, like Hazor and Gezer, had indeed been encircled by a casemate wall attached to a six-roomed city gate.

Yadin applied the same kind of reasoning to develop a theory which challenged long-held judgements about the Megiddo water system. He tested and confirmed it during his trial digs. He was prompted to do so by something that had eluded him during his full-scale dig at Hazor. He had completed that four-season excavation in 1958 with one major problem unsolved: how the people of Hazor ensured their water supply in time of siege. It did not seem logical that so well-fortified and strategic a city would have lacked the means of access to its water source when under attack. Moreover, as the biblical record shows, for most of its existence, especially from the beginning of the ninth century BC until its destruction in 732 BC by Tiglath-pileser III, Israel and her neighbours were menaced by the Aramaeans and Assyrians. And the Israelites assuredly knew that however strong the defences of a walled city in the heat of the Middle East, it could withstand siege only as long as its water supply lasted. Yet Yadin had found no clue at Hazor to the presence of any installation which would guarantee that supply.

When he came to Megiddo in 1960 to investigate the Solomonic fortifications, he also made some scrapings near its water system. He thought it might shed light on his problem at Hazor. The earlier archaeologists had unearthed at Megiddo an ingenious water installation which is one of the most remarkable examples of the skilled engineering of ancient days. To ensure a regular supply of fresh water from a spring outside the city walls even during siege, the engineers had sunk a shaft into the ground inside the city to a depth of 120 feet, and from the bottom of the shaft had cut a 215-foot tunnel to the spring. They had then blocked the outside entrance to the spring by a wall, and camouflaged it with a covering of earth. Thus, when Megiddo was besieged, the inhabitants had access to the spring down the steps inside the shaft and along the tunnel, unseen and uninhibited by the enemy. The enemy for their part were denied access to the water source. The earlier scholars had ascribed this water system to the twelfth century BC.

In his probe in 1960, Yadin found enough to suggest that it was installed at a much later date, and in 1966 he returned for a more thorough examination. He then discovered from the pottery, the masonry, the architectural style, and above all from the stratigraphy, that the Megiddo water system was part of a rebuilding programme, including the stables and solid city wall, that was carried out on the ruins of the Solomonic city, and belonged certainly to the ninth century BC and probably to the reign of Ahab.

Yadin was now convinced that a similar water system must have been built at the same time at Hazor – for the same reason – and in 1968 he returned for a fifth season of excavation, after an interval of ten years, to try and find it. He proceeded on the assumption that there would be a shaft and tunnel, as at Megiddo, and that these would have been quarried and constructed as near as possible to the source of water. But where was that water source? As Yadin stood on the tel and surveyed the area at the edge of the lower city compound, he noticed a ravine which he remembered had been covered by green shrubs throughout the year, clearly nourished by an abundant and continuous supply of water. The source indeed proved to be several natural springs. The local shepherds in fact watered their flocks there in the hot summer months. He therefore decided to start excavating in that area, and after long and arduous labours he reaped a spectacular reward. He found a magnificently engineered system consisting of a well-built entrance to a broad square shaft which tapers down through the rock to join a tunnel which is not horizontal, as at Megiddo, but has a gentle slope and ends in a pool. The archaeological evidence puts its date definitely as the first half of the ninth century BC, contemporary with the system at Megiddo. The depth of the entrance and shaft is $97\frac{1}{2}$ feet, and the gradient of the sloped tunnel, just over 80 feet long, adds another $32\frac{1}{2}$ feet to the depth. Running down each of the four sides of the shaft is a flight of handsome rock-cut steps, broad enough for comfortable simultaneous ascent and descent. A fifth flight at the bottom merges with the staircase of the tunnel. Here, the steps were of soft stone, and the ancient engineers had given them a thick coating of plaster for protection. The last eight steps, however, which would be under water when the level rose, were fashioned from more resistant basalt slabs.

After his comprehensive investigation of Hazor and brief post-mortems at Megiddo, which added much to our knowledge of the material culture of the land of the Bible in biblical times, Yadin wrote: 'For the kings of Israel and Judah, the ability to hold out in face of a prolonged siege was the only hope for survival.' It was imperative, therefore, to develop engineering skills, which they did, and they created 'fortifications and underground water systems unsurpassed by any other nation' at the time.

Yadin's Hazor excavation, though the first carried out on so large a scale, did not inaugurate archaeological activity in the new State. Several modest digs were started soon after the 1948–9 fighting ended, and each year saw more and more archaeological teams engaged in digging up the Bible at numerous sites throughout the country. Archaeology rapidly became not only a prized field of study for university students but also the subject of most popular interest, third only to politics and military affairs. Israel is probably the only country in the world where almost any archaeological discovery, not necessarily of prime importance, makes front-page news. One practical result is that the announcement of a forth-coming excavation draws applications from thousands of amateur volunteers for the non-professional jobs – which make the digs less expensive and enable more to be carried out. The idea of inviting volunteers was conceived by Yadin for one of his later excavations, and there was a large response, not only from Israel but from many parts of the world. This practice has become a standard feature of all Israeli digs.

No period has been as fruitful for biblical archaeology as the three decades of Israel's renewed independence. Excavations have been undertaken throughout the country, adding much to our knowledge of the Bible and of the land and the lives of the people in biblical times. Among the biblical sites that have yielded their secrets are Dan and Beersheba, Arad and Ashdod, En-gedi and Jaffa, Shikmona and Tel-Aviv and Afek. Sites of importance in the post-biblical history of the country have also been excavated, not-ably Tiberias and Acre, Caesarea, Avdat, Shivta, Baram, and the area round the Sea of Galilee.

The two most remarkable ones have been the dig at Masada, the spectacular hill-top site with a dramatic history, and the ten-season excavation at the foot of the Temple Mount in Jerusalem – the dream of archaeologists for more than a hundred years. It took a war to make it possible.

8 Jerusalem and Masada

The Arab-Israel Six Day War of 1967 ended with a divided Jerusalem re-united, and brought once again within the control of a people bound to it by a unique, unbroken, three-thousand-year-old bond. The opportunity was now offered for extensive archaeological excavation to recover the material remains of the city's turbulent past.

The sites of deepest interest to the archaeologists were those inside the walled Old City of today, notably the Temple Mount and its environs. It was there that the most dramatic events in Jerusalem's history were enacted, from the time of Solomon in the late tenth century BC onwards. Yet that was the very area where hitherto, as we have seen, it had not been possible to undertake a comprehensive excavation, only surface exploration and archaeological probes by tunnelling. This, indeed, was the reason why most of the periodic digs since the days of Wilson and Warren had been at the more accessible sites outside the city walls. From those investigations, particularly from the important one by Kathleen Kenyon, the modern scholars already knew that they would find nothing inside the Old City associated with the man who had started Jerusalem on its phenomenal course of history – King David. What the archaeologists had found was that the Jerusalem of David's day lay outside the present walls.

David captured the Jebusite enclave, which had not been taken during the Joshua conquest, in the opening years of the tenth century BC. He established it as 'the strong hold of Zion' (2 Sam. 5:7) and the capital of the united Israelite kingdom. It was to become great in stature and to generate a spiritual and national influence that was everlasting. Yet it was small in size, confined to a narrow spur on what archaeologists consider to have been the biblical hill of Ophel covering the southern part of a ridge. (It was the higher, northern part of this very ridge that was to be the site of

OPPOSITE A Herodian pool which had been re-used in the Byzantine period, discovered at excavations in the Jewish quarter of the Old City of Jerusalem undertaken by Nahman Avigad after the 1967 Six Day War.

Solomon's Temple and to be known thereafter as the Temple Mount.) David's city was well sited, close to a source of water, the Gihon spring, and protected by valleys on three sides, Kidron on the east, Hinnom on the south, and the valley that would much later be known as the Tyropoeon on the west. Only its northern boundary was unprotected by a steep incline, and David fortified it by a rampart which ran a few hundred yards to the south of the subsequent Temple Mount and today's southern city wall. The biblical record shows that David's building activities were modest. 'And David built round about from Millo and inwards.' (2 Sam. 5:9.) It is now generally held that Millo was not a place-name but the Hebrew word for 'filling', and referred to the earthworks supporting his strengthened defences and the few structures he erected, such as his 'house of cedar' and stone (2 Sam. 7:2), barracks for his garrison, and accommodation for his family, the priests and royal officials. He was far too busy fighting, neutralizing his enemy neighbours, and welding the Israelite tribes into a united nation to have engaged in any large construction projects.

The builder in the family was his son Solomon, and if the archaeologists were to find the earliest structural remains inside Jerusalem's present walls, these would belong to his reign. For he extended his father's city northwards across the Ophel and carried out a huge building programme on the high ground that lies within today's Old City. This was 'the threshing floor of Araunah the Jebusite' (2 Sam. 24:18), which David had bought and 'built there an altar unto the Lord', hoping to erect a permanent shrine. But this privilege was given not to him but to his son, and it was here, on the highest point of the ridge, that Solomon built the Temple. In it rested the Ark of the Covenant that had accompanied the Children of Israel on their trek through the wilderness following the climactic Law-giving ceremony on Mount Sinai. Henceforth, Jerusalem, the city of the Temple, would be vested with a unique mystic power as the geographical centre of the Jewish religion and nationhood.

Below the Temple, in a series of descending terraces, Solomon built his palace and the subsidiary royal buildings, each set in its own court, and the entire complex was encircled by a wall of stone. This cluster of handsome buildings, the spectacular architectural feature of Jerusalem, stood for almost four hundred years. All was destroyed when the Babylonian king Nebuchadnezzar ravaged the city in 587 BC and exiled the Jews to Babylon. The Temple was rebuilt fifty years later – and known from then on as the Second Temple – when the Persian king Cyrus the Great vanquished the Babylonian empire and helped the Jews to return to Jerusalem. In the following century, Nehemiah, a descendant of the Jewish exiles, arrived in Jerusalem as governor of Judea and rebuilt the city walls. The Persian period had been followed by the Hellenistic, when the country was ruled first by the Ptolemies and then the Seleucids. It was during the oppressive reign of Seleucid emperor Antiochus IV Epiphanes in the second century BC that the Maccabees led their successful revolt, regained and purified the desecrated Temple, and restored Jewish independence, the leadership continuing with the Hasmoneans, descendants of the original Maccabee family. The Books of the Maccabees record the public buildings they erected.

Then came the Roman period, and it was under Herod, whom the Romans had installed in 37 BC as the puppet 'king of the Jews', that the next ambitious building project was initiated. It is known that Herod, largely to gain favour with his hostile people, applied his hand to glorify Jewry's central shrine. He reconstructed the Temple, retaining the original ground-plan and interior arrangements as laid down in the Old Testament. But he doubled its height, amplified its porch, and added terraces with huge colonnaded courts. He set all these buildings on a great rectangular platform supported by substructures and formidable buttress walls rising from the ravines that bounded the Temple Mount. With an eye to internal security, Herod erected a massive castle at the north-west corner of the Temple compound which he called the Antonia fortress (in honour of Mark Antony). It was manned by a Roman infantry unit who, with a commanding view of the Temple worshippers, could watch for signs of popular discontent. The third major structure built by Herod was his magnificent palace, on the other side of the city from the Temple, in the west, the site of the present Citadel adjoining today's Jaffa Gate.

Was there the hope that the archaeologists might find the remains of any of the buildings constructed during this thousand-year BC period? If Jerusalem had been an isolated and abandoned tel, unoccupied for the last 2,000 years like so many of the biblical sites in the country, it would have been possible to undertake a thorough excavation, peeling off layer after layer, and trace its development from Solomon to Herod. But Jerusalem has a record of uninterrupted settlement – and there was more to come, more destruction and construction.

The opening years of the first century AD were times of tension and conflict, and it was in this atmosphere of rebellion against the rule of imperialist Rome that Jerusalem was the scene of the last ministry of Jesus. It would be three centuries before great monuments would arise in Jerusalem to mark the events of his life and crucifixion, and the foundations of many of them would be discovered by the archaeologists of our own day.

le roy enthiocus

Jherusalem

The pillage of Jerusalem by Seleucid emperor Antiochus IV Epiphanes in 167 BC, an illustration from a fifteenth-century illuminated manuscript of *The Jewish Wars* by Josephus. It was this action which sparked the Jewish revolt under the banner of the Maccabees, who regained and purified the Temple three years later.

The Jewish Temple in Jerusalem as reconstructed by Herod in the first century BC. A scale-model by Professor Michael Avi-Yonah in the garden of the Holyland Hotel, Jerusalem.

Less than four decades after the crucifixion, the Jews of Israel rose against the Romans, but were crushed after a five-year war of resistance. In AD 70, Rome's Titus captured Jerusalem, destroyed the Temple, and exiled most of the Jewish survivors. The archaeologists had little hope of finding the material evidence of that destruction – they would be surprised when they came to dig – for they knew what had happened sixty-five years later, in AD 135, when the heavy hand of the Roman emperor Hadrian had descended upon the land, and crushed the desperate Jewish insurrection led by Bar Kochba. Hadrian razed Jerusalem, built it anew, and renamed it Aelia Capitolina.

The emperor Constantine in the fourth century AD restored the name Jerusalem and erected great Christian edifices. The most important was the Church of the Holy Sepulchre, which still stands on its original site, though most of its surviving structure is from Crusader times. Constantine also built the Church of Eleona on the Mount of Olives, and the remains of its foundations have been found. Remnants of other fourth-century churches discovered by archaeologists are the Church of the Apostles on Mount Zion, the traditional site of the Last Supper; the Church of the Ascension on the Mount of Olives; and a church built by the emperor Theodosius I in Gethsemane, where Jesus and his

210

disciples spent the night before his arrest. Incidentally, no Christian monument, whether church, convent or monastery, was erected close to the Temple Mount.

It was the Moslems who took over the site of the Jewish shrine as their own. Omar entered Jerusalem in AD 638, swept away Christian rule, and inaugurated the first Moslem period in the Holy Land. At the end of the seventh and beginning of the eighth century AD, the Moslems erected the Dome of the Rock and the Mosque of El-Aksa on the compound where Solomon had built the Temple some 1,700 years earlier; and the rectangular Herodian platform on which the two mosques stood – and stand to this day – was named the Haram esh-Sharif, Arabic for 'Noble Sanctuary'. With this Moslem construction, the secrets of the past that lie buried beneath it remain inviolable.

The Crusaders captured the city in 1099. They were formidable builders, and they erected a host of churches and hospices, monasteries and convents. The best preserved is the Church of St Anne, and much of their reconstruction of the Church of the Holy Sepulchre is also visible today. The remains of other Crusader structures have been found at small-scale archaeological excavations, notably those of a monastery on the Mount of Olives and another near Mary's Tomb in the Kidron valley; buildings on the site of the Citadel; a chapel near St Stephen's Church and one near Gethsemane; and the Church of St Thomas.

Saladin recaptured Jerusalem in 1187, and thereafter, except for a fifteen-year reversion to Crusader rule early in the thirteenth century, Jerusalem remained under Moselm control for the next seven centuries, first under the Mamelukes and then the Ottoman Turks. It was the Ottoman emperor Suleiman the Magnificent who left his mark on Jerusalem by restoring its ramparts. The walls surrounding the Old City which we see today are the very walls he rebuilt, completing the work in about 1540.

Turkish rule came to an end in 1917 when the Allied Forces under General Allenby entered Jerusalem, and until 1948 Palestine was governed by a British Administration. When that terminated on 14 May 1948 and the State of Israel was established, Transjordan (later called the Hashemite Kingdom of Jordan) was one of the five neighbouring Arab countries whose armies invaded the new-born State. This put Jerusalem on the firing line, and when the war ended with the signing of an armistice in April 1949, Jerusalem was a divided city. The eastern half, which included the Old City, was under Jordan, the western part under Israel. During the fighting, the crowded Jewish Quarter in the Old City, close to the Temple Mount and isolated from the main Jewish community in west Jerusalem, fell to the Jordanian Arab Legion in bitter house to house combat, and many dwellings, synagogues and religious academies were destroyed. For the next nineteen years, Israelis were barred from their holy places.

This all changed on the morning of Wednesday, 7 June 1967, the third day of the Six Day War, when east Jerusalem fell to the Israelis after a grim battle. Within days, Jerusalem became a re-united living city, with anti-sniping walls torn down and barriers and barbed wire removed. Arabs visited the western part and Jews the eastern part, meeting each other in homes, in the streets, in shops and markets, and the holy places of all three faiths were now accessible to all their members.

Though the now re-unified city was under a regime passionately interested in its history, the archaeologists were under no illusion that they would be completely free of the objective difficulties encountered by their predecessors, who had found the most promising sites occupied by buildings. But those scholars had also been sorely troubled by a suspicious local population and the hostility of the Ottoman government who always delayed and often refused permits to dig. There would be none of that now. Moreover, the rehabilitation of areas devastated by war offered possibilities for the archaeologist that had not existed before. This was the case in the destroyed Jewish Quarter of the Old City. There were also areas which had been cleared near the Western Wall and alongside the southern wall of the Temple compound.

However, because of the repeated massive destruction of Jerusalem in the earlier centuries, the archaeologists could not be hopeful of finding much about the very periods which were of special interest, those of the Israelite kings and prophets. They expected that their major finds would be those belonging to the time of Herod. This was understandable, not only because he had built so extensively – from the Temple Mount in the east of the city to his palace in the west – but because the remains of some of his structures still stood. The massive stones in the lower courses of the Western Wall, for example, are part of the wall Herod built to buttress the great platform of the Temple compound. Remains of his Antonia fortress may still be seen. (The site is now occupied by the Umariya boys' school, about 300 yards from the Lions' Gate.) And adjoining the Citadel is part of a tower (the 'tower of Phasael'), one of three constructed by Herod at the northern end of his palace. It was likely, therefore, that excavation would bring to light further Herodian remains and artefacts.

The first and most dramatic of the excavations undertaken after the 1967 war was the one started by Professor Binyamin Mazar of the Hebrew University in the spring of 1968. The site he chose was the area round the south-western corner of the Temple Mount. His expectation of Herodian finds proved justified three months later, when he discovered a wide street from the first century BC which had clearly been part of Herod's Temple reconstruction project. It had led up to the main entrance to the Temple compound from what was in those days the Tyropoeon valley which skirted the Mount and which had long since been filled in by the debris of centuries. The street was beautifully paved with well-shaped slabs of Jerusalem stone. Adjoining it was a broad plaza laid down at the same time. What excited the archaeologists was not so much the discovery of a Herodian street as the huge chunks of Herodian building stones which they found strewn about its surface. This immediately evoked the scene of slaughter and havoc in AD 70 as the Jewish defenders fought their bitter losing battle against the Roman troops of Titus who had fired and breached the walls of the Temple compound. The chunks of stone had been part of those walls and had fallen onto the street below, the force of the impact cracking some of the paving slabs.

To reach this Herodian stratum, Mazar had dug down forty feet through the levels of later settlement, and he found valuable pottery and stone utensils, as well as an abundance of Jewish coins ranging from the time of the Hasmoneans – these coins bore dates between 135 to 37 BC – right down to the final months before the destruction of the Temple and of Jerusalem. These later coins belonged to the special group that were struck by the Jewish authorities during the five years of their revolt against the Romans, from AD 66 to 70, as a symbolic demonstration of Jewish sovereignty over their land. They took the form of silver shekels, half- and quarter-shekels, so that adult males could pay the annual offering, in accordance with the biblical injunction (in Exodus 30:13). One side of the coin bore the Hebrew inscription 'Jerusalem the Holy', 'Freedom of Zion', or 'For the Redemption of Zion'. The other side carried the words 'Shekel of Israel' and was stamped with the year of the revolt in which it was minted. Thus, 'Year One' belonged to the first year of the revolt, namely, AD 66–67. The last coins found on this site bore the date 'Year Four', corresponding to AD 69–70.

Mazar's next structural find in this Herodian level was a staircase of monumental dimensions which led up to large gates in the southern wall of the Temple compound, and for the first time one could picture the authentic Temple scene during the Jewish Festivals. The broad stretch of steps ran along the foot of the southern wall for some 350 feet, so that thousands upon thousands could follow each other slowly and comfortably up the stairs, through the wide gates, and onto the outer court of the Temple. Adjoining the

Veteran Israeli archaeologist Binyamin Mazar at his important excavations near the south-west corner of the Temple Mount in Jerusalem, the first large-scale dig to be carried out inside the city walls.

213

The broad Herodian staircase unearthed by Mazar which led up to the main entrance to the Temple compound through gates in the southern wall.

staircase was a massive plaza, which Mazar unearthed. It was almost as broad as the Temple compound itself, and there the crowds of pilgrims from all over the country would congregate before entering the Temple precincts, after purifying themselves in the ritual baths of a building in the centre of the plaza, which was found at the same time.

Curiously enough, it was in this very area of the stairway and plaza below the southern wall that Mazar discovered other Herodian remains beneath the ruins of handsome Moslem buildings erected seven centuries later, which had been lost to Moslem memory for hundreds of years. Herodian pillars from the Temple courts above had been used for the foundation of a large palace complex built during the Umayyad dynasty (AD 660–750). The palace and its ancillary buildings had been constructed round central courts, and were served by an elaborate water and sewage system. But these structures did not last long. They were destroyed by earthquake in AD 747 and never restored, and this is probably why their very existence was unknown even to Moslem historians.

The ruins in their turn became a quarry for later builders, and in the eleventh century the site was used as a cemetery.

Of other Herodian finds, the broad platform which had been supported by Robinson's Arch near the Western Wall has already been referred to in an earlier chapter. Mazar made an illuminating discovery in the same area, but belonging to a later period, when he dug out further courses of the Herodian wall below the projecting springer to Robinson's Arch. This was a fourth-century AD inscription in Hebrew, etched in the stone, of a verse from the prophet Isaiah. It is considered that this was made during the three-year reign (AD 361–3) of the Roman emperor Julian. He is usually referred to as Julian the Apostate, for he disavowed the Christian faith of his uncle, Constantine the Great, and embarked on a policy of universal toleration. For those three years, Jerusalem had again been opened to Jewish settlers and pilgrims. Before that, since the AD 135 edict of Hadrian, Jews had been banned from entering Jerusalem, on pain of death. The Jews seem to have taken full advantage of Julian's benevolence, and their joy shines forth in the verse they had chosen to inscribe on the stone which the archaeologists discovered. They had written the opening words of Isaiah's verse 14, chapter 66, which follows the phrase 'ye shall be comforted in Jerusalem'. They read: 'And when ye see this, your heart shall rejoice, and your bones shall flourish like an herb.'

Mazar found no remains of early structures, but he unearthed two well-preserved rock-cut tombs belonging to the eighth–seventh century BC about a hundred yards south-west of the Western Wall. Other seventh-century BC finds among the potsherds of this era of the Judean monarchy were jar-handles bearing the inscription 'la-melech', Hebrew for 'the king's'. Most of the other inscriptions found on this dig belonged to the latter part of the Second Temple period. One was the word 'Korban', Hebrew for 'sacrifice', which was incised on a decorated stone utensil used in the Temple service and referred to in the Mishnah. Another, also belonging to the first century BC, was the more interesting 'Le'beth Hatekiah' – 'To the place of the blowing [of the ram's horn, the ritual shofar]'. This was a most revealing find, for it matches the narrative by the historian Josephus of the destruction of Jerusalem in AD 70. The stone had fallen from a balcony at the Temple compound wall during the fighting, and had been part of a structure which Josephus mentioned in describing the Jewish fortifications on Temple Mount. He wrote that one of the Jewish defence towers was built onto the roof of the priests' quarters, and on Friday evenings a priest would step to the balcony – marked 'the place of the blowing' – to proclaim by a blast of the ram's horn the advent of the Sabbath, when all work should cease.

Digs at several other archaeological sites in and around the Old City were undertaken after 1967, some with surprising results. Ruth Amiran and Avraham Eitan excavated in the Citadel, the site of Herod's palace, on the other side of the city from the Temple Mount. Their unexpected discovery was the remains of buildings belonging to the seventh century BC. It came as a surprise to scholars that there should have been any construction at all so far to the west during the reigns of the Judean kings. We have seen that Jerusalem had developed northwards from David's city in Solomon's days, the tenth century BC, and it was known that some time later it had spread westwards; but no-one knew exactly when, or how far in each period. It had now been established by the accumulated wisdom from the post-1967 excavations of Mazar, Avigad, Amiran and Eitan, and of Magen Broshi, who has been digging on Mount Zion and nearby sites, that Israelite settlement on the hill to the immediate west of the Temple Mount began probably as early as the eighth century BC, when it was still unwalled, and certainly by the seventh century, when it was bounded by a rampart. This western hill, called by Josephus the Upper City, and the site today of the Jewish and Armenian Quarters of the Old City, was part of a ridge that ran parallel to the eastern ridge occupied by the Temple Mount in the north and David's city in the south.

The latest excavations have also shown that the valley between these two ridges lay outside the city until the eighth century BC. Desolation marked the years that followed Nebuchadnezzar's destruction in 587 BC, and with the return of the exiles from Babylon to a Jerusalem in ruins, life was confined once again to the eastern hill. Renewed expansion westward was gradual until the Hasmonean period, when the western hill was again enclosed within Jerusalem's walls. The archaeologists found ample evidence of this in the remains of formidable buildings, a massive tower abutting a Hasmonean wall as far west as the Citadel, and the wall itself continuing outside the Citadel beyond the present walls.

A current Jerusalem dig, started in 1978 and expected to last five seasons, is in the area of David's city, due south of the Temple Mount, in a section of the spur above Siloam which was not included in Kathleen Kenyon's comprehensive excavation. The director, Yigal Shiloh of the Hebrew University, like every archaeologist, no doubt hopes to discover what earlier scholars may have missed, particularly structural ruins and possibly inscriptions from the reign of David. His first season has already yielded fruitful finds from the period of the kings of Judah. He has unearthed a section of the city wall belonging to the eighth or seventh century BC; a stratum of the sixth century BC which covers the beginnings of

216

Remains of a large Herodian house (foreground) excavated by Avigad in the Jewish Quarter of the Old City, located on the hill to the immediate west of the Temple Mount.

resettlement by the returning Jewish exiles from Babylon; ruins of fortifications from the First and Second Temple periods; and part of a water tunnel. His most important discovery was a fragment of ancient Hebrew writing, chiselled in stone on the wall of an eighth-century public building. The examination of this inscription was not yet completed when this book went to press; but it is already known that the script is the same as that of the Hebrew Siloam Inscription of the same century, on the rock wall of the conduit built by king Hezekiah.

A Jerusalem excavation of high importance which followed soon after the start of Mazar's dig at the foot of Temple Mount was undertaken in the destroyed Jewish Quarter of the Old City. It was directed by Nahman Avigad, like Mazar and Yadin a professor of archaeology at the Hebrew University. He began and continued his operations during the rehabilitation of the Quarter. He was more fortunate than Mazar in finding remains belonging to the period before the destruction of the First Temple, unearthing the foundations of a city wall, the plastered floor of a house, part of an olive press, and much pottery, all belonging to the seventh century BC. Here was evidence that settlement under the Judean monarchy had spread several hundred yards west of the Temple Mount at so early a period. The house may well have been one of the first to be built in the area; and the wall presumably marked the western boundary of the city at that time. It is possible that this was the very 'broad wall' mentioned in the Book of Nehemiah as having been repaired by the fifth-century BC returnees from Babylon, among them 'Uzziel the son of Harhaiah, of the goldsmiths' and 'Hananiah the son of one of the apothecaries'. Under the direction of Nehemiah, 'they fortified Jerusalem unto the broad wall'. (3:8.)

While the Temple had been rebuilt in the previous century, the city walls were still in ruin from the time of the Nebuchadnezzar destruction when Nehemiah arrived. What prompts the suggestion that the wall unearthed by Avigad was the one they repaired was that it was indeed broad – more than twenty-one feet thick. And it was built on bed-rock.

By the first and second centuries BC, particularly during the Hasmonean period, this quarter was well developed and built up. Avigad found the remains of spacious structures, water cisterns and drainage channels. Pottery, artefacts and many coins attested to the date. There were also many Herodian finds in the late first-century BC stratum. Perhaps the most outstanding was not a structure but the representation of a seven-branched candelabrum, the celebrated menorah, incised on plaster. The menorah, today the symbol of the State of Israel, stood in the Temple at that time, and Avigad's discovery might well have been a true portrayal of the Temple original. Since it differs in certain details from the one depicted on the Arch of Titus in Rome, it raises the kind of problem which scholars enjoy: which of the two is an authentic copy of the Temple menorah?

Of special Christian interest was Avigad's discovery, at his excavations in the Jewish Quarter, of the remains of a splendid church known to have been built by the emperor Justinian I in the sixth century AD. It was called the New Church ('Nea' in Greek). Justinian was the last of several Byzantine rulers to follow the practice inaugurated by Constantine in the fourth century AD of building Christian monuments. Emperor Theodosius I had erected a church in Gethsemane in AD 385. And the wife of Theodosius II built the Church of St Stephen in the following century. (Its remains were found at excavations just north of the Damascus Gate.) She was the remarkable empress Eudocia. Separated from her husband, she left the court of Byzantium and came to live in Jerusalem, where she also concerned herself with the restoration of the city. It was she who repaired and extended the city wall so that it enclosed Mount Zion (which today abuts, but is outside, the south-west corner of the Old City). It was she, too, who was responsible for securing the abolition of the ban on Jews to enter Jerusalem freely. The total ban had been lifted slightly in the previous century when the Jews were allowed in once a year, on their fast day, the Ninth of Ab, to visit the site of the Temple and mourn over its ruins. Thanks to the intercession of Eudocia, they could, in the fifth century AD, settle in the city.

The builder of Christian monuments in the next century was Justinian, and historians had long known the details of his structures, for they had been carefully described in a six-volume treatise by the Byzantine historian Procopius called *The Buildings of Justinian*, written, no doubt, at the command of the emperor. It was known, therefore, that the New Church was consecrated in November of the year AD 543. It had long been lost to sight when, in 1914, a hospital in the Jewish Quarter was being enlarged, and the builders came across some ancient masonry. This was inspected by Louis Hugues Vincent, a French Dominican monk and archaeologist, one of the heads of the École Biblique et Archaéologique Française in Jerusalem, and it seemed to him, as he wrote, that the remains were those of the bases of arches which had supported Justinian's New Church, as described by Procopius. Digging not far from this site but outside the city wall in 1963, Kathleen Kenyon uncovered structural remains which were tentatively ascribed to the hospital which had been attached to this church. Avigad's excavation unearthed the massive foundations of the church itself.

Of all the discoveries at the post-1967 Jerusalem digs, the most poignant was that made by Avigad in the Jewish Quarter when he brought to light further evidence of the AD 70 destruction by Rome. He unearthed a ruined house, and found it in the very state in which it had been left when destroyed by fire. The date was established by the character of the havoc, and the pottery, artefacts and Jewish coins from the period of the revolt that lay amidst the ashes. The last of these coins was marked 'Year Four' (AD 69–70). The four rooms and kitchen on the ground floor still stood, though badly charred, buried beneath the heap of collapsed walls, ceilings, and burnt wooden beams from the upper storeys. For some reason this pile of destruction had remained uncleared and undisturbed for 1,900 years, so that the scholars found among the debris in the kitchen the usual cooking pots, jars and bowls of the period, as well as stoves and grinding stones. What was by no means usual, and, particularly moving for Israeli archaeologists who had witnessed the rebirth of Israel in our own time, were human bones stuck to the kitchen wall – the bones of the forearm of a young woman. One could imagine her going about her domestic duties as the battle raged nearby. She had paused, perhaps, her arm against the wall, as the sounds of the enemy came suddenly close, and with them the flames. She was caught in the fiery trap and entombed when the house collapsed.

The fall of Jerusalem, made vivid by the discoveries of Mazar and Avigad, marked the formal end of the five-year war of the Jews against Rome. But it was not the end of the fighting. That came

Kathleen Kenyon, seen here at her dig on a spur south-east of the Jerusalem city wall, close to the site of the city in David's time.

219

three years later with the fall of the last outpost of Jewish resistance, and a startling and dramatic end it was, too. The evidence of that final episode was dug up by Yadin in a fascinating excavation at the bleak eastern edge of Judea.

Slaughter, enslavement or exile was the fate of the Jews when the Romans eventually broke through their defences and charged into Jerusalem. But a small group of Jewish fighters led by Eleazar ben Yair managed to escape. Determined to continue the battle for freedom, these zealots made their way with the surviving members of their families across the rugged Judean wilderness to Masada, an immense flat-topped rock that rises 1,300 feet above the western shore of the Dead Sea. The main access trail wound its way up the sharp eastern slope, and was described by the contemporary historian Josephus as 'the snake path', because it had – and still has – 'the narrowness and constant windings' of a snake. 'Walking along it is like balancing on a tightrope. The least slip means death; for on either side yawns an abyss so terrifying that it could make the boldest tremble.' One hundred years earlier, when Herod had good reason to fear that he might need a refuge, he had fortified the summit with a casemate wall round the perimeter and a series of towers. It was from this stronghold base that Eleazer and his men now set forth on raiding forays against Rome's occupation troops, and harried them for the next two years. Routine enemy attempts to dislodge them from their fortress height were beaten off.

In AD 72, Rome resolved to wipe them out. Realizing by now that this was no simple task, General Silva, the Roman commander, headed a large expedition and marched on Masada, prepared for a long campaign if need be. His force consisted of the redoubtable Tenth Legion and auxiliary troops, and thousands of prisoners of war to carry water, provisions and equipment across the Judean desert. The Jews at the top of the rock were well prepared for defence. They could make use of Herod's fortifications and storehouses, and the ingenious water-system he had devised to keep the cisterns full.

General Silva tried an immediate assault when he arrived, on the outside chance of a swift victory. But when his men attempted to scale the heights they were greeted by a hail of rocks from above, and were forced to retire. He thereupon reverted to his original plan and embarked on elaborate siege arrangements until he was in a position to reach and crush the resisters. He spent several months erecting a three-mile wall encircling the base of Masada, punctuated at intervals by camps, to prevent flight or raiding sorties by the Jewish zealots. At the same time he set his men to the construction of a ramp upon a spur which meets the western slope of the fortress closer to the summit, so that he could move up battering-rams to breach the defenders' casemate wall. To keep them away from that wall while the ramp was being built and to give cover to his men when they launched the critical assault, he threw up a siege tower from which arrows and catapult stones could be directed at the summit.

Silva went into action as soon as the ramp was completed. The battering-rams were brought up and the casemate wall was breached. The defenders countered by improvising an inner wall above the ramp consisting of earth-filled wooden breastworks, so that the blows of the rams beat the earth into a compact barrier. Silva responded by setting fire to the new wooden wall. What happened next is related by Josephus – it is from his report alone that the Masada episode has come down to us: the wood 'immediately took fire, and the flames raged with the utmost violence.' Suddenly, however, the wind veered in the opposite direction, blowing the flames back on the troops and their siege engines, and 'plunging the Romans into despair'. Spirits rose anew among the Jewish zealots. They had been fighting continuously since leaving Jerusalem, a mere handful holding the Roman army at bay, gaining confidence with each successful engagement. They were hopeful that they might hold out. Providence was with them. Then Silva had appeared with his powerful force, and they watched with anxiety the culmination of his designs to get his troops onto the summit. However, they maintained their alertness, doing all possible, however dim the prospect, to keep them out. Thus, they plugged the breach in their defences, while recognizing that it could only be temporary. Then came the fire. The end was surely near, but it had been followed by the miraculous change of wind. Providence had not abandoned them after all. Rescue had come at the last moment.

Joy died quickly – as quickly as the wind which changed again and resumed its former direction, thrusting the flames against the wall and turning it into a blazing mass. It was now the Romans who exulted, and, as Josephus relates, they 'returned to their camp full of spirits, and with a fixed determination to attack the enemy by break of day on the following morning; and, in the meantime, to place strong guards, that their opponents might not escape in the night.' But Eleazar ben Yair had no thought of escaping – at least not in the way the Romans might have expected. Instead, as darkness fell, he assembled his band of patriots, 960 in all, men, women and children, illumined only by the dying embers; and what followed was an unforgettable drama on the summit of Masada.

They had fought the brave fight for Jewish freedom. It was now

OVERLEAF The rock of Masada, overlooking the Dead Sea.

221

about to end in Roman triumph. The Lord had indeed abandoned them, and the Lord's will was not to be questioned. Nothing now stood between them and Silva's legions, who would come storming through the gap at dawn. Every zealot fighter would willingly face them and give his life in battle. But what of those who survived? What of their women and children? At best, slain; at worst, paraded in shame and enslaved. Was there nothing they could do in the few hours left to them to pluck victory from the Romans? That was the problem with which Eleazar had grappled as the flames consumed his defensive wall. He had now found a grim solution. They had lived by the conviction that 'a death of glory was preferable to a life of infamy'. They could now demonstrate the force of that conviction by the manner in which they died. He would propose to his people that 'the most magnanimous resolution would be to disdain the idea of surviving the loss of liberty'.

This was the spirit in which Eleazar now rose to address the comrades gathered around him on this anguished night. His words were subsequently related by two women who failed to go through with his plan:

Will anyone who is not destitute of the common spirit of man wish to view the rising of another sun? Nay, would he wish it even if he might live in safety? Can anyone have so little regard to his country, so mean, so contracted a soul as not to regret that he has survived to behold this fatal day? Happy would it have been for us if we had all been sacrificed, rather than to have witnessed this sacrilegious destruction and to have beheld Jerusalem itself become a pile of ruins.

While hope remained, however, our courage did not fail, and we despaired not of a happy change in our affairs. But as we have now no further reason to expect so auspicious a circumstance . . . it becomes us to have some regard to our wives, our children and ourselves; and in the plan of our proceeding we should be expeditious, while the means are yet in our power.

All men are equally destined to death; and the same fate attends the coward as the brave. . . . While freedom is our own, and we are in possession of our swords, let us make a determined use of them to preserve our liberties. Let us die free men. . . . Eternal renown shall be ours by snatching the prize from the hands of our enemies, and leaving them nothing to triumph over but the bodies of those who dared to be their own executioners.

Thus spake Eleazer. So long as there was hope, they had fought. Now, with disaster inevitable, they would die by their own hand. They had little time. They moved without delay to the performance of their plan.

While they embraced their wives and children for the last time, they

wept over and stabbed them in the same moment, taking comfort however that this work was not to be performed by their enemies. . . . There
was not one man who was wanting in the necessary courage. . . . Those
who had been the principal agents in this slaughter, smitten as they were
with grief . . . collected all their effects together and set them on fire. They
then cast lots for the selection of ten men out of their number to destroy
the rest. These being chosen, the devoted victims embraced the bodies of
their deceased families and then, ranging themselves near them, resigned
themselves to the hands of the executioners. When these ten men had
discharged their disagreeable task, they again cast lots as to which of the
ten should kill the other nine. . . . The nine devoted victims died with the
same resolution as their brethren had done. And the survivng man,
having surveyed the bodies and found that they were all dead, threw
himself on his sword, among his companions. . . .

At dawn the next day, the Romans prepared themselves for the
final assault. They were astonished at the lack of opposition – and
then they saw the bodies and heard the story from the two women
who had hidden themselves. Josephus writes:

Far, however, from exulting in the triumph of joy that might have been
expected from the enemies, they united to admire the steady virtue and
dignity of mind with which the Jews had been inspired, and wondered at
the generous contempt of death by which such numbers had been bound
in one solemn compact.

Restoration work on the
murals in the palace-villa of
Herod at Masada.

It was this dramatic event, and the prodigious archaeological prospects offered by the site where it occurred, that prompted Yadin to
undertake a comprehensive excavation of Masada in 1963–5. And,
indeed, he brought to light the grim remains of Eleazar's patriot
band in the opening months of the dig. One of the moving features
of the finds was the stark contrast between the lavish structures
built by luxury-living Herod and the makeshift improvisions of the
embattled zealots. It was one of the rare excavations where the
archaeologist could recapture not only the varied patterns of life
but also the very mood of each of the peoples who had occupied the
rock at different periods.

Yadin was not the first investigator to be drawn to Masada by the
colourful account in the writings of Josephus. There had been some
minor probes in the previous decades. And in the mid-1930s
Shmaryahu Gutman together with professors Michael Avi-Yonah,
Nahman Avigad and Yohanan Aharoni carried out brief, modest
but very valuable surveys and an examination of the visible structures. They would have wished to follow this up with an exhaustive excavation. But funds were lacking at the time, and the
manpower equipped to tackle the tough topographic and logistic
problems could not be spared. A large-scale expedition became

possible only in the 1960s, headed by Yadin, again aided by the Israel Army, and also by volunteer diggers from Israel and overseas.

Yadin first had to decide where to establish his base camp. The likeliest spot seemed to be at the foot of the 'snake path' on the eastern slope, for it was close to a good access road and to the water and electricity networks. However, it was ruled out. The frequent climb up the tortuous path would be tiring and time-wasting for the expedition members; and the haulage of heavy excavation equipment posed too many difficulties. Yadin finally selected a site at the foot of the spur to the western slope, adjoining the camp established by another general, the Roman Silva, nineteen centuries earlier. The summit would now be reached in a ten-minute walk by a footpath of general gradient along the Roman ramp. Army engineers soon bulldozed the site, set up the archaeologists' base camp, blasted a long stretch of access track through the Judean wilderness, and constructed, with no little danger, a staircase on the steep face of the Masada rock to cover the gap between the top of the ramp and the edge of the summit. A four-mile pipeline brought water, and generators supplied the electricity. Equipment was carried to the excavation area by cable ferry between girders erected on the summit and at the camp below.

The dig could now begin, and evidence was soon unearthed to confirm the historical report by Josephus, as well as his description of the buildings. The most striking structural remains were those of Herod's three-tiered palace-villa at the northern tip of the summit. It was a marvel of architecture and engineering, with living quarters giving on to courts bounded by pillars topped by handsome capitals, and huge terraces projecting from each of the three levels, looking in profile like gigantic steps, and offering an all-round view of the Dead Sea, the mountains and the desert. Decorative wall paintings and mosaic floors were found there in a good state of preservation.

At the stratum when this hanging palace had been used as a communal building by the resistance group, Yadin found a thick layer of ashes, with Jewish coins of the period, matching the Josephus account that the zealots of Masada had burned the buildings before taking their lives. Most moving was the find in Herod's private bath-house. On the steps leading to the pool lay the remains of three skeletons, those of a young man, a young woman and an infant. The ground appeared to be blood-stained. At the side of the male skeleton were scales of armour, arrow-heads, parts of a Jewish prayer shawl, and a piece of pottery with a Hebrew inscription. The scalp of the young woman was still attached to the skull, and flowing from it were beautifully plaited locks of brown

The three-tiered palace-villa of Herod at the northern edge of the Masada summit. (The wall paintings in the foreground, the lowest terrace, are now shielded by protective glass.)

hair. Nearby lay her sandals. Josephus had written that, on the final night, the last survivor set fire to the palace and then killed himself at the side of his slain family. It is tempting to speculate that the bones were those of that very fighter, his wife and their child.

To the immediate south of the palace-villa Yadin found and cleared the substantial ruins of Herod's storerooms. They had clearly served the zealots as their central commissary. The jars bore Hebrew inscriptions stating that the contents had been tithed. Like the Bar Kochba rebels sixty years later, the devoutly religious zealots scrupulously observed the Jewish laws even under the pressures of battle.

The expedition brought to light remains of the Jewish defenders in all the Herodian buildings they excavated. The most notable of these structures were an extensive working palace, several small villas Herod built for his family and friends, a classic Roman-style bath-house, a large garrison building, and the casemate wall which encircled the summit perimeter. The chambers in this double wall had served as the principal dwellings of the zealots, and here were found their cooking stoves and vessels, coins, tools, leather and cloth fragments. Also unearthed within the casemate wall were the ruins of zealot construction, the most important of which were a synagogue and a Jewish ritual bath (*mikve*), more ancient than any discovered so far. A find in almost every one of the zealot rooms, which brought vividly to life the scene and mood of the final hours, was a small heap of ashes. Bits of clothing, sandals and domestic utensils lay amidst the embers. As Josephus reported, each family had collected together its humble effects and set them on fire. They were of little intrinsic worth; but denying them to the Romans, like the taking of their lives, was an act of defiance.

The discovery of ancient writings was high on Yadin's agenda of expectation when he started the Masada dig. It seemed evident that the zealots, orthodox Jews, would have carried with them from Jerusalem their sacred writings – handwritten scrolls of biblical works, prayers, and other religious texts. They would surely have hidden them, to prevent their falling into the profane hands of the Romans. Such writings would be of special archaeological significance since, unlike other Dead Sea scrolls, they could be dated with the certainty that they were no later than AD 73!

The archaeologists were not disappointed. By the end of the final season, they had found portions of no less than 14 scrolls and some 700 ostraca. Two of the scrolls had been hidden beneath the floor of the synagogue. One was found by sifting the rubble covering a large wall behind the palace-villa; another was unearthed in a tower near the working palace; the other ten had been secreted in the dwelling chambers of the casemate wall. These scrolls are of considerable value to scholars of religious history, the literature of the period and paleography. Most of them are biblical, containing texts which were later (about AD 100) included in the canon of the Old Testament. There were chapters of Deuteronomy, Leviticus, Ezekiel and Psalms, almost identical with the Hebrew biblical texts in use today. The non-biblical scrolls were writings held sacred by the Jews at the time, which failed, however, to be accepted into the Old Testament. They therefore ceased 'publication' in their original Hebrew version, namely, they were no longer copied by Hebrew scribes to be perpetuated by succeeding Jewish generations. However some of those works which only narrowly missed being included in the canon were preserved in their Greek and (later) Latin translations, and formed what is known as the Old Testament Apocrypha, which is part of the Septuagint and the Vulgate. One of the Masada scrolls turned out to be such a work – but in its extremely rare original Hebrew text. It is 'The Wisdom of Ben Sira', written in Hebrew at the beginning of the second century BC and translated into Greek later in that century by Ben Sira's grandson. It had been included in the pre-canonical Septuagint, and passed to the Christian Church as a book of the Apocrypha,

The synagogue at Masada, built between the double walls that encircle the summit. These are the earliest synagogue remains ever discovered. A pit beneath the floor of an adjacent chamber yeilded sacred scrolls which the zealots of Masada had hidden before ending their lives.

bearing the Greek title Ecclesiasticus (not to be confused with the biblical Book of Ecclesiastes). It is to this day part of the Roman Catholic liturgy.

The ostraca discovered at Masada were also of great value. Most of them belonged to the brief period when Eleazar's group occupied the fortress height. Almost 300 found near the storerooms were marked with Hebrew letters, and may have been used in a rationing system during the siege. The stratum from the reign of Herod yielded several ostraca with the rare inscription of a specific date, attested in the customary Roman fashion by reference to the consul of the year. These potsherds were parts of wine jars sent from Italy, and the consul's name on the jars was C. Sentius Saturninas, who served in the year 19 BC. Some were also inscribed 'To king Herod of Judea', a discovery which would have given the clue to Herod's association with Masada even if no record had been left by Josephus.

Though all the writings, both the scrolls and the inscribed potsherds, were of scholarly importance, the most intriguing were a group of eleven small ostraca, each bearing a Hebrew name. Yadin proposed the theory that these may have been the lots drawn by the final ten men to determine which one 'should kill the other nine'. Why, then, would there be eleven and not ten ostraca? Yadin points out that one of the potsherds bore the name 'ben Yair', the Masada commander himself, and he suggests that the other ten were Eleazar's 'commanders who had been left to the last, after the decision had been wholly carried out, and who had then cast lots among themselves'.

Thus ended the lives of the fighters of Masada in their final stand against the Romans. Today, newly-enlisted troops in the Armoured Corps of the Israel Defence Forces take their oath of allegiance at the top of Masada. They make the ascent up the ancient 'snake path' in the late afternoon and parade on the summit as darkness falls, by the light of flaming torches. There they vow that 'Masada shall not fall again'.

Select Bibliography

Y. Aharoni, *The Land of the Bible*, London 1967

Y. Aharoni and M. Avi-Yonah, *The Macmillan Bible Atlas*, Jerusalem and New York 1968

W. F. Albright, *The Archaeology of Palestine and the Bible*, New York 1935; *The Archaeology of Palestine*, London 1954, 1963; *From the Stone Age to Christianity*, New York 1957; *The Amarna Letters from Palestine* (Chap. 20, Vol II of Cambridge Ancient History, new ed.), Cambridge 1966

M. Avi-Yonah, ed. *Encyclopaedia of Archaeological Excavations in the Holy Land*, Jerusalem 1975

D. Bahat, *Carta's Historical Atlas of Jerusalem*, Jerusalem 1973

F. J. Bliss, *A Mound of Many Cities*, London 1898; *The Development of Palestine Exploration*, London 1906

P. E. Botta, *Letters on the Discoveries of Nineveh*, London 1850

J. H. Breasted, *Ancient Records of Egypt*, Chicago 1906–7

J. Bright, *A History of Israel*, London 1960

J. L. Burckhardt, *Travels in Syria and the Holy Land*, London 1822

M. Burrows, *What Mean these Stones?*, New Haven 1941; *The Dead Sea Scrolls*, New York 1955; *More Light on the Dead Sea Scrolls*, New York 1958

C. W. Ceram, *Gods, Graves, and Scholars*, London 1952; ed. *The World of Archaeology*, London 1966

C. Clermont-Ganneau, *Archaeological Researches in Palestine during the Years 1873–4*, London 1896–9

J. Comay, *The World's Greatest Story*, New York 1978

C. R. Conder and H. H. Kitchener, *The Survey of Western Palestine*, Vols. I–III: *Galilee; Samaria; Judea;* London 1881–3

L. Cottrell, *Digs and Diggers*, London 1966

J. W. Crowfoot, K. M. Kenyon, E. L. Sukenik, *The Buildings at Samaria*, London 1942

F. M. Cross, *The Ancient Library of Qumran and Modern Biblical Studies*, New York 1961

G. E. Daniel, *A Hundred Years of Archaeology*, London 1950

W. G. Dever and others, *Gezer* I and II, Jerusalem 1970, 1974

A. Dupont-Sommer, *The Jewish Sect of Qumran and the Essenes*, New York 1956

H. J. Franken and C. A. Franken-Battershill, *A Primer of Old Testament Archaeology*, Leiden 1963

H. Frankfort, *The Birth of Civilization in the Near East*, New York 1956

J. Garstang, *Joshua Judges*, London 1931

N. Glueck, *The Other Side of the Jordan*, New Haven 1940; *The River Jordan*, Philadelphia 1946; *Rivers in the Desert*, New York 1959

C. H. Gordon, *Introduction to Old Testament Times*, New Jersey 1953; *Forgotten Scripts*, London 1968

H. V. Hilprecht, *Explorations in Bible Lands during the 19th Century*, Philadelphia 1903

C. H. Irwin, *The Bible, the Scholar and the Spade*, London 1932

K. M. Kenyon, *Digging up Jericho*, London 1957; *Archaeology in the Holy Land*, London 1960, 1979

R. Koldewey, *The Excavations at Babylon*, London 1914

S. N. Kramer, *History Begins at Sumer*, London 1958

R. S. Lamon and G. M. Shipton, *Megiddo* I (1925–34), Chicago 1939

A. H. Layard, *Nineveh and its Remains*, London 1850; *Discoveries in the Ruins of Nineveh and Babylon*, London 1853

G. C. Lewis, *An Historical Survey of the Astronomy of the Ancients*, London 1862

W. F. Libby, *Radiocarbon Dating*, New York 1955

S. Lloyd, *Foundations in the Dust*, London 1947

G. Loud and others, *Megiddo* II (1935–39 seasons), Chicago 1948

R. A. S. Macalister, *A Century of Excavation in Palestine*, London 1925

A Malamat, ed. *The Age of the Monarchies: Culture and Society* (in the series *The World History of the Jewish People*), Jerusalem 1979

B. Mazar, *The Mountain of the Lord*, New York 1975; ed. *Patriarchs* (Vol. II in *The World History of the Jewish People*), 1970; *Judges* (Vol. III in *The World History of the Jewish People*), Jerusalem 1971

S. A. B. Mercer, *The Tell el-Amarna Tablets*, Toronto 1939

A. T. Olmstead, *The History of the Persian Empire*, Cambridge 1949

H. M. Orlinski, *Ancient Israel*, New York 1954, 1960

A. Parrot, ed. *Nineveh and the Old Testament*, London 1956; *Nineveh and Babylon*, London 1961

W. M. F. Petrie, *Ten Years' Digging in Egypt*, London 1892; *Methods and Aims in Archaeology*, London 1904; *Researches in Sinai*, London 1906; *Seventy Years in Archaeology*, London 1932, 1969

M. Pope, *The Story of Archaeological Decipherment*, London 1975

J. M. Pritchard, *Archaeology and the Old Testament*, Princeton 1958; ed. *The Ancient Near East*, Princeton 1958

H. C. Rawlinson, *The Persian Cuneiform Inscriptions of Behistun*, London 1846

G. Rawlinson, *A Memoir of Major-General Sir Henry Creswicke Rawlinson*, London 1898

G. A. Reisner, C. S. Fisher, D. G. Lyon, *Harvard Excavations at Samaria, 1908–10*, Cambridge (Mass.) 1924

R. W. Rogers, *A History of Babylonia and Assyria*, New York 1915

A. Rowe, *The Topography and History of Beth-shan*, Philadelphia 1930

H. H. Rowley, *The Re-discovery of the Old Testament*, London 1946

J. A. Sanders, ed. *Near Eastern Archaeology in the Twentieth Century* (Essays in honour of Nelson Glueck), New York 1970

G. A. Smith, *The Historical Geography of the Holy Land*, London 1894, 1903; *Jerusalem from the Earliest Times to* AD 70, London 1907

E. A. Speiser, *Mesopotamian Origins*, Pennsylvania 1930; ed. *At the Dawn of Civilization* (in the series *The World History of the Jewish People*), Jerusalem 1964

J. L. Starkey, *Excavations at Tell ed-Duweir* [Lachish], London 1934

E. L. Sukenik, *The Dead Sea Scrolls of the Hebrew University*, Jerusalem 1955

H. Torczyner (Tur-Sinai), *The Lachish Letters*, Oxford 1938

M. F. Unger, *Archaeology and the Old Testament*, Grand Rapids 1954

C. Warren, *Underground Jerusalem*, London 1876

C. Warren and C. R. Conder, *The Survey of Western Palestine: Jerusalem*, London 1884

G. Waterfield, *Layard of Nineveh*, London 1963

R. E. M. Wheeler, *Archaeology from the Earth*, Oxford 1954, 1968

W. W. Williams, *The Life of General Sir Charles Warren*, London 1941

C. W. Wilson, *Picturesque Palestine, Sinai and Egypt*, London 1881. (Two sections of this book were reprinted in Jerusalem in 1975, under the titles *Jerusalem the Holy City* and *The Land of Galilee and the North*, with an introduction by Zev Vilnay.)

C. W. Wilson and C. Warren, *The Recovery of Jerusalem*, London 1871

C. L. Woolley, *Excavations at Ur*, London 1926; *Digging up the Past*, London 1930, 1961

C. L. Woolley and T. E. Lawrence, *The Wilderness of Zin*, London 1915, 1936

G. E. Wright, *Biblical Archaeology*, London 1957; ed. *The Bible and the Ancient Near East* (Essays in Honour of William Foxwell Albright), Jerusalem 1961

G. E. Wright and F. V. Filson, *The Westminster Historical Atlas to the Bible*, London 1957

Y. Yadin, *The Art of Welfare in Biblical Lands*, New York and Jerusalem 1963; *The Message of the Scrolls*, London 1957; *Masada*, London 1966; *Bar Kochba*, London 1971; *Hazor*, London 1975

Acknowledgments

The author and publisher would like to thank the following museums, private collections and individuals by whose kind permission the illustrations are reproduced. The page numbers of the colour pictures are italicized.

Bibliothèque Nationale, Paris, 208–9
Bodleian Library, Oxford, 81 below
Werner Braun, Jerusalem, 104
British Museum, London, 68, 74, 90, 92, 96, 97, 139, 194
Mike Busselle, 148–9
Camera Press, London, 113 (Werner Braun), 170, 177 (Werner Braun and David Harris), 219 (Werner Braun), 222–3 (Werner Braun)
Cooper-Bridgeman Library, London, 25 below (given by Mr J. Pierpoint Morgan), 161 above
Dr Peter G. Dorrell, 143
Fotomas Index, London, 15
A. B. Glik, Jerusalem, 39, 214
David Harris, Jerusalem, endpapers, 2–3, 30, 31, 46, 61, 109, 131, 136, 144, 149, 150, 176, 179, 181 above, 188, 199, 204, 227
Israel Exploration Society, Jerusalem, 217
Israel Government Tourist Office, London, 154, 173, 192, 225
Israel Department of Antiquities and Museums, Jerusalem, 56–7, 102, 127, 135
Israel Museum, Jerusalem, 63 (David Harris), 189
A.F. Kersting, London, 6, 34, 69, 117, 184
Gemma Levine, London, 26–7, 23, 88
Mansell Collection, London, 14, 18–19, 20, 91, 94–5, 112, 141
National Portrait Gallery, London, 87, 125
Oriental Institute, Chicago University, 81 above
Palestine Exploration Fund, London, 1, 133
Pierpoint Morgan Library, New York, 181 below
Popperfoto, London, 50, 65
Radio Times Hulton Picture Library, London, 82, 106
Zav Radovan, Jerusalem, 210
Roger-Viollet, Paris, 79
Royal Geographical Society, London, 22
David Rubinger, Jerusalem, 213
Ronald Sheridan, Harrow, 25 above, 28, 53, 70 above and below, 100, 161 below, 162–3, 182–3, 196
Shrine of the Book, Jerusalem, 158 (Helene Bieberkraut), 167
Sopritendenza alle antighita, Egittologia, Torino, 84
Spectrum, London, 98, 99
Staatliche Museeun zu Berlin, 66
Topham Picture Archives, Ederbridge, 142, 174
Weidenfeld Archives, 10, 13, 42–3, 110, 120, 138, 151, 228
Yigael Yadin, 164, 166

Index

Temple Israel

Minneapolis, Minnesota

In Honor of the Bar Mitzvah of
MICHAEL STEWART RUBENS
by
Alan & Donna Rubens

May 16, 1981